By Divine DESIGN

By Divine DESIGN

BEST PRACTICES FOR FAMILY SUCCESS & HAPPINESS

EDITED BY

BRENT L. TOP AND MICHAEL A. GOODMAN

RELIGIOUS STUDIES CENTER
BRIGHAM YOUNG UNIVERSITY

DESERET
BOOK

Published by the Religious Studies Center, Brigham Young University, Provo, Utah, in co-operation with Deseret Book Company, Salt Lake City.
http://rsc.byu.edu

Printed in the United States of America by Sheridan Books, Inc.

Deseret Book is a registered trademark of Deseret Book Company.
Visit us at DeseretBook.com.

ISBN 978-0-8425-2850-4
Retail US $27.99

Cover design by Tiffany Simmons and Juliana G. Cox
Interior design by Juliana G. Cox

Cover photo by Rhonda Richins
Cloud texture by Lost & Taken

Library of Congress Cataloging-in-Publication Data

By divine design : best practices for family success and happiness / Brent L. Top and Michael A. Goodman, editors.
    pages cm
Includes index.
ISBN 978-0-8425-2850-4 (hard cover : alk. paper) 1. Families--Religious aspects--Church of Jesus Christ of Latter-day Saints. 2. Mormons--Conduct of life. I. Top, Brent L., editor of compilation. II. Goodman, Michael A., 1963- editor of compilation.

BX8643.F3B9 2014
248.4'89332--dc23

2013036712

Contents

BRENT L. TOP & MICHAEL A. GOODMAN

Preface

Ɪɴ a revelation given to the Prophet Joseph Smith in 1832, the Lord stated, "And as all have not faith, seek ye diligently and teach one another words of wisdom; yea, seek ye out of the best books words of wisdom; *seek learning, even by study and also by faith*" (D&C 88:118; emphasis added). Latter-day disciples of Christ are commanded in the same revelation not only to diligently "teach one another the doctrine of the kingdom" (D&C 88:77) but also to study many other subjects and disciplines (see vv. 78–79) "that ye may be prepared in all things . . . to magnify the calling whereunto I have called you" (v. 80). It is our hope that this book, in some measure, helps readers gain new and important knowledge through an appropriate combination of the "words of wisdom" from both spiritual and scriptural sources (faith) and from the findings of solid social science research (study) about our most important responsibility throughout time and eternity—our families. Prophets, seers, and revelators have long reminded us that "the most important of the Lord's work [we] will ever do will be within the walls of [our] own homes" (Lee, 1973, p. 91), and "no success can compensate for failure in the home" (McKay, 1935, p. 116). So important is the family to our Heavenly Father's plan that the First Presidency and Quorum of the Twelve Apostles issued a solemn proclamation to the world in 1995. "The family is central to the Creator's plan for the eternal destiny of His children," the proclamation declared. "Happiness in family life is most likely to be achieved when founded upon the teachings of the Lord Jesus Christ. Successful marriages and families are established and maintained on principles of faith, prayer, repentance, forgiveness, respect, love, compassion, work, and wholesome recreational activities" (First Presidency and Council of the Twelve Apostles, 1995, p. 102).

Although the inspired teachings of latter-day prophets and apostles need no empirical validation, there is much, however, in the world of academic research that corroborates those teachings and provides us with additional insights and practical applications. The Prophet Joseph Smith taught that "one of the grand fundamental principles of 'Mormonism' is to receive truth, let it come from whence it may" (Smith, 1980, p. 229). Therefore, whether truth comes from revelation, science, philosophy, or any other branch of knowledge, we are commanded to seek after it. Truth seekers do not pit science against religion or reason against faith, but rather, embrace the truths of each that will bless our lives, strengthen our families, and bring us all closer to God, who is the source of all truth. "Religion and science have sometimes been in apparent conflict. Yet, the conflict can only be apparent, not real, for science seeks truth, and true religion is truth," declared President Ezra Taft Benson (1988). "The two are meeting daily; science as a child; true religion as the mother. Truth is truth, whether labeled science or religion" (118). In an effort to better understand and apply essential truths relating to marriage and family, this volume seeks to combine revelation and reason—the scientific as well as the spiritual methods of learning.

Our objective for this project was to make available to a broader LDS audience solid scholarship in the field of family studies in a format that would not be like an academic journal article or a textbook. We desire to provide a gospel-centered, "best practices" book for husbands and wives, fathers and mothers that is founded on prophetic teachings and substantiated by good science. Just as the objective of this book is a "marriage," so to speak, of disciplines—gospel knowledge and application combined with academic, social-science scholarship—so too is the collection of contributors to this volume. Each of the chapters is written by faithful Latter-day Saint scholars from Brigham Young University who have strong academic credentials, having studied at some of the best universities in the country. Each has extensive experience in teaching, researching, and publishing on the subjects related to marriage enrichment, child development, and parenting skills. While all of the contributors come from Brigham Young University, each has unique insights and experiences. Some teach LDS marriage and family classes in Religious Education. Others teach classes in child development, family studies, sociology, or psychology in the School of Family Life and the College of Family, Home, and Social Sciences. Some have extensive experience in marriage and family counseling. Some write primarily to the Latter-day Saint audience. Others are recognized nationally and internationally for their scholarly contributions to the academic community. All are wives or husbands, mothers or fathers, and devoted members of The Church of Jesus Christ of Latter-day Saints. Bringing together these different voices—each speaking from his or her unique vantage point—combined with a common faith in the eternal nature of families—is the objective of this book. It is our hope that their voices will inform and inspire.

Although each of the chapters is a "stand alone" contribution—not directly related to the previous or succeeding chapters, there is a logical "flow" of the chapters—moving from general principles to more specific suggestions, from marriage to parenting, and from parenting young children to parenting older children. Neither this book nor any book could adequately address every issue related to marriage and family life or every problem than any couple or parent may encounter in life. As a result, this book is not intended to be a comprehensive or exhaustive study of the family. Rather, we have selected those topics that address common but important issues. The contributors to this volume were selected because of their expertise in researching, writing, and teaching about these issues. With the overarching objective being the faithful blending of social science and gospel principles, the authors were not only allowed to select the topic they wanted to address in their chapter but also the approach they wanted to take in their writing of it. Amazingly, the topics that were proposed by the respective authors were not redundant and touched upon all of the main issues of marriage and family that we wanted addressed. Giving the individual authors that much latitude, however, does have some downside. There is some overlap among the concepts taught in the various chapters. This is to be expected when dealing with such a broad topic as family relationships. Also, the approach taken by the authors is not correlated or consistent. One author may have more social science citations than another. One may address the social science first and the gospel applications at the end. Another may reverse the order. Some seamlessly blend them together. Some authors will highlight the main points of their chapters with many different studies cited in the family science literature, whereas others may focus almost exclusively on their own studies, the accompanying statistical results, and what generalizations can be made therefrom. Rather than being a weakness, the diversity of experts and their own unique approaches to the topics provide academic strength and a broad gospel perspective.

It is our hope that readers of this book will be both *informed* and *inspired* by what we have included in this volume—informed by what we can learn from scientific studies of the family and inspired by what we can learn from the scriptures, modern-day prophets, and spiritual insights. Combined, these can provide important gospel-centered solutions and applications for Latter-day Saint families.

Each of the authors is solely responsible for the ideas and applications expressed in his or her own chapter. While we have diligently sought to ensure that which is written herein represents good scholarship and ideas and teachings in harmony with the scriptures and teachings of the prophets, we recognize that our words do not represent the official doctrine or positions of The Church of Jesus Christ of Latter-day Saints. We do not speak for the leadership of the Church or Brigham Young University. This book is not an official publication of either. We hope that this work will contribute in some way to blessing families—which will in turn further the Father's plan for the immortality and eternal life of his family.

Brent L. Top
Editor

Michael A. Goodman
Editor

References

Benson, E. T. (1988). *Teachings of Ezra Taft Benson*. Salt Lake City: Bookcraft.

First Presidency and Council of the Twelve Apostles. (1995, November). The family: A proclamation to the world. *Ensign, 25*(11), 102.

Lee, H. B. (1973, September 11). Be loyal to the royal within you. *Speeches of the Year, 1973*. Provo, UT: Brigham Young University, 1974.

McKay, D. O. (1935, April). In Conference Report. 116.

Smith, J. (1980). *Words of Joseph Smith: The contemporary accounts of the Nauvoo discourses of the Prophet Joseph*. A. F. Ehat & L. W. Cook (Eds.). Provo, UT: Religious Studies Center, Brigham Young University.

Acknowledgments

As with any project like this, there are many "moving parts" and many people involved to ensure that all those parts fit together like they are supposed to. We wish to acknowledge and express our appreciation to them for the respective contributions to this book. A special thanks goes to Linda Godfrey, secretary of the Department of Church History and Doctrine, and her student assistants Karra King, Emily Matson, Rachel Thompson, and Kimberly Pellegrini, who devoted much time to source checking, proofreading, and other important tasks.

We are grateful for the able assistance of the editorial and production staff of the Religious Studies Center: Joany Pinegar, publications coordinator; Brent Nordgren, production supervisor; Devan Jensen, executive editor; and their team of editors and designers. We express particular thanks to Aleesha Bass, Rachel Ishoy, Tiffany Simmons, and Juliana G. Cox for their work on this project.

We deeply appreciate the partnership with Deseret Book and express thanks to Sheri Dew, Cory Maxwell, and Laurel Christensen for their support and suggestions. This book is better because of their guidance.

E. JEFFREY HILL

I

Finding Life Harmony as We Struggle to Juggle

The happiest people I know are those whose life-styles center around the home. Work is very important, and success in one's profession or business is also essential to happiness, but remember what we say so often: "No other success can compensate for failure in the home."
—*N. Eldon Tanner (1978, p. 2)*

"THE Family: A Proclamation to the World" teaches that we are responsible to both provide for and nurture our families in the context of the gospel of Jesus Christ (First Presidency, 1995, p. 102). Being fully involved as a spouse and parent on top of adequately providing and being a reliable employee can feel like a burden. "As we meet with Church members around the world, one challenge seems universal: having enough time to do everything that needs doing," stated Bishop Keith B. McMullin (2002, p. 94).

As we struggle to juggle our employment, our home duties, and our Church callings, we may often feel out of balance and stressed. We may wrestle with deciding whether to work late or to leave on time to attend a child's activity. We agonize about whether to miss out on a previously planned family outing because an unexpected church assignment has come up. We wonder if we should stay up late to go the extra mile in preparing a Sunday lesson or to go to bed and get much-needed rest. Sometimes it seems like work, home, and church are in a tug-of-war, fighting for our personal time and energy. Juggling may eventually exhaust us and cause us to lose interest in the very things we love most. We may even begin to feel inadequate, pessimistic, and discouraged.

Perhaps it is beneficial to view the situation from a different perspective. Recent social science research proposes that work, family, and other life domains can actually be complementary—not competing—priorities. Success in the work place often contributes to one's success outside of the work place and vice versa. Data from a large, multinational survey reveal that relationships and social interaction, physical and psychological benefits, and improved skills are examples of aspects of work that can enhance home life and vice versa (Hill et al., 2007). The key to harmony is to invest our time in activities that enhance multiple domains that we value in our lives.

This concept of enhancement utilizes a music metaphor and has been called *life harmony* (Hill & Anderson, 2004). Just as the different voices in a well-composed piece of music unite in harmony, the different facets of our lives can be coordinated in peace. Using the perspective of life harmony, we no longer see work, family, and church as fighting for our scarce time. We see mortality as a great symphony with the many different voices in our own lives united harmoniously to the glory of God (Hill & Martinengo, 2005).

There is no one formula for creating greater life harmony because each individual faces different constraints based on local economies, job opportunities and policies, family situations, cultural settings, and personal preferences. But there are a variety of strategies that can help individuals in any circumstance. Employing any of these strategies can help us experience greater joy as we bring the demands of job, family, and church into greater harmony. In this chapter we focus on seven suggestions: (a) enhance energy, (b) increase quality time, (c) learn to bundle, (d) focus on the most important things, (e) work flexibly, (f) simplify your life, and (g) center on the Savior.

Enhance Energy

A self-report questionnaire taken by employees among 10 state agencies recently revealed that it is the depletion of energy—rather than time spent on the job—that is the main factor in whether a person feels like there is conflict between work and the rest of his or her life (Carlson, Kacmar, & Stepina, 1995). It is very possible that 50 hours per week in a job that is invigorating may have a less negative impact on the home than a 40-hour per week job that is depressing. When an individual feels that employment is sapping strength, there is little energy left for service at home or in the Church.

One suggestion to increase your energy without reducing work hours is to make a list of all the things you do at work that either drain or energize you. To create more work-family harmony, see if you can arrange to do the energizing things right before you go home so that you can carry more of that energy home to your family. For example, perhaps you are an engineer who loves design work and hates paperwork and meetings. You could choose to get onerous paperwork tasks done earlier in the day, and save the energizing design work for the hours right before you go home.

Another way to increase energy is to choose to make time to do things that are personally renewing. Physical exercise often creates physical energy. Peaceful music may soothe the soul. Talking to a friend can be energizing to some. A short nap is often invigorating. Having a few minutes alone in quiet solitude can rejuvenate the heart. Taking time for rejuvenating activities may appear to only add more to a to-do list full of high-priority tasks, but such moments can add the extra physical and spiritual strength we need to accomplish everything. Even the Savior took time for this kind of replenishment (see Matthew 14:23). It is important to see personal renewal as an investment instead of a waste of time.

Commuting to and from work can also be a time of energy renewal rather than depletion. One mother reviews scriptures she has memorized as she walks to work. She arrives on the job with a clear and active mind.

Physical exercise creates physical energy and can be personally renewing. Tamra Ratieta, © Intellectual Reserve, Inc.

Another parent, a father, listens to conference talks as he drives home from work. By the time he greets his family he has forgotten about aggravating experiences during the workday and is ready for his most important work. After the incessant staccato of many jobs, we often need a peaceful larghetto for renewal before returning to our home.

An often-overlooked method of increasing energy at work is prayer. We are repeatedly counseled in the scriptures to "pray always" (see 2 Nephi 32:9; 3 Nephi 18:15, 18; Luke 21:36; 2 Thessalonians 1:11; D&C 10:5; 19:38; 20:33; 31:12; 32:4; 61:39; 88:126; 90:24; 93:49–50), but prayer may be forgotten on the job. Indeed, we are counseled in the scriptures to "cry over the flocks of [our] fields, that they may increase" (Alma 34:25). One father has related that he prays frequently at work, sometimes on his knees and sometimes silently and is blessed with spiritual light (energy) that guides him in how to be more effective in his job. As the Spirit helps him solve work problems, he feels he has more time and energy for his family and church service.

As we open our minds to better see ways to enhance energy, we may discover activities that foster harmony in our lives without requiring additional time. We may find ourselves with less fatigue, conflict, and stress while actually doing more. Additionally, we may find that as we seek physical and spiritual renewal, we allow ourselves access to the enabling power of the Atonement, helping us on a day-to-day basis to accomplish more than we thought we could on our own.

Increase Quality Time

All time is not created equal. In seeking to obtain life harmony we must find ways to put each moment to its best use. When Elder Oaks (1975) was in his third year of law school and involved in church responsibilities, he had to make the most of limited time with his daughters. He recalls, "My favorite play activity with the little girls was 'daddy be a bear.' When I came home from my studies for a few minutes at lunch and dinnertime, I would set my books on the table and drop down on all fours on the linoleum.

Praying at work increases energy and effectiveness. © *Luca Bertolli.*

Then, making the most terrible growls, I would crawl around the floor after the children, who fled with screams, but always begged for more" (pp. 7–8). No doubt this was quality time spent!

In his occupation as an airline pilot, President Dieter F. Uchtdorf was required to travel away from home for long periods of time. He found family harmony by seeking quality time. His son Guido remembers, "When Dad returned home, we played, we talked, and we laughed together. . . . That was quality time!" (Nelson, 2008, p. 19).

Family mealtime is a great opportunity for high-quality time. President Ezra Taft Benson (1987) taught, "Happy conversation, sharing of the day's plans and activities, and special teaching moments occur at mealtime because mothers and fathers and children work at it." A recent life-harmony study of a parental subsample of US IBM employees revealed that regular family mealtime protected individuals from conflict between work and family life when they had to work long hours (Jacob, Allen, Hill, Mead, & Ferris, 2008). In addition, extensive social science research has documented that regular family mealtime is associated with less adolescent risk for a variety of internalizing behaviors such as depression, weak self-esteem, suicidal thoughts, attempted suicide, withdrawn or distressed behavior, and behavioral problems (Eisenberg, Olson, Neumark-Sztainer, Story, & Bearinger, 2004; Fiese, Foley, & Spagnola, 2006; Hofferth & Sandberg, 2001).

To be together for mealtime is a challenge, especially in large families. It requires careful planning. One family holds a family council each Sunday and carefully selects a dinnertime each evening when everyone can be there. The time varies according to the activities of the week. Another family chose to share the big meal of the day at 3:00 p.m. each afternoon, right when the children came home from school. In this family the father came home early from work for dinner with the family, and then finished his workday at home, via telecommuting.

Bedtime may also be a time of extraordinary quality. Children rarely want to go to sleep when parents want them to, but will often give parents undivided attention at bedtime. In an experimental study consisting of

405 mothers and their infants or toddlers, it was found that having a consistent bedtime routine led to better sleep for children and a better mood for their mothers (Mindell, Telofski, Weigand, & Kurtz, 2009). Parents can read or tell stories, pray, cuddle, sing songs, read the scriptures, and do many other things. This is also an ideal time to teach the gospel. The peaceful feelings associated with bedtime stay with children throughout the night. Likewise, these bedtime interactions with children may be just what a parent needs to forget the frustrations of the day and to sleep peacefully.

The specific ways to increase quality time are many. One may focus on creating time for carefree play with the children, carefully plan a time when all family members can be available for family dinner, or make it a priority to be available during the bedtime hour. The specifics may vary, but the principle is the same: when we make the effort to engage in meaningful activities with those we care about, we create harmony in our lives.

Learn to Bundle: Do Two or More Things at the Same Time in Harmony

Bundling, according to life-harmony research, is when one activity simultaneously serves purposes in two or more aspects of life (Sandholtz, Derr, Bruckner, & Carlson, 2002). Successful bundlers are often able to do two or more things at the same time in harmony. In many cases, each facet of a bundled activity is of greater value than if it were done as its own activity. For example, when a couple chooses to walk together, they may get needed exercise, relax and be rejuvenated, share ideas about Church callings, express their affection, talk about their children, brainstorm solutions to problems at work, and so on. This one bundling activity is of great value because it may contribute to many facets of life.

A few years ago my wife gave me a tandem bicycle for my birthday. This proved to be our best tool of bundling ever. We often ride together on a bike path up a beautiful canyon next to the Provo River. By doing so, we

Bundling can also include doing chores together and having fun as a family when the work is done. Matt Reier, © Intellectual Reserve, Inc.

can both get as much exercise as we want. We stay close, so it easy to talk to one another and strengthen our marriage as we exercise. We are invigorated by the beautiful scenery on the trail. We greet and sometimes talk with members of the community. This list could go on and on. Riding a tandem with a family member accomplishes so much more than riding alone.

Another example of bundling is when a parent takes a child with them to run errands. A mother may take her child with her to purchase groceries. While shopping she has the opportunity to connect with her child one-on-one and engage in relationship-building conversation. She can also teach principles of provident living by showing her child how to save money by comparison shopping.

In today's world, many parents transport their children to school, sports practice, and a myriad of other activities. This may be an excellent time to bundle travel time with meaningful conversation. Elder Robert D. Hales (2010) counseled parents, "As you drive or walk children to school or their various activities, do you use the time to talk with them about their hopes and dreams and fears and joys? Do you take the time to have them take the earplugs from their mp3 players and all the other devices so that they can hear you and feel of your love?" (p. 95).

We may also bundle church service time with family time. A bishop with a young family in a ward with numerous widows related that he brings one or more children with him each time he makes a non-confidential visit. The widows have learned to love his children and the children are able to see their father ministering.

When we do two or more things at the same time in harmony, we give that time period greater value. As we examine our lives, we will find many such activities that will enable us to struggle less with juggling and claim greater harmony in our lives.

Focus on the Most Important Things

Bundling does not always work. There are many times when it is better to set firm boundaries and not let paid work's *basso profundo* overpower the gentle melodies of home life. Keeping the Sabbath day holy may be a key to focused harmony. Bob Egan, a successful IBM executive, told my work and family class at BYU that he made a promise never to work on Sunday, and he never has. He said it feels good to tell his children, "Sunday is a special day, a day different than other days of the week. Daddy doesn't go to work on Sunday."

Weekly family home evening is also sacred family time around which firm boundaries should be set. Outside friendships, work, and church service should not encroach upon this activity. This might be a great time to turn the phones off completely, avoiding even the intrusive buzz of an incoming text message. It is a time to say "no" to activities (however worthy they might be) that intrude upon having a faith-promoting family home evening.

Family vacation may be another time for muting work completely. In today's wireless world of smartphones, tablets, iPads, and laptops, it is easy to let work bring dissonance to the delicate tunes of vacation renewal. A few years ago, I took my wife and three of our children to enjoy the Big Island

Family time is more important than most other things in life. Matt Reier, © Intellectual Reserve, Inc.

of Hawaii for an eight-day vacation. I brought my laptop with the thought that I could log on a few minutes each day and keep up with my e-mail. However, the few minutes turned into a few hours each day. It seemed that even when playing with the kids at the beach I would become distracted by thinking about a work project or by becoming irritated because of something I read in an e-mail. It is true that where the mind is, the heart is soon sure to follow. A few days into our vacation, my boss firmly demanded (via e-mail) that I join an important 9:00 a.m. conference call the next morning. After replying that I would attend, I realized that the 9:00 a.m. call in New York would be 3:00 a.m. Kona time. Sitting in on that tense conference call in the wee hours of the morning, with the sound of the waves crashing in the background, was the straw that broke this camel's back. I asked myself, "What am I doing? I'm supposed to be on vacation!" So after the call I locked up the laptop, put away the calling card, and crawled back into bed. I made a resolution from then on that I would throw off my "electronic leash" whenever I went on vacation (Hill, 1999).

Part of focusing on the most important things is recognizing that the family takes priority over other life domains. The First Presidency (1999) wrote: "However worthy and appropriate other demands or activities may be, they must not be permitted to displace the divinely-appointed duties that only parents and families can adequately perform." Sometimes we erroneously place Church service arbitrarily above family responsibilities. President Dieter F. Uchtdorf (2009) taught, "Even some programs of the Church can become a distraction if we take them to extremes and allow them to dominate our time and our attention at the expense of things that matter most. We need balance in life" (p. 60). Certainly our employment and Church callings are important, and should be fulfilled diligently. However, on occasion, we may need to remember what Elder Dallin H. Oaks (2007) counseled: "We have to forego some good things in order to choose others that are better or best because they develop faith in the Lord Jesus Christ and strengthen our families" (p. 107).

Work Flexibly

Research has consistently shown that those with workplace flexibility are better able to manage the competing demands of paid work and family life. Workplace flexibility is defined as "the ability of workers to make choices influencing when, where, and for how long they engage in work-related tasks" (Hill et al., 2008, p. 152). Some examples of workplace flexibility include telecommuting (working electronically from home), flextime (being able to modify start times, meal breaks, and ending times), part-time work (working reduced hours for reduced pay), and leave (taking time off without pay for family responsibilities).

A large body of research documents the benefits of this flexibility to both work and family life. For example, one study in a large multinational corporation compared 279 mothers working part-time in professional positions with 250 mothers working full-time. Those working part-time reported that they used their extra discretionary time to care for and nurture their dependent children. They reported less work-to-family conflict, as well as greater work-family success, childcare satisfaction, and family success (Hill & Anderson, 2004). Another study compared 441 telecommuters who worked primarily from home to 4,315 workers who worked primarily from the office. Those who worked from home reported greater job motivation, career opportunity, work-life balance, and personal/family success. They also reported that they were less likely to be thinking about leaving the company (Hill, Ferris, & Martinson, 2003). Several other studies have revealed that those who have workplace flexibility are able to work longer hours without experiencing work-family conflict (Hill, Hawkins, Ferris, & Weitzman, 2001; Hill, Erickson, Ferris, & Holmes, 2010).

Over the years I have personally used each of these options to facilitate work and family harmony. The strategy that probably helped the most was when I worked from home for IBM instead of commuting to and from the office each day. In 1990, I became one of IBM's first telecommuters. For nearly ten years, I worked from my home in Logan, Utah—more than 2,000 miles from my coworkers in New York. This enabled me to live in a quiet community, forego the stressful 45-minute commute each morning and evening, and be at home within earshot of my family for most of our waking hours. I found myself much more involved in the everyday activities of the home, and much more in tune with the individual needs of my children. I also found that flexibility and autonomy of telework enabled me to do my job more effectively and efficiently. However, working with so many children in the background sometimes made it difficult to maintain professional boundaries between work and home life. Let me share one humorous story that appeared in a *Wall Street Journal* article on telecommuting:

One morning while I recorded my daily voice mail greeting, my wife Juanita was folding clothes in the laundry room across the hall. My six-year-old daughter Emily had just taken a shower upstairs and could not find the clothes she wanted to wear. She came downstairs draped in nothing but a towel. When Juanita saw her, she said in a loud, giggly female voice, "Look at you! You have no clothes on!" After several colleagues commented with a chuckle about my voice mail greeting, I listened to it, and this is what I heard:

> *Male Voice:* This is Dr. Jeff Hill with IBM Global Employee Research . . .
> *Giggly Female Voice:* Look at you! You have no clothes on!
> *Male Voice:* I'm not available right now . . .
> (Shellenbarger, 1997, p. B1)

The many electronic tools available in the digital age opens up many possibilities for when, where, and how long work is performed. Most large companies and many smaller ones offer these flexible work options. Whether it is flextime, telecommuting, part-time work, or leave, a key component for achieving life harmony is to choose to work flexibly. Those who are successful at this see their life as a whole and choose to work when it makes sense to work and to be with family members when it makes sense to be with family.

Simplify Your Life

Voluntary simplicity—deliberately choosing to accumulate fewer possessions and engage in fewer activities—aids in creating life harmony (Brophy, 1995). Elder L. Tom Perry (2008) counseled, "In our search to obtain relief from the stresses of life, may we earnestly seek ways to simplify our lives" (p. 10). King Benjamin's counsel is applicable to many of us today: "And see that all these things are done in wisdom and order; for it is not requisite that a man should run faster than he has strength" (Mosiah 4:27). In directing members to follow this counsel, Elder Neal A. Maxwell (1994) challenged every member of the Church to give up one outside activity in order to have more time for the family. Many of us seek diligently to please and help those around us. Sometimes we agree to do too many things that are not part of our primary mission. If we really want to focus on those activities with value, then we need to learn how to kindly but firmly say "no."

This may be easier said than done, especially for those of us who want to please others. I have learned a simple way to do this. When someone asks me to do something I respond, "Thank you very much for this invitation. I appreciate it. Let me think it over and I'll get back to you tomorrow." If, after consideration, I decide it is an invitation I'd rather not accept, I think of others who might want to do it. Then when I get back to the person I say something like, "I thank you again for the invitation, but with what's going on right now I am not going to be able to accept it. However, you might want to contact Thom Curtis or Wally Goddard. One of them might be interested and they would probably do a better job than I would." Using such a dialogue, I can say no without a twinge of regret.

In order to obtain life harmony, we must also look for a way to compose a life of modest means. We live in a materialistic world, and when we have too much we run the risk of obscuring the simple but powerful life melody we hope to compose. One important way to simplify life is to follow the counsel of the prophets to stay out of debt. Elder Joseph B. Wirthlin (2004) promised great blessings to those who pay an honest tithing, spend less than they earn, learn to save, honor financial obligations, and teach children sound financial principles.

There are many ways to simplify by planning together to reduce the number and time demands of out-of-home activities. For example, a father may choose to go golfing with the office group every other week instead of every week. A bishop may decide to reduce the length and frequency of ward leadership meetings. A Relief Society instructor may choose to spend a little less time making fancy handouts for her lesson. Youth may choose to reduce the number of extracurricular activities in which they are engaged during the school year and the amount of time they spend hanging out with friends. Though the ways to do this vary, the principle is to reduce the time spent engaging in low-value activities.

Center on the Savior

Perhaps the most important key for successfully orchestrating a life of harmony is to center on the Savior. President Howard W. Hunter (1997) said, "I am aware that life presents many challenges, but with the help of the Lord, we need not fear. If our lives and our faith are centered on Jesus Christ and his restored gospel, nothing can ever go permanently wrong" (p. 40). The concept of life harmony is embodied in the scripture, "And we know that all things work together for good to them that love God, to them who are the called according to his purpose" (Romans 8:28). When the primary focus of our life is to become a disciple of Jesus Christ, everything else—employment, home, and church—falls into place.

We create harmony as we center on the Savior by building spiritual patterns in the home (Newell & Newell, 2005). There are many ways of doing this. Many families choose to start the morning each day by pursuing the pattern of reading and discussing the scriptures and holding family prayer. In addition, we have been counseled to hold a meaningful family home evening every week. Elder David A. Bednar (2009) gave several suggestions about how to center our lives on the Savior by being "more diligent and concerned at home." He counseled parents to frequently bear their testimony in informal settings in the home. He also advised parents to be consistent in these spiritual patterns, for "our consistency in doing seemingly small things can lead to significant spiritual results" (pp. 17–20).

There are numerous other small and simple things that can be done to more effectively center on the Savior. Fathers' blessings provide a way to partner with the Savior in rearing children in love and righteousness. Beginning and ending a sincere fast together as a family is another way to be centered. Parents can read faith-filled inspirational stories at bedtime

We can teach our children by example to center their lives on the Savior. One way to do this is through regular family prayer. Matt Reier, © Intellectual Reserve, Inc.

to help in this regard. Whatever the specific path, the key is to create an environment that centers on the Savior.

Summary

Finding harmony in our lives may appear to be an unrealistic ideal when it seems the best we can do is "struggle to juggle" our extensive demands. However, utilizing strategies such as enhancing energy, increasing quality time, learning to bundle, focusing on the important things, working flexibly, simplifying our lives, and centering our lives on the Savior can lighten the burden and bring greater joy and purpose in the work of life. As we seek life harmony, we are better able to both provide for and nurture our families and compose our lives into a magnificent symphony.

Appendix: The Mexican Fishing Village Story
Author Unknown

An American entrepreneur was standing at the pier of a small coastal Mexican village when a small boat with just one fisherman docked. Inside the small boat were several large yellowfin tuna. The American complimented the Mexican on the quality of his fish.

"How long did it take you to catch them?" the American asked.

"Only a little while," the Mexican replied.

"Why don't you stay out longer and catch more fish?" the American then asked.

"I have sufficient to support the needs of our home," the Mexican said.

"But," the American then asked, "What do you do with the rest of your time?"

The Mexican fisherman smiled and with a twinkle in his eye said, "I do a lot at home, señor. I play with my niños, lend a hand with the comida, and then take a siesta with my wife, Maria. After helping the kids with their homework, we stroll to the plaza in the evening where we listen to the guitar and sing with our amigos. I have a full and wonderful life, señor."

The American scoffed, "I am a Harvard MBA and could help you. You should spend a lot more time fishing, and with the proceeds you can buy a bigger boat, and with the proceeds from the bigger boat you could buy several boats, eventually you would have a fleet of fishing boats . . . Instead of selling your catch to a middleman, you would sell directly to the consumers, eventually opening your own can factory. You would control the product, processing, and distribution. You would need to leave this small coastal fishing village and move to Mexico City, then LA, and eventually New York, where you will run your expanding enterprise."

The Mexican fisherman asked, "But señor, how long will this all take?"

To which the American replied, "Not long, maybe fifteen to twenty years."

"But what then, señor?"

The American laughed, "That's the best part. When the time is right, you will sell your company stock to the public and become very rich; you will make millions."

"Millions, señor? Then what?"

The American said slowly, "Then you would retire and move to a small coastal fishing village where you could do a lot at home. You play with your grandkids, help with the comida, take a siesta with your wife, and stroll to the plaza in the evenings where you could listen to the guitar and sing with your amigos . . ." (Yen, 2002; Hill and Anderson, 2004, pp. 150–151).

References

Bednar, D. A. (2009, November). More diligent and concerned at home. *Ensign*, 39(5), 17–20.

Benson, E. T. (1987, February). To the mothers in Zion. Address given at a fireside for parents; published as a pamphlet. Salt Lake City: The Church of Jesus Christ of Latter-day Saints.

Brophy, B. (1995, December 11). Stressless—and simple—in Seattle. *U.S. News and World Report, 11,* 96–97.

Carlson, D. S., Kacmar, K. M., & Stepina, L. P. (1995). An examination of two aspects of work-family conflict: time and identity. *Women in Management Review, 10*(2), 17–25.

Eisenberg, M. E., Olson, R. E., Neumark-Sztainer, D., Story, M., & Bearinger, L. H. (2004). Correlations between family meals and psychosocial well-being among adolescents. *Archives of Pediatrics and Adolescent Medicine, 158,* 792–796.

Fiese, B. H., Foley, K. P., & Spagnola, M. (2006). Routine and ritual elements in family mealtimes: Context for child well-being and family identity. In Larson, R. W., Wiley, A. R., Branscomb, K. R. (Eds.). *Family mealtime as a context of development and socialization.* In *New Directions for Child and Adolescent Development,* 111. Ann Arbor, MI: Wiley Periodicals.

First Presidency. (1999, February 27). Letter regarding parents teaching children. *Church News.* Retrieved from http://www.ldschurchnews.com/articles/35284/Letter-regarding-parents-teaching-children.html

First Presidency and Council of the Twelve Apostles. (1995, November). The family: A proclamation to the world. *Ensign, 25*(11), 102.

Hales, R. D. (2010, May). Our duty to God: The mission of parents and leaders to the rising generation. *Ensign, 40*(5), 95.

Hill, E. J. (1999). Put family first—work will be there when you return. *Deseret News.* Retrieved from http://www.deseretnews.com/article/729646/Put-family-first----work-will-be-there-when-you-return.html?pg=1

Hill, E. J., & Martinengo, G. (2005). Harmonizing paid work and home life. In S. K. Klein & E. J. Hill (Eds.). *Creating home as a sacred center: Principles for everyday living.* Provo, UT: BYU Academic Publishing.

Hill, E. J., & Anderson, R. (2004). Life harmony: Helping clients find peace in a busy life. *AMCAP Journal, 29,* 143–151.

Hill, E. J., Allen, S., Jacob, J. I., Bair, A. F., Bikhazi, S. L., Langeveld, A. V., . . . Walker, E. (2007). Work-family facilitation: Expanding theoretical understanding through qualitative exploration. *Advances in Developing Human Resources, 9*(4). 507–526.

Hill, E. J., Erickson, J. J., Holmes, E. K., & Ferris, M. (2010). Workplace flexibility, work hours, and work-life conflict: Finding an extra day or two. *Journal of Family Psychology, 24*(3). 349–358.

Hill, E. J., Ferris, M., & Martinson, V. (2003). Does it matter where you work? A comparison of how three work venues (traditional office, virtual office, and home office) influence aspects of work and personal/family life. *Journal of Vocational Behavior, 63*(2), 220–241.

Hill, E. J., Grzywacz, J. G., Allen, S., Blanchard, V. L., Matz-Costa, C., Shulkin, S., & Pitt-Catsouphes, M. (2008). Defining and conceptualizing workplace flexibility. *Community, Work, and Family, 11*(2), 152.

Hill, E. J., Hawkins, A. J., Ferris, M., & Weitzman, M. (2001). Finding an extra day a week: The positive effect of job flexibility on work and family life balance. *Family Relations, 50*(1), 49–58.

Hofferth, S. L., & Sandberg, J. E. (2001, May). How American children spend their time. *Journal of Marriage and the Family, 63,* 295–308.

Hunter, H. W. (1997). *The Teachings of Howard W. Hunter.* Salt Lake City: Bookcraft.

Jacob, J. I., Allen, S., Hill, E. J., Mead, N. L., & Ferris, M. (2008). Work interference with dinnertime as a mediator and moderator between work hours and work and family outcomes. *Family and Consumer Sciences Research Journal, 36*(4), 310–327.

Maxwell, N. A. (1994, May). Take especial care of your family. *Ensign, 24*(5), 88–91.

McMullin, K.B. (2002, November). Come to Zion! Come to Zion! *Ensign, 32*(11), 94.

Mindell, J. A., Telofski, L. S., Weigand, B., & Kurtz, E S. (2009). A nightly bedtime routine: Impact on sleep in young children and maternal mood. *SLEEP, 32*(5), 599–606.

Nelson, R. M. (2008). President Dieter F. Uchtdorf: A family man, a man of faith, a man foreordained. *Ensign, 38*(7), 19.

Newell, K., & Newell, L. D. (2005). Building spiritual patterns in the home. In Hart, Craig H., Newell, Lloyd D., Walton, E., & Dollahite, D. C. (Eds.). *Helping and Healing our Families.* Salt Lake City: Deseret Book.

Oaks, D. H. (1975, September). The student body and the president. *BYU Speeches.* Retrieved from http://speeches.byu.edu/reader/reader.php?id=6076

Oaks, D. H. (2007, November). Good, better, best. *Ensign, 37*(11), 107.

Perry, L. T. (2008, November). Let him do it with simplicity. *Ensign, 38*(11), 10.

Sandholtz, K., Derr, B., Bruckner, K., & Carlson, D. S. (2002). *Beyond Juggling.* San Francisco: Berrett-Koehler.

Shellenbarger, S. (1997, September 24). Work and family: These telecommuters just barely maintain their office decorum. *The Wall Street Journal*, p. B1.

Tanner, N. E. (1978, June). Happiness is home centered. *Ensign, 8*(6) 2–5.

Uchtdorf, D. F. (2009, May). We are doing a great work and cannot come down. *Ensign, 39*(5), 59–62.

Yen, Duen Hsi (2002). The American tourist and Mexican fisherman. Retrieved from http://www.noogenesis.com/pineapple/fisherman.html

Wirthlin, J. B. (2004, May). Earthly debts, heavenly debts. *Ensign, 34*(5), 40–43.

MICHAEL A. GOODMAN

2

The Influence of Faith on *Marital Commitment*

ELIGION significantly influences many American marriages. Ninety-five percent of married couples in the United States report a religious affiliation (Mahoney, Pargament, Tarakeshwar, & Swank, 2001). Not only is a religious affiliation almost universal, but around 60% of Americans report that religion is important or very important to them (McCullough, Larson, Hoyt, Koenig, & Thoresen, 2000). Over half of American married couples say they attend religious services at least monthly (Heaton & Pratt, 1990, p. 196). Even with a tendency to exaggerate religious participation, these statistics indicate that religious involvement is an important part of American marriage and family life (Christiano, 2000), so it seems logical that religious beliefs affect marital relationships. However, it is not universally accepted that religious people actually connect their religious beliefs to their marital relationships. One recent academic review suggested that connection between religious beliefs and practices "appear more heterogeneous [varied] and tenuous than family scholars have expected, with conservative religious beliefs not necessarily translating into conservative familial behavior" (Bulanda, 2011). However, some highly religious people do strongly connect their religious faith to their family life. This chapter

Divorce rates drop dramatically among active Latter-day Saints who were married in the temple. John Luke, © Intellectual Reserve, Inc.

will examine the research connecting religious beliefs to marital commitment and will examine specific doctrines held sacred by members of the Church of Jesus Christ of Latter-day Saints that seem to influence their marital commitment.

Current State of Marriage

By most accounts, the institution of marriage is in serious decline. The most recent trends regarding the state of marriage are ominous. The latest update by the National Marriage Project includes the following information: From 1970 to 2007, the number of marriages for women 15 and older has dropped by almost half, the number of divorces in the same group has increased by 15%, and the number of cohabiting couples has increased twelve-fold. The percentage of children under the age of 18 living with a single parent has increased by over 100%, whereas the percentage of children living with two married parents has decreased by 20% and the percentage of births to unmarried women has increased by about two and a half times (University of Virginia, 2008).

Members of The Church of Jesus Christ of Latter-day Saints are not immune to these troubles. Most members of the Church have firsthand knowledge of broken homes and broken hearts among those they love. Research shows that the overall divorce rate among Latter-day Saints is actually very close to the divorce rate in the general population. However, among active Latter-day Saints, especially those married in the temple, the divorce rate drops dramatically (Heaton, Bahr, & Jacobson, 2005). According to three national data sets, Mormons have a divorce rate 25% lower than the national averages. This is true if there is no differentiation between active and less-active members of the Church. Mormon couples in which at least one spouse attends church weekly have divorce rates which are 36% lower than the national averages. If both spouses attend church weekly they estimate the divorce rate is 40% lower than the national average, and finally, the estimated divorce rate for those who were married in the temple would be 70% lower than the national average at the highest. This is only an estimate based on several past studies, as the national data sets that were used for the current analysis did not contain information on temple marriage (Heaton, Bahr, & Jacobson, 2005).

Marital Commitment

For years scholars have tried to figure out what leads some couples to stay together and others to separate. One of the primary constructs used to predict whether a person will stay in their marriage is marital commitment. Studies have found that lifetime commitment to marriage is one of the most frequently mentioned attributes considered important by participants in successful, long-term marriages (Robinson, 1994, pp. 210–211). A national survey found that 73% of respondents indicated that divorce occurred because of lack of commitment (National Fatherhood Initiative, 2005, p. 32).

Though there are numerous definitions and scales used to measure a person's or couple's commitment to a relationship, most commitment constructs fall under what Stanley and Markman (1992) call *personal dedication* or *constraint commitment*. According to these researchers,

> personal dedication refers to the desire of an individual to maintain or improve the quality of his or her relationship for the joint benefit of the participants. It is evidenced by a desire (and associated behaviors) not only to continue in the relationship, but also to improve it, to sacrifice for it, to invest in it, to link personal goals to it, and to seek the partner's welfare, not simply one's own. In contrast, constraint commitment refers to forces that constrain individuals to maintain relationships regardless of their personal dedication to them. Constraints may arise from either external or internal pressures, and they favor relationship stability by making termination of a relationship more economically, socially, personally, or psychologically costly. (pp. 595–596)

Couples with a lifetime commitment to marriage are more likely to stay together. Matt Reier, © Intellectual Reserve, Inc.

Though Stanley and Markman (2011) have continued to refine the tool they use to measure these forms of commitment, the Commitment Inventory Scale, it maintains the same basic constructs. One interesting definition Stanley came to a decade later was that commitment is "a choice to give up other choices" (Stanley, 2002, "Why Commitment Develops," para. 1). Others use different terms to capture similar ideas. For example, Adams and Jones (1997) used six studies involving 1,787 participants to empirically test different ways of conceptualizing marital commitment. "Results suggested the existence of three primary dimensions of marital commitment: an attraction component based on devotion, satisfaction, and love; a moral-normative component based on a sense of personal responsibility for maintaining the marriage and on the belief that marriage is an important social and religious institution; and a constraining component based on fear of the social, financial, and emotional costs of relationship termination" (p. 1177).

Johnson, Caughlin, and Huston (1999) divide commitment into three similar components: personal commitment, moral commitment, and structural commitment. The concept of moral commitment adds another important component: commitment to the institution of marriage itself. Though by Stanley and Markman's definitions, moral commitment would normally be considered a part of dedication commitments, it is possible that it acts as a constraint as well. Wilcox found that a couple's commitment to the institution of marriage plays a strong role in marital stability (Wilcox & Nock, 2006). Regardless of which terms are used to define marital commitment, there seems to be three key elements to marital commitment (though Stanley and Markman combine the first and second into one). However conceptualized, most researchers agree that commitment to each other and to the institution of marriage are essential aspects of marital stability.

Exactly how marital commitment impacts couples is debated. Murray and Holmes (2008) conjecture that relational commitment is of value only when there are problems in the relationship. Others, including Clements and Swensen (2000), argue that relational commitment is related not only to relational stability but also to marital quality as well. Stanley (2005) found that increased marital commitment was related to better communication, increased happiness, and more constructive coping within marital relationships. It seems logical that couples who are more committed to their marriages are willing to work harder to make their relationship work. This effort would likely lead not only to greater marital stability but to greater satisfaction and meaning in their marriages. Several researchers have theorized that as long as a couple is satisfied with their relationship, structural or constraint commitment plays little to no part in a couple's day-to-day interactions and decisions. It is only when the first two aspects of commitment begin to wane that structural or constraint commitment comes into play. According to this theory, commitment acts like a seatbelt—it is really only noticed when one makes an attempt to leave. Ultimately though, as Amato (2010) points out, the theoretical and empirical underpinnings of how commitment impacts relationships are still in need of further development.

Religion and Marital Commitment

Several studies have shown that religiosity has been linked with increased marital satisfaction and stability (Bahr & Chadwick, 1985). Greater religiosity has repeatedly been related to reduced risk of divorce (Breault & Kposowa, 1987). Mahoney, Pargament, Tarakeshwar, and Swank (2001) found that the divorce rate for those who attended church was 44% compared to 60% for those who did not attend. This difference was true even after controlling for a broad range of confounding variables. A confounding variable is another known cause of divorce such as financial challenges and lower educational levels. It is important to note that none of these studies claimed to show causality. They simply confirmed that those who are more religious are more likely to have a strong commitment to their marriage and less likely to divorce. But these studies don't explain why or how religion impacts marital commitment and stability.

A few studies have specifically sought to understand how religion influences marital commitment (Larson & Goltz, 1989). However, most studies have only been able to demonstrate the correlation between religion and marital commitment. One study by Allgood, Harris, Skogrand, and Lee (2009) specifically investigated marital commitment among members of The Church of Jesus Christ of Latter-day Saints. The researchers conducted the study using a random sample of over 1,000 people, out of which over 70% were Latter-day Saints. The researchers specifically looked at the three different aspects of marital commitment. They found that Latter-day Saints had much higher-than-average marital commitment, especially among those who were most active in their faith. This study is one of the only quantitative studies that focused on marital commitment among Latter-day

Couples who consider religion to be important are less likely to divorce. Christina Smith,
© Intellectual Reserve, Inc.

Saints. Yet, the focus on more distal aspects of religion (affiliation and
church attendance) prevented the researchers from determining how the
Latter-day Saint religion specifically impacted the couple's marital commitment. However, in the last 10 years, several studies based on the American
Families of Faith Project have specifically sought to understand which religious beliefs and practices have influence on a couple's marital commitment
level (Brown, Lu, Marks, & Dollahite, 2011; Dollahite & Marks, 2009;
Lambert & Dollahite, 2008; Dollahite & Lambert, 2007; Goodman &
Dollahite, 2006; Lambert & Dollahite, 2006; Marks, 2005; Marks, 2004).

American Families of Faith Project

The American Families of Faith Project is an ongoing research project led by David Dollohite and Loren Marles that entails in-depth interviews with family members of the three Abrahamic faiths: Christianity, Judaism, and Islam. So far over 50 peer-reviewed articles have been published from this study. Couples and their children are interviewed to ascertain how they connected their faith with their family life. The sample was purposive, meaning that the participants are prototypical of the variables being studied; in this case highly religious couples with happy marriages. As such the sample is not random and therefore not immediately generalizable. However, information gained from purposive samples such as these often provide the nuanced information needed for further study of the variables of interest.

As of 2011, 445 individuals from 184 families have been interviewed as part of the project. All of the families had a high level of religious commitment (as reported by both referring clergy and the participants themselves. There were 133 Christian families (including Catholic, Mainstream Protestant, Evangelical Protestant, Orthodox, and New Christian Religious Traditions), 31 Jewish families (including Hasidic, Orthodox, Conservative, and Reformed Traditions), and 20 Muslim families (both Sunni and Shia). Slightly more than half of the families (51%) represent an ethnic or racial minority. There were 32 African American families, 13 Latino, 11 Middle Eastern, 4 East Indian, 17 Asian American, 15 Native American, and 1 Pacific Islander, with the balance of the families (90) being Caucasian. Couples were typically in their mid-forties and had been married on average for 20 years. All couples had at least one child (mean = 3.3 children). The couples interviewed resided in all eight regions of the United States.

Several of the interview questions pertained specifically to the concept of marital commitment. These questions allowed the interviewees to explain in their own words and according to their own beliefs exactly how their faith had impacted their marital commitment and how their marital commitment had impacted their family life. Analysis followed the grounded theory

Jewish (left), Christian (top right), and Islamic (bottom right) families participated in the American Families of Faith Project. © Kai Chiang (left), Dmitriy Shironosov (top right), and szefei (bottom right).

approach explicated by Strauss and Corbin (1998) as well as the analytic induction approach advocated by Gilgun (2001). These approaches allowed the researcher to look at the data without attempting to make the data fit a pre-conceived theory. Analysis revealed several themes that shed light on the possible processes by which religious faith can impact marital commitment and how increased marital commitment impacts marriage and family life.

Findings from the American Family of Faiths Project regarding Commitment

In one of the first studies published from the American Families of Faith Project, Loren Marks (2004) conducted in-depth interviews with 38 couples in order to understand how three dimensions of religion (beliefs, practices, and community) influenced the couples' marriages. Couples identified religious beliefs more often than specific practices or community as having the greatest impact on their marriages, and three themes where found among the responses: a belief supporting marriage and discouraging divorce, a belief in the importance of belief homogamy (husband/wife agreement) and the belief that God is a support to marriage. When asked how these beliefs impacted their marriages, couples listed three outcomes: stability and unity, growth and motivation to succeed, and greater happiness and peace. These outcomes match tightly to the concept of personal dedication commitment explicated by Stanley and Markman (1992), attraction and moral-normative commitment as defined by Adams & Jones (1997), and personal and moral commitment as defined by Johnson (Johnson, Caughlin, & Huston, 1999).

Next, in a study of 32 couples, Goodman and Dollahite (2006) analyzed what role these couples believed God played in their marital relationship. About 74% of the couples believed that because of God's influence on their marriages, their marriages were more stable and unified. This finding was the most frequently mentioned outcome of all. Findings also indicated that couples who believed that marriage was part of God's plan and that God was involved in their marital life perceived the greatest benefits from their religious faith. Interestingly, though the main question of this study was different from the Marks 2005 study, both studies found that these couples felt that their religious faith produced the exact same outcomes: stability and unity, growth and motivation to succeed, and greater happiness and peace.

In 2006, Lambert and Dollahite released their study of 57 couples, in which they had tried to determine how the religious faith of these couples helped them prevent, resolve, and overcome marital conflict. Couples reported that religiosity affected their marriages at three phases of the conflict process: problem prevention, conflict resolution, and relationship reconciliation. Though this study did not specifically investigate commitment, two aspects of this study add to our understanding of marital commitment. Like the Marks 2005 study, couples in this expanded sample stated that their religious beliefs were a strong influence on their family life and that their beliefs lead to greater levels of marital commitment. Specifically, couples reported that their religious beliefs increased their commitment to relationship permanence. "God hates divorce" or "marriage is forever" were some of the common expressions couples made regarding commitment to relationship permanence. This commitment generated a desire within couples to reconcile with each other and work through difficult times. Those interviewed emphasized being "committed to the relationship no matter what problems might arise." (p. 445)

Using the same sample, Dollahite and Lambert (2007) published another study that examined how the religious faith of a couple promoted marital fidelity. The research pointed to four ways that religion impacted a couple's commitment to remain faithful: (a) religious belief and practice sanctified their marriage and thereby improved marital quality that indirectly promoted fidelity; (b) religious vows and faith involvement fortified marital commitment to fidelity; (c) religious belief strengthened couples' moral values, which promoted fidelity in marriage; and (d) religious involvement improved spouses' relationship with God, which encouraged them to avoid actions such as infidelity that they believed would displease God. Notice again the tight match to earlier findings from the original samples in this project as well as to the earlier conceptualizations of marital commitment by Stanley and Markman, Adams and Jones, and Johnson.

A 2008 study by Lambert and Dollahite examined how the faith of couples impacted their marital commitment. Analysis indicated that these couples' religious beliefs and practices lead to three specific processes by which their commitment to their marriage was strengthened. These processes involved including God as the third cord in their marriage, an inclusion that binds couples to each other with strong ties; believing in marriage as a religious institution that can and should last; and finding meaning in committing to marriage. Overall, Lambert and Dollahite were able to show several connections between the couples' beliefs and practices and their marital commitment by researching how couples' religion helps them resolve conflict, how their religious faith promotes fidelity, and how their faith directly impacts their marital commitment.

Based on the data from the American Families of Faith Project, Marks and Dollahite (2011) analyzed data from all 184 couples. In their analysis of the interviews, they found eight specific ways these couples saw their religious faith impacting their marriages.

1. Sacred, meaningful family rituals and practices that unify the marriage and family
2. A shared belief system and worldview
3. A view of God as the "third cord" in their marriage which binds couples to each other with strong ties
4. A specific belief in marriage as a religious institution that can and should last
5. A focused effort to find meaning in committing to marriage
6. A desire to work to prevent problems in the relationship
7. An ability to draw on sacred beliefs and practices to resolve conflict
8. A religiously based motivation to work toward relational reconciliation" (p. 191)

As can be seen, these eight connections match the findings from all of the other studies thus far, which indicates a fair amount of theoretical and conceptual saturation.

Also based on the data from the American Families of Faith Project, Goodman, Dallahite, and Marks (2012) researched using data from 24 LDS couples located in seven states. This study pointed to specific beliefs such as the eternal nature of marriage and specific practices such as temple attendance, prayer, scripture study, and church attendance, which impacted these couples marital commitment. The following section will take a closer look at specific LDS beliefs that are connected to marital commitment.

Latter-day Saint Religious Beliefs and Marital Commitment

As the above literature review demonstrates, some highly religious couples perceive religious beliefs as having a strong influence on their marital behavior. In several studies cited above, religious beliefs were more likely to be specifically associated with marital commitment than other aspects of religiosity were, including religious practices and religious community. In addition, as noted earlier, Goodman and Dollahite (2006) found that couples who believed marriage was part of God's plan experienced more benefits from their religious involvement, including greater marital commitment. This belief appeared to be a gateway that determined the extent of influence religion would play in their marital relationships.

Latter-day Saints mentioned the eternal nature of marriage in relations to marital commitment more frequently than couples of other religious affiliations. Though Latter-day Saints were not the only highly religious couples who believed that marriage can last beyond death, they made the vast majority of such references in the American Families of Faith project. In fact, Goodman, Dollahite, and Marks (2012) noted that all 24 Latter-day Saint couples who were part of the American Families of Faith Project specifically mentioned that their belief that families not only can but should last forever was a strong influence on their personal marital commitment.

The following quotations from this study illustrate some possible pathways by which this fairly distinctive Latter-day Saint belief could impact marital commitment (Goodman, Dollahite, & Marks, 2012). First, several couples reported that they felt greater security in their relationship because divorce was simply not an option. One Latter-day Saint wife stated:

> Well, one of the things that [my husband] and I were talking about just the other day is that we know that we are gonna be married forever. Divorce is not an option; just being married until one of us dies isn't part of the plan. So, we know that neither one of us is

going anywhere, you know, even if we are having a miserable day, or week, or month, if it comes to that, we are not worried that the other person is gonna take off, and we are not worried that our marriage is falling apart. (p. 564)

The belief that divorce was not an option lead some couples to say they approach serious problems with the understanding that they must find the solution because failure was not an option. Another Latter-day Saint wife explained:

No matter what happens . . . because we believe in the eternities, and that marriage is forever, that no matter how bad, or whatever happens to us, we're going to make it work no matter what. We like to say that the "D" word [divorce] . . . never come[s] up in the house. (p. 564)

A Latter-day Saint husband described how the belief in eternal marriage helped him and his wife focus on long-term solutions even if those solutions were more difficult than an easier quick fix.

The decisions you make, if you know they are going to affect your eternal future are different than the decisions you make if you knew it was just till you die. . . . If you are looking at long range instead of short range, just here on earth, the decisions you make are different.

Finally, some couples pointed out that their marital commitment went beyond their commitment to their spouses and marriages and extended to their actual commitment to God. Realizing that marriage is part of God's plan for their eternities meant that they were not only accountable to each other but also to God for their relationship. One Latter-day Saint husband stated that "we are committed to the institution I think even more than to one another" (564–565).

Understanding the importance of marriage in God's plan of happiness may help husbands and wives focus on long-term solutions and approaches within their marriage. Craig Dimond, © Intellectual Reserve, Inc.

As is evident by the above examples, the doctrine of eternal marriage has a potentially powerful effect in the lives of Latter-day Saints who believe it. Latter-day Saint theology on the eternal nature of marriage and family life is extensive, deep, and nuanced. Given the space constraints in most scholarly journals as well as the secular audience, only brief references can be made to the specifics of this doctrine. However, the audience for this volume and the fact that each chapter explicitly seeks to wed current social science research together with specific Latter-day Saint doctrines and beliefs allow a much more nuanced exploration of the doctrines involved here.

The Doctrine of Eternal Marriage

President Boyd K. Packer (2004) has repeatedly taught that "true doctrine, understood, changes attitudes and behavior. The study of the doctrines of the gospel will improve behavior quicker than a study of behavior will improve behavior" (p. 79). This statement seems to be born out in the lives of the highly religious couples interviewed as part of the American Families of Faith Project. Almost all of the Christian, Jewish, and Muslim couples linked specific religious beliefs to different aspects of their marital lives. The Latter-day Saint couples universally did. As mentioned above, the doctrine referred to most frequently by the Latter-day Saint couples was the eternal nature of marriage. They felt that this doctrine had tremendous impact on their marital commitment and on how they worked through the difficulties of married life. There are several aspects of the doctrine of eternal marriage which might have an impact on a couple's commitment. The following discussion will highlight some of these important aspects. This exploration will illustrate why in the gospel of Jesus Christ, marriage is not a tangential issue relating to couple's' commitment to their relationship but rather is an integral part of the Latter-day Saint definition of exaltation.

Prophets, seers, and revelators have spoken for millennia regarding the divine origin and centrality of marriage and family in the gospel plan. President Joseph Fielding Smith (1966) taught that marriage involves "an eternal principle ordained before the foundation of the world and instituted on this earth before death came into it" (p. 25). Bruce R. McConkie (1995) taught that "marriage and the family unit are the central part of the plan of progression and exaltation. All things center in and around the family unit in the eternal perspective. Exaltation consists in the continuation of the family unit in eternity. Those for whom the family unit continues have eternal life; all others have a lesser degree of salvation in the mansions that are prepared" (p. 546). Brigham Young (1973) taught that marriage "lays the foundations for worlds, for angels, and for the Gods; for intelligent beings to be crowned with glory, immortality, and eternal lives. In fact, it is the thread which runs from the beginning to the end of the holy Gospel of salvation."

In the lifetime of most married Latter-day Saints, no document has had a more central role in shaping what members believe about the doctrine of eternal marriage than "The Family: A Proclamation to the World." The very first paragraph makes clear the preeminent position of marriage and family in Latter-day Saint doctrine: "We the First Presidency and the Council of the Twelve Apostles of The Church of Jesus Christ of Latter-day Saints, solemnly proclaim that marriage between a man and a woman is ordained of God and that the family is central to the Creator's plan for the eternal destiny of His children" (First Presidency, 1995). The document ends with this solemn warning: "We warn that individuals who violate covenants of chastity, who abuse spouse or offspring, or who fail to fulfill family responsibilities will one day stand accountable before God. Further, we warn that the disintegration of the family will bring upon individuals, communities, and nations the calamities foretold by ancient and modern prophets."

Statements like these and countless others that could be cited leave very little ambiguity as to the importance of marriage in God's plan of happiness. In fact, President Spencer W. Kimball (1973) taught that marriage and family are not only central to Heavenly Father's plan but that "family is the great plan of life as conceived and organized by our Father in Heaven" (p. 15). As discussed earlier, couples who believe that marriage is part of God's plan and that God is deeply concerned about marriage approach their marriages differently. Their commitment level rises, and their approach to marital challenges becomes more purposeful. As can be seen from the above doctrinal statements, Latter-day Saints have many reasons to believe the marriage is part of God's plan and that it is imperative as part of their relationship to him. This belief, in and of itself, may go a long way to explaining why active, believing Latter-day Saints are so committed to their marriages.

Many of these statements hint at the centrality of marriage and family to God's plan for his children. However, they do not explain *why* marriage and family are so central to the plan of salvation and why President Kimball

(1973) would say "Family *is* the great plan of life." To understand the reason for such an emphasis, it is necessary to take a closer look at what Latter-day Saint doctrine teaches about the plan itself. When we understand the plan according to Latter-day Saint beliefs, we can see why active members of the Church have a tendency to have very strong commitment to marriage as both a general concept and a personal reality.

The Plan of Salvation and the Nature of God

Like members of virtually every Christian church, members of The Church of Jesus Christ of Latter-day Saints believe Jesus Christ died so that they can one day live with God in heaven. Most Christians would refer to this as being saved. This answer is well supported by Latter-day Saint scripture (see 2 Nephi 2:25; Matthew 5:3; 10, 12, Luke 18:22; Mosiah 2:41; Alma 11:37; D&C 6:37; D&C 20:24; Moses 7:21). Sometimes the scriptures refer to this aspect of our eternal destiny as "everlasting life" (see John 3:16; 3 Nephi 5:13; D&C 45:5). If members of the Church were asked why they are here on earth, the answer would, in part, likely refer to *returning* to live with Heavenly Father in His kingdom since they believe we already lived with him once before. We sometimes refer to being saved as inheriting everlasting life. Although the term everlasting life is descriptive of the duration of our destiny, it is less descriptive of the quality.

Doctrine and Covenants 14:7 uses a more descriptive term: "If you keep my commandments and endure to the end you shall have eternal life, which gift is the greatest of all the gifts of God." We learn from Doctrine and Covenants 19:10–12 that eternal is another name for God. Therefore, eternal life is another way of saying God's life, or the kind of life that God lives. God's work and glory is to bring to pass not only our immortality (or our everlasting life) but our eternal life—life like his. Both concepts, duration and quality, are brought together in Moses 1:39: "For behold, this is my work and my glory—to bring to pass the immortality and eternal life of man." Though living forever is an important part of our destiny, it is important to make a distinction between immortality and eternal life. Satan and all who follow him are immortal inasmuch as they will have no end, but they certainly don't enjoy eternal life. We seek eternal life—life like God's.

However, such a belief does not propose becoming equal to God. Latter-day Saints believe that he is our Heavenly Father and will always be our Heavenly Father. We worship him as our Creator and our God. That relationship will never change. We will never be his equal and we will always worship him as our God. However, we believe that God intends to make us as he is. We believe that God is truly our Heavenly Father and that we are his offspring (Acts 17:29). Latter-day Saints take seriously, and quite literally, the words of Paul that "the Spirit itself beareth witness with our spirit, that we are the children of God: And if children, then heirs; heirs of God, and joint-heirs with Christ; if so be that we suffer with him, that we may be also glorified together" (Romans 8:16–17). Again this does not mean equal to, but instead like unto God, or as he is. But if we are meant to be like God, what is God like?

We must come to better understand the nature of our Heavenly Father and what it means to become like him if we are to fulfill our ultimate destiny. It is obviously beyond our knowledge as well as the scope of this chapter to seek to exhaustively define the nature of our Father in Heaven. The entire canon of scriptures is woefully inadequate for such a task. God's character is made up of all that is beautiful, virtuous, and perfect in infinite measure. If you were to list every attribute that is "virtuous, lovely, or of good report or praiseworthy" (Articles of Faith 1:13), and place the word "all" in front of it, it would be but a beginning of a description of God. As the thirteenth article of faith finishes, "we seek after these things." Developing these attributes in perfection is completely outside of our ability to do on our own. However, we believe that through Jesus Christ, "[we] can do all things" (Philippians 4:13). We believe it is not only possible for us to develop these attributes but that God wants, even commands, us to do so.

To summarize, Heavenly Father is perfect and he wants us to become perfect also. However, what does becoming perfect have to do with marriage and the plan of salvation? Further, what does becoming like God have to do with Latter-day Saint commitment to marriage? To answer these question, it is necessary to examine not only what God is like but also what God does. What is God's purpose? Why does he do what he does? These questions get to the very definition of what it means to a Latter-day Saint to be like God. What does our Father in Heaven do with his perfection? A most succinct answer is found in the verse of scriptures quoted earlier from the book of Moses: "For behold, this is my work and my glory—to bring to pass the immortality and eternal life of man" (Moses 1:39).

Christians throughout the world would likely agree that God is seeking to save his children, or to help them achieve eternal life. However, for members of The Church of Jesus Christ of Latter-day Saints, this truth takes on added meaning because, as was stated above, we believe eternal life is synonymous with living a life like God's. This flows from how Latter-day Saints view God's relationship with His children. Besides viewing God as an all-powerful, perfected being, we view God as our literal Father in Heaven. We believe we are the children, the offspring, of God.

And we believe that God does what righteous earthly parents try to do—help their children grow to be all that they can be. This connection begins to illuminate what President Kimball meant when he said family is the great plan of life. God is a full-time, totally dedicated parent. His work and glory is raising his children. What's more, he is not alone. As is obvious in the natural process of procreation in mortality, you cannot have a father without a mother. So it is in eternity. Our Father in Heaven is not alone in his work. He has an equally glorious and perfected companion—our Heavenly Mother. In other words, God is married. President Harold B. Lee (1996) explained that "that great hymn 'O My Father' puts it correctly when Eliza R. Snow wrote, 'In the heav'ns are parents single? No, the thought makes reason stare! Truth is reason; truth eternal tells me I've a mother there.' Born of a Heavenly Mother, sired by a Heavenly Father, we knew Him, we were in His house . . ." (p. 22).

God is not only married, but the very definition of godhood or exaltation is dependent on his relationship with Heavenly Mother. We learn in

Doctrine and Covenants 131:1–4 that "in the celestial glory there are three heavens or degrees; and in order to obtain the highest [to be exalted like our heavenly parents], a man must enter into this order of the priesthood (meaning the new and everlasting covenant of marriage); and if he does not, he cannot obtain it. He may enter into the other, but that is the end of his kingdom; he cannot have an increase." In other words, eternal marriage is a necessary precondition of exaltation. There is no such thing as an unmarried god. Doctrine and Covenants 132:19 teaches that those who enter into the new and everlasting covenant of marriage and are faithful to it will "pass by the angels, and the gods, which are set there, to their exaltation and glory in all things, as hath been sealed upon their heads, which glory shall be a fulness and a continuation of the seeds forever and ever." It is only through the union of man and woman, eternally married, that a "continuation of the seeds forever and ever" is possible.

Though we know very few details regarding Heavenly Father and Heavenly Mother's marriage, there can be few things more central to their nature. All that they do is for the welfare and eternal salvation of their children. Elder Oaks (2001) taught that "the work of God is to bring to pass the eternal life of His children (see Moses 1:39), and all that this entails in the birth, nurturing, teaching, and sealing of our Heavenly Father's children. Everything else is lower in priority" (pp. 83–84). As Elder Dennis E. Simmons (2004) explained, "He [God] has already achieved godhood. Now His only objective is to help us—to enable us to return to Him and be like Him and live His kind of life eternally" (p. 73).

This very doctrine is at the foundation of our understanding of eternal marriage. The destiny of mankind is to become like our heavenly parents. This capacity is part of our premortal, mortal, and postmortal nature. The First Presidency of Heber J. Grant, Anthony W. Ivins, and Charles W. Nibley taught that "man is the child of God, formed in the divine image and endowed with divine attributes, and even as the infant son of an earthly father and mother is capable in due time of becoming a man, so that undeveloped off-spring of celestial parentage is capable, by experience through ages and aeons, of evolving into a God" (Clark, 1965–1975, p. 244). Elder Dallin H. Oaks (1995) taught that "the purpose of mortal life and the mission of The Church of Jesus Christ of Latter-day Saints is to prepare the sons and daughters of God for their eternal destiny—to become like our heavenly parents" (p. 7).

Through understanding the nature of God and our relationship to him, we come to understand that our nature is his nature in embryo. God is by nature a relational being, eternally married to his coequal: Heavenly Mother. By eternal destiny we too have the seeds of that same nature within us. If our eternal destiny depends on our being eternally married, our deepest, most innate spiritual nature must be in line with this destiny. As Howard W. Hunter (1997) taught, "My spiritual reasoning tells me that because God is an exalted being, holy and good, that man's supreme goal (and destiny) is to be like him" (p. 15).

The Prophet Joseph Smith taught that "God himself was once as we are now, and is an exalted man, and sits enthroned in yonder heavens! That is the great secret. If the veil were rent today, and the great God who holds this world in its orbit, and who upholds all worlds and all things by His power, was to make himself visible—I say, if you were to see him today, you would see him like a man in form—like yourselves in all the person, image, and very form as a man" (Roberts, 1971, p. 304). President Lorenzo Snow (1919) completed this thought with the famous couplet "As man now is, God once was. As God now is, man may be" (p. 656).

Being like God means that our supreme goal and destiny is linked to our relationship with our eternal companion. As Elder Henry B. Eyring (1998) explained, "the requirement that we be one is not for this life alone. It is to be without end. The first marriage was performed by God in the garden when Adam and Eve were immortal. He placed in men and women from the beginning a desire to be joined together as man and wife forever to dwell in families in a perfect, righteous union" (66). Though the Lord has not revealed many details of how this will be in the afterlife, we know of a surety that it will be. We know that we are destined to become like he is. We are destined to be married for all eternity.

This doctrine, as shown through both the studies mentioned above, and the daily lives of millions of Latter-day Saints, guides the thoughts and actions of Latter-day Saints who understand the beliefs of the Church in relation to marriage and family. Other than Jesus Christ and his Atonement, it would be hard to find anything more central to the beliefs of members of the Church of Jesus Christ of Latter-day Saints than eternal marriage. Because Latter-day Saints believe it is both our nature and our destiny to become as God is now, we naturally feel a great commitment to marriage and family. Thus marriage and family are much more than social constructs to believing Latter-day Saints. They are the central organizing constructs of our existence. In some ways, they epitomize the concept of sanctification as defined by Annette Mahoney and colleagues. Marriage and family become endowed with sacred qualities and Latter-day Saints believe that God is not only interested in but also integrally involved in their marriages. They believe that their eternal destiny depends on it. Without eternal marriage, Latter-day Saints do not believe it possible to realize their true nature and divine destiny. For these reasons, Latter-day Saints who understand the basics of their own theology are prone to show a profound and deep commitment to their marriages. Thus marital commitment is not only a social value, it is a divine mandate backed up by divine design and upheld through divine means.

References

Adams, J. M., & Jones, W. H. (1997). The conceptualization of marital commitment: An integrative analysis. *Journal of Personality and Social Psychology, 72*(5), 1177–1196.

Allgood, S. M., Harris, S., Skogrand, L., & Lee, T. R. (2009, January). Marital commitment and religiosity in a religiously homogenous population. *Marriage and Family Review, 45*(1), 52–67.

Amato, P. R. (2010, June). Research on divorce: Continuing trends and new developments. *Journal of Marriage and Family, 72,* 650–666.

Bahr, H. M., & Chadwick, B. A. (1985, May). Religion and family in Middletown, USA. *Journal of Marriage and the Family, 47*, 407–414.

Breault, K. D., & Kposowa, A. J. (1987, August). Explaining divorce in the United States: A study of 3,111 counties, 1980. *Journal of Marriage and Family, 49*, 549–558.

Brown, T., Lu, Y., Marks, L. D., & Dollahite, D. C. (2011). Meaning-making across three dimensions of religious experience: A qualitative exploration. *Counseling and Spirituality, 30*(2), 11–36.

Bulanda, J. R. (2011, September). Doing family, doing gender, doing religion: Structured ambivalence and the religion-family connection. *Journal of Family Theory & Review, 3*, 179.

Christiano, K. J. (2000). Religion and the family in modern American culture. In S. Houseknecht & J. Pankhurst (Eds.), *Family, Religion, and Social Change in Diverse Societies* (pp. 43–78). New York: Oxford University Press.

Clark, J. R. (comp.). (1965–1975). *Messages of the First Presidency of The Church of Jesus Christ of Latter-day Saints* (vol. 5). Salt Lake City: Bookcraft.

Clements, R., & Swensen, C. H. (2000). Commitment to one's spouse as a predictor of marital quality among older couples. *Current Psychology, 19*(2), 110–119.

Darwin, T., & Cornwall, M. (1990). Religion and Family in the Eighties: Discovery and Development. *Journal of Marriage and the Family, 52*, 983–992.

Dollahite, D. C., & Lambert, N. M. (2007). Forsaking all others: How religious involvement promotes marital fidelity in Christian, Jewish, and Muslim couples. *Review of Religious Research, 48*, 290–307.

Dollahite, D. C., & Marks, L. D. (2009). A conceptual model of family and religious processes in a diverse, national sample of highly religious families. *Review of Religious Research, 50*, 373–391.

Eyring, H. B. (1998, May). That we may be one. *Ensign, 28*(5), 66.

First Presidency and Council of the Twelve Apostles. (1995, November). The family: A proclamation to the world. *Ensign, 25*(11), 102.

Gilgun, J. F. (2001). Case-based research, analytic induction, and theory development: The future and the past. Paper presented at the 31st Theory Construction and Research Methodology Workshop, National Council on Family Relations, Rochester, New York.

Goodman, M. A. & Dollahite, D. C. (2006). How religious couples perceive the influence of God in their marriage. *Review of Religious Research, 48*(2), 141–155.

Goodman, M. A., Dollahite, D. C, & Marks, L. D. (2012). Exploring transformational processes and meaning in LDS marriages. *Marriage & Family Review, 48*(6), 555–582.

Heaton, T. B., & Pratt, E. L. (1990). The effects of religious homogamy on marital satisfaction and stability. *Journal of Family Issues, 11*(2), 191–207.

Heaton, T. B., & Goodman, K. L. (1985). Religion and family formation. *Review of Religious Research, 26*, 343–359.

Heaton, T. B., Bahr, S. J., & Jacobson, C. K. (2005). Mormon families over the life course. In *A Statistical Profile Of Mormons: Health, Wealth, And Social Life*, pp. 79–121. Lewiston, NY: Edwin Mellen.

Hunter, H. W. (1997). *The teachings of Howard W. Hunter: Fourteenth president of the Church of Jesus Christ of Latter-day Saints*. C. J. Williams, (Ed.). Salt Lake City: Bookcraft.

Johnson, M. P., Caughlin, J. P., & Huston, T. L. (1999, February). The tripartite nature of marital commitment: Personal, moral, and structural reasons to stay married. *Journal of Marriage and the Family, 61*, 160–177.

Kimball, S. W. (1973). The family influence. *Ensign, 3*(7), 15.

Lambert, N. M., & Dollahite, D. C. (2007). Forsaking all others: How religious involvement promotes marital fidelity in Christian, Jewish, and Muslim couples. *Review of Religious Research, 48*(3), 290–307.

Lambert, N. M., & Dollahite, D. C. (2006, October). How religiosity helps couples prevent, resolve, and overcome marital conflict. *Family Relations, 55*, 439–449.

Lambert, N. M., & Dollahite, D. C. (2008). The threefold cord: Marital commitment in religious couples. *Journal of Family Issues, 29*, 592–614.

Larson, L. E., & Goltz, J. W. (1989). Religious participation and marital commitment. *Review of Religious Research, 30*(4), 387–400.

Lee, H. B. (1996). *The teachings of Harold B. Lee: Eleventh president of The Church of Jesus Christ of Latter-day Saints*, ed. Clyde J. Williams, Salt Lake City: Bookcraft.

Mahoney, A., Pargament, K., Jewell, T., Swank, A., Scott, E., Emery, E., & Rye, M. (1999). Marriage and the spiritual realm: The role of proximal and distal religious constructs in marital functioning. *Journal of Family Psychology, 13,* 321–338.

Mahoney, A., Pargament, K., Tarakeshwar, N., & Swank, A. (2001). Religion in the home in the 1980s and 1990s: A meta-analytic review and conceptual analyses of links between religion, marriage, and parenting. *Journal of Family Psychology, 15*(4), 559–596.

Marks, L. D. (2004). Sacred practices in highly religious families: Christian, Jewish, Mormon, and Muslim perspectives. *Family Process, 43*(2), 217–231.

Marks, L. D. (2005). Religion and bio-psycho-social health: A review and conceptual model. *Journal of Religion and Health, 44*(2), 173–186.

Marks, L. D., & Dollahite, D. C. (2011). Mining the meanings from psychology of religion's correlation mountain. *Journal of Psychology of Religion and Spirituality, 3,* 181–193.

McConkie, B. R. (1994). *Doctrinal New Testament commentary,* (vol. 1). Salt Lake City: Bookcraft.

McCullough, M. E., Larson, D. B., Hoyt, W. T., Koenig, H. G., & Thoresen, C. (2000). Religious involvement and mortality: A meta-analytic review. *Health Psychology, 19*(3), 211–222.

McDonald, G. W. (1981, November). Structural exchange and marital interaction. *Journal of Marriage and Family, 44,* 825–839.

Murray, S. L., & Holmes, J. G. (2008). The commitment-insurance system: Self-esteem and the regulation of connection in close relationships. In M. P. Zanna (Ed.), Advances in experimental social psychology (Vol. 40, pp. 1–60). Amsterdam: Elsevier Press.

National Fatherhood Institute. (2005). With this ring: A national survey on marriage in America. Retrieved from http://www.smartmarriages.com/nms.pdf.

Oaks, D. H. (1995, October). Same-gender attraction. *Ensign, 25*(10), 7.

Oaks, D. H. (2001, May). Focus and priorities. *Ensign, 31*(5), 83–84.

Packer, B. K. (2004, May). Do not fear. *Ensign, 34*(5), 79.

Roberts, B. H. (1971). *History of the Church of Jesus Christ of Latter-day Saints* (Vol. 6). Salt Lake City: Deseret News.

Robinson, L. C. (1994, March). Religious orientation in enduring marriage: An exploratory study. *Review of Religious Research, 35*(3), 207–218.

Sherkat, D. E., & Ellison, C. G. (1999). Recent developments and current controversies in the sociology of religion. *Annual Review of Sociology, 25*, 363–394.

Shrum, W. (1980). Religion and marital instability: Change in the 1970's? *Review of Religious Research, 21*, 135–147.

Simmons, D. E. (2004, May). But if not . . . *Ensign, 34*(5), 73.

Smith, J. F. (1966). *The way to perfection.* Salt Lake City: Deseret Book.

Snow, L. C. (1919, June). *Improvement Era, 12*(8), 656.

Stanley, S. M. (2002, July). What is it with men and commitment, anyway? Keynote address to the 6th Annual Smart Marriages Conference. Washington, DC. Retrieved from http://www.smartmarriages.com/stanley.men.anyway.html.

Stanley, S. M. (2005). *The power of commitment: A guide to active lifelong love.* San Francisco: Jossey-Bass.

Stanley, S. M., & Markman, H. J. (1992, August). Assessing commitment in personal relationships. *Journal of Marriage and Family, 54*(3), 595–608.

Stanley, S. M., & Markman, H. J. (2011). The revised commitment inventory: Psychometrics and use with unmarried couples. *Journal of Family Issues, 32*(6), 820–841.

Strauss, A. C., & Corbin, J. M. (1998). *Basics of qualitative research: Techniques and procedures for developing grounded theory.* Newbury Park, CA: Sage.

University of Virginia. (2008). National Marriage Project. Retrieved from http://www.stateofourunions.org/pdfs/2008update.pdf.

Wilcox, W. B., & Nock, S. L. (2006, March) What's love got to do with it? Equality, equity, commitment and women's marital quality. *Social Forces, 84*(3), 1321–1345.

Young, B. (1973). *Discourses of Brigham Young.* Comp. J. A. Widtsoe. Salt Lake City: Deseret Book.

MARK D. OGLETREE

3

Healing the Time-Starved Marriage

Time flies on wings of lightning;
We cannot call it back.
It comes, then passes forward
Along its onward track.
And if we are not mindful,
The chance will fade away,
For life is quick in passing.
'Tis as a single day.
(*Hymns*, no. 226)

No matter how wealthy we are or how poor, no matter how intelligent we are or how ignorant, no matter whom we are related to or how attractive we are, each one of us has the same amount of time allotted to us each day. We cannot purchase extra minutes, create extra hours, or trade rainy days for sunny ones. One of the greatest challenges and opportunities of this life is to learn to manage the twenty-four hours a day that each one of us has been given. How we allocate our time is driven by what we value the most, who we love the most, and duties and responsibilities that demand our attention. President Brigham Young taught that we should be "indebted to God for the ability to use time to advantage, and he will require of us a strict account of [its] disposition" (*Teachings*, 1997, p. 286).

One of the most significant challenges in modern marriage is balancing the demands and pressures that are placed upon husbands and wives. Family expert Judith Wallerstein explained:

> In today's marriages, in which people work long hours, travel exten-
> sively, and juggle careers with family, more forces tug at the rela-
> tionship than ever before. Modern marriages are battered by the
> demands of her workplace as well as his, by changing community
> values, by anxiety about making ends meet each month, by geo-
> graphical moves, by unemployment and recession, by the vicissitudes
> of child care, and a host of other issues. (Wallerstein & Blakeslee,
> 1995, p. 7)

Latter-day Saints are not immune from these time-related challenges. Indeed, perhaps one of the most significant trials in the lives of contemporary Latter-day Saint couples is the apportionment of time. With so much to do, how can husbands and wives find time for each other? Careers, church responsibilities, children's activities, household duties, and community involvement often interfere with maintaining a close connection with one's spouse. Many contemporary couples seem to spend the bulk of their time in other pursuits, neglecting what should be their highest priority—their sacred, covenantal marriage. It seems that the longer people are married, the less time they spend together (Kingston & Nock, 1987). Yet the amount of time couples spend together in face-to-face interaction is critically important to marital happiness and satisfaction (Glorieux, Minnen, & Tienoven, 2010).

Unfortunately, too many ancillary activities can keep couples distracted from each other. Today, being hyperbusy is the new status symbol; the social prizes no longer go to the wealthiest, but the busiest. As contemporary couples attempt to "keep all the balls in the air," marital connection and intimacy are often placed on the sacrificial altar. Marriage expert Michele Weiner-Davis (1992) argues that the most significant contributor to the breakdown in marriages today is the lack of time together.

Since husbands and wives are often pulled in different directions, the strength of their relationship and marital satisfaction often suffers. In fact, research confirms that couples who experience a lack of time together report lower marital satisfaction (Umberson, Williams, Powers, Liu, & Needham, 2005). In the National Survey of Marital Strengths, spending time together was identified as one of the top ten strengths for happily married couples; 71% of happy couples agreed with the statement, "We have a good balance of leisure time spent together and separately" (Olson, 1980, p. 3). Conversely, only 17% of unhappy couples felt that they spent a healthy dose of leisure time together (p. 3). In the same study, researchers identified the lack of time together as one of the top ten stumbling blocks for married couples. Over 80% of husbands and wives who were having struggles in their marriage identified insufficient couple time as a significant problem (p. 5). Finally, in measuring couple connection and closeness, 97% of happy couples reported that they enjoy spending free time together (p. 17). For couples who reported they were unhappy in their marriage, only 43% reported that they enjoyed spending time together (p. 17). If couples want to strengthen their marital bonds, spending time together is not optional! President Dieter F. Uchtdorf (2010) recently reminded us that when it comes to family relationships, "love is really spelled t-i-m-e" (p. 22).

Most couples are not likely to admit that their marriage relationship ranks at the bottom of their priority list. If they were asked, most adults would contend that their marriages and families are the most important priorities in their lives (Stinnett, 1985). However, how much time couples actually spend with each other and their families may indicate how they feel about their true priorities. Our priorities are driven by (a) what is scheduled and (b) whom we are accountable to; hence, what screams the loudest is going to receive the most attention. Doctors Les and Leslie Parrott (2006) have stated, "Time is made whenever we decide what matters most. A top priority gets more time. If you decide that collecting stamps is the most important thing in your life, you will begin to schedule your day around it, you will spend your money on it, and you will talk about it. Because you prioritize it, you'll make decisions that create more time for it" (p. 65).

What can be said, then, of Latter-day Saint couples who seem to have little time for their marriage relationships? What if they have strong desires to spend time together, but logistically it is practically impossible? For example, LDS husbands and wives may feel committed and responsible to their daughter's traveling soccer team, their son's elite baseball team, the Parent Teacher Association, their professional work schedules, and, of course, their church callings, long before their marriage or family responsibilities demand their time. After all, what would happen if a father didn't take his son to the final game of a seven-game championship series? Or what if a mother, who also happened to be the stake young women's camp director, simply refused to plan young women's camp? On the other hand, what would happen if a husband failed to take his wife out to dinner on a Friday evening? The consequences could be quite different. Unfortunately, marriages often get whatever is left over after everything else has been said, done, and accounted for, which often isn't much (Doherty, 2003). When couples fail to put their marriages first, they risk the possibility of having significant marriage complications down the road.

Meanwhile, couples who engage in meaningful activities and validate each other in the marriage are most often happy people (Gager & Sanchez, 2003). Nevertheless, even though most couples understand the value of time together, they have a difficult time managing their priorities. Most active Latter-day Saint husbands and wives are busy people. Aside from the regular duties that most couples are responsible for, members of The Church of Jesus Christ of Latter-day Saints have the extra weight of Church assignments and callings, often more children than non-Latter-day Saint parents, and

The happiest marriages are those where the couples engage in meaningful activities and validate each other. By putting the welfare of our spouse as one of our highest priorities, we can create a celestial marriage. Welden Andersen, © 2006 Intellectual Reserve, Inc.

additional financial obligations that having children entails (food, lessons, missions, college, and weddings). With increasing responsibilities and pressures, Latter-day Saint couples risk facing the consequences sure to follow when their most sacred duties and covenants are neglected. On the other hand, when we esteem the welfare of our spouses among our highest priorities, a celestial marriage can be created—celestial in this life and in the life to come (Nelson, 2008)!

This chapter will explore the time famine that many Latter-day Saint couples struggle with, common distractors that pull husbands and wives away from each other, and the rituals that can help couples reconnect and build a strong marriage.

The Time Famine

Elder Russell M. Nelson (2006) taught: "Marriage brings greater possibilities for happiness than does any other human relationship. Yet some married couples fall short of their full potential. They let their romance become rusty, they take each other for granted, allow other interests or clouds of neglect to obscure the vision of what their marriage really could be. Marriages would be happier if nurtured more carefully" (p. 36). Couples who allow their "romance [to] become rusty" or "allow other interests or clouds of neglect" to interfere with their marriages have misplaced their priorities and have limited the amount of time they spend together. Marriage is difficult enough—even without such sins of omission.

Happy and successful marriages are not easily created—they take time and effort. Elder Dean L. Larsen (1985) once explained: "I repeatedly encounter the illusion today, especially among younger people, that perfect marriages happen simply if the right two people come together. This is untrue. Marriages don't succeed automatically. Those who build happy, secure, successful marriages pay the price to do so. They work at it constantly" (p. 20).

If successful marriages take work, time, and effort, what can be said of marriages where couples have little time to devote to nurturing the marriage? Such marriages will struggle to thrive in our current time-starved environment. Contemporary marriage and family therapists often hear treatment-seeking couples make the following statements:

- "This relationship isn't working for me anymore."
- "Our needs are just so different."
- "We just grew apart."
- "Everyone else's marriage is so much better than ours."
- "He's not the same person I married."

- "After the children left home, I realized I had nothing in common with her—we had nothing."
- "Our relationship has gone stale. There is nothing exciting about being married anymore."

Although there are many potential reasons for such marriage problems, a common denominator points to a "time-starved" marriage. When couples fall in love, they spend substantial amounts of time together, supply each other with healthy doses of compliments and praise, and shower each other with physical affection. Ironically, time-starved couples cease doing the very things that propelled them towards marital bliss. Once couples decrease the amount of time they spend together, they become disconnected physically, emotionally, and spiritually. Connection in marriage reenergizes the relationship; likewise, disconnection kills it off. Over time, nurturing is replaced with nagging, and praise is supplanted with pessimism. Simply put, no marriage will survive without nurturing. Without proper nourishment, the marriage will ultimately wither—just as a lawn will without sunlight, water, or fertilizer. President Spencer W. Kimball (1976) explained further:

> Love is like a flower, and, like the body, it needs constant feeding. The mortal body would soon be emaciated and die if there were not frequent feedings. The tender flower would wither and die without food and water. And so love, also, cannot be expected to last forever unless it is continually fed with portions of love, the manifestations of esteem and admiration, the expressions of gratitude, and the consideration of unselfishness. (p. 6)

Some faithful marriage partners have time for each other only at the end of the day—when both are completely worn out and exhausted. It is difficult to build a marriage when both husband and wife are running on vapor; nevertheless, most couples continue to buy into the notion that next week will be much better. They tell themselves, "If we can just get through this week, then things will slow down," only to discover that things never change unless they put some kind of intervention in place.

About ten years ago, I interviewed over twenty middle-aged Latter-day Saint women, (interview notes in possession of the author) asking them about their most significant family challenge. These women were active, temple-attending, covenant-keeping Saints. However, they were honest enough to admit that they still had marital challenges to deal with. One woman said:

> After 46 years of marriage and raising six children, I think hyper-busyness robs LDS couples of time together. You become like pre-schoolers who engage in parallel play. . . . Just going on your personal treadmills, thinking you are doing the Lord's work, but much too busy to do the most effective work—which is relationships, talking, listening, pondering, and loving. Now, I see the same busy patterns in my own married children's lives. We are running too fast for our own good.

Another woman responded:

> My husband thinks that one of the greatest challenges for active Latter-day Saint couples is to learn to grow together, and not sepa-rately. When you and your husband are involved in children, church responsibilities, and work, it seems that you are constantly going in different directions. How do you find the time to grow together? How do you make it so that when the children leave home, you and your spouse are not complete strangers? I know several couples who were not able to work through these challenges. Now, as older couples, their marriages are hollow and unfulfilling. They spent the majority of their time on everything else except their marriages.

These women are not alone in their reflections. Many happily married Latter-day Saint couples have the desire to spend more time together—they simply do not know how to do it. They ask, "Where will the extra time come from?" In my counseling practice, I once met with a couple who were having challenges spending time together. As the wife complained to me that her husband was rarely home, and when he was home, he was exhausted. The husband responded, "What would you like me to do, quit my job so we can have more time together?" The frustrated husband then explained to his wife that he *could* quit his job, but that they would be living under a bridge instead of in a nice home. His wife rolled her eyes, feeling completely exasperated. Answers to these issues do not come easily.

Lost Priorities

Marriage requires much more than half-hearted compliance. Elder Jeffrey R. Holland (2000) taught that couples "cannot succeed in love if you keep one foot out on the bank for safety's sake. The very nature of the endeavor requires that you hold on to each other as tightly as you can and jump in the pool together." A healthy marriage requires whole-souled devotion, dedication, and commitment—and that is exactly the problem. It seems that many couples today either don't have the time, or are not able to invest the time to give such commitment to their marriages. Marriage expert Michele Weiner-Davis (2009) explained:

> I'm convinced that the single biggest contributor to the breakdown of relationships today is the fact that couples aren't spending enough time together. They aren't making their relationships a number one priority. The relationship gets put on the backburner. Everything else seems more important—careers, children, hobbies, community involvement, and personal pursuits. And when relationships aren't attended to as they should be, trouble sets in.
>
> People who don't prioritize their relationships tell me that they often end up fighting during the little time they do have together. They argue about day to day issues; unpaid bills, uncleaned

If your marriage is a priority, you make time for each other. You can find ways to spend time with each other amidst the day-to-day grind. Craig W. Dimond, © Intellectual Reserve, Inc.

houses, unruly children. And it's no wonder. It's difficult to do what needs to be done to keep life moving in a productive direction, let alone try to coordinate your efforts with your partners when you're under a time crunch. But the truth is, arguing about "who's doing what around the house," is really just a symptom of deeper problems—isolation, loneliness and resentment. You argue about the mundane issues when your emotional needs aren't being met. The [soda] can left in the living room becomes a symbol of a lack of caring for you. (para. 2–3)

Contention increases when marital needs are not met, and thus the downward spiral begins. The lack of time and nurturing erodes positive communication, bonding time, intimacy, conflict resolution, and meeting each other's marital needs. A marriage that lacks nurturing and time together will ultimately be suffocated by the demands of work, family, community, and even church. And when the marriage suffers, the entire family will be negatively impacted. Molehills can be made into mountains as each member of the family feels emotionally cheated. In a short period of time, parents and children in time-starved relationships never get their emotional cups filled. Ultimately, happiness, family satisfaction, and nurturing become nonexistent.

Origins of the Time Famine for LDS Couples

There are many distractors that can pull Latter-day Saint couples apart. Do you find, as a couple, that you have very little time for each other? When was the last time that you did something fun together as a couple? Do you remember your last date with each other? Can you remember the last time you did something spontaneous together? When was the last time you sent a love note to your spouse, or did something special for him or her? Do you feel that your children's schedules dominate your life? Do you have something going every night of the week, and even on weekends? Does your family ever have time to relax or talk, or simply "chillout"? Although there are many distractions that can drive a wedge between LDS couples, three significant distractors will be addressed.

Work Time

The demands at the office are colliding with marriage and family responsibilities "and placing a tremendous time squeeze on many Americans" (Gerson & Jacobs, 2004, p. 29). Working men and women spend 14 more hours per week at work than their cohorts did 30 years ago (Sayer, 2005). Today's working American man averages 49.4 hours of work per week while today's working woman averages 42.4 hours of work per week (Brandt, 2003). In fact, more than one-third of male managers and professionals work more than 50 hours per week (Gerson & Jacobs, 2004, p. 31).

Moreover, there are currently more women in the labor force than at any other time in our nation's history. In 1970, only 43% of women were employed. However, in 2008, that number increased to 77% of mothers with older children, and 63% of women with younger children (US Bureau of Labor Statistics, 2011). Furthermore, for the first time in the history of the United States, women now hold the majority of the nation's jobs. And, of the 15 job categories projected to grow in the next decade, all but two will be primarily occupied by women (Rosin, 2010).

According to a religiosity and life satisfaction study, 56% of Latter-day Saint women between the ages of 24 and 44 are working. However, of married Latter-day Saint women with children at home, only 23% work full-time. Another 22% work in part-time jobs (Johnson, 2005, p. 205). It appears that not as many Latter-day Saint women are in the workforce when compared to the national average. However, these statistics point to almost half of all LDS women working, which is a huge disrupter for marriage and family life.

Meanwhile, men are working longer hours, traveling more with their jobs, and spending much more time at the office than they initially signed up for. Today, 65% of all fathers work more than 40 hours a week, compared to 36% of working mothers. Furthermore, 25% of working fathers work more than 50 hours per week (National Fatherhood Initiative, 2007, p. 121). Of course, more time at work translates into less time as a couple, and of course, less time as a family.

If couples want to experiences happiness and satisfaction in their relationships, they will need to make their marriages a top priority. President Ezra Taft Benson (1987) taught the brethren of the priesthood, "Nothing except God himself takes priority over your wife in your life—not work, not recreation, not hobbies. . . . What does it mean to 'cleave unto her'? It means to stay close to her, be loyal and faithful to her, to communicate with her, and to express your love for her" (p. 50).

Media

Perhaps the most significant distraction in marriages today is time spent with media. Approximately 2.5 billion (not million) people view television programs daily. In the average American home, the television set is on approximately seven hours per day (Ballard, 1989). According to researchers Robinson and Godbey (2000), television viewing now occupies 40% of the free time of the average American adult (p. xv). One study documented that American men spend 15 hours per week watching television, while women spend almost 17 hours per week in front of the tube (Fisher & Robinson, 2009, pp. 2–3).

It wasn't too long ago that solely television or videos could rob a couple of precious time. However, in today's world, there are enough media options to distract us for a lifetime. Of course, there still are interruptions of time caused by television and movies. But on top of that, there are distractions such as smartphones, Internet surfing, gaming, e-mail, and social networking. Who would have thought that with all the technology designed to give us more time that we would be cramming all those "extra moments" we've saved with even more time-consuming wizardry? The problem is that, with all the gizmos and gadgets, we feel more frenzied, more harried, and more out of breath than ever before. It seems ironic, but the very things we think are going to save us time often end up stealing it (Parrott, 2006, p. 85).

According to the US Census Bureau (2011), over 75% of American homes had a computer, and almost 72% had Internet access. The percentages of home computer use increases with education, income, and employment. Furthermore, 90% of people with college degrees had a computer at home, and almost 87% of them had Internet access. Today, almost 50% of the colleges educated have smartphones, allowing them to access the internet almost anywhere. With such easy accessibility, more and more men and women spend a large quantity of their discretionary time on the computer. Brad Stone (2005) of *Newsweek* reported that 75% of Americans spend an average of three hours a day online.

According to a recent Nielsen survey, men between the ages of 18 and 34 are now the most prevalent users of video games, with 48.2% of all American men using a video console each day, averaging over 2.5 hours daily (Bennett, 2011, p. xxii). The average age of a gamer is now 32 years old (Online Education). A recent study conducted by researchers at Brigham Young University reported that 75% of gamers' spouses wish their spouse would put more time and effort into the marriage (Sifferlin, 2012). Moreover, 82% of gaming occurs between 6:00 p.m. and 11:00 p.m. Of those who play online role-playing games, 36% are married, and 22% have children (Jabr, 2012). Many wives and children are being ignored during prime family time. The use of media during prime family time is a marriage killer.

In a recent interview (interview notes in author's possession), a middle-aged mother from Idaho stated:

> I hate electronic media, all of it. I feel that so much time is wasted on unimportant facts and information. I will admit that when my husband gets a new computer, iPad, iPhone, or other gadget, I get jealous. I want his time and attention. The truth is that our family only has a few short hours a day together. So, when my husband comes home, I do not like competing with media devices for his time. I want us focusing together on our family; cooking dinner, eating dinner, doing homework, and cleaning up together—with both parents engaged.

Many family members feel ignored due to a family member's choice to play video or computer games or use other media during prime family time. Jonathan Hardy, © 2012 BYU Photo.

Men are not the only media junkies in marital relationships. Contemporary women can spend inordinate amounts of time in media usage. Several years ago in my counseling practice, I saw a distressed husband who didn't know what to do about his wife. She was involved in online gaming and social networking half of the day—and most of each night. Because of her media addiction, she could not change her behavior—nor did she desire to. Their marriage ultimately ended in divorce.

Elder Ian S. Ardern (2011) recently spoke pointedly about the dangers that are sure to accompany those who spend too much time in media-related activities. He declared, "I know our greatest happiness comes as we tune into the Lord (Alma 37:37) and to those things which bring a lasting reward, rather than mindlessly tuning in to countless hours of status updates, Internet farming, and catapulting angry birds at concrete walls. I urge each of us to take those things which rob us of precious time

Couples who never spend time together because they are constantly tending to the needs of their children will also be discouraged in the marriage. © *Cathy Yeulet.*

and determine to be their master, rather than allowing them through their addictive nature to be the master of us" (p. 32).

Do you spend time watching television when your spouse is home with you? Do you watch television together as a family or couple activity, or is it a separate activity? How many hours per day do you spend on your home computer? Do you find yourself engaged in social networking and other media activities on your phone or computer that takes you away from your spouse? Elder Russell M. Nelson (1991) has taught, "If marriage is a prime relationship in life, it deserves prime time" (p. 23).

Children's Schedules

Marriage, children, and family relationships lie at the core of the plan of salvation. A happy marriage and family life brings joy and fulfillment into the hearts and homes of faithful Latter-day Saints. However, sometimes husbands and wives can become unbalanced in the time they devote to their children in proportion to the time they spend with each other.

Marriage expert Dr. John M. Gottman explained that in child-centered marriages, "couples often use their parenting obligations as an excuse for neglecting their relationship with each other. . . . The sad irony is that in striving to create the perfect life for their children, these parents fail to provide what kids need most—a happy home" (Gottman, Gottman, & DeClaire, 2006, pp. 232–233).

Parenthood can be stressful, and children can become one of the largest drains on their parents' time. The presence of children in the home increases the time demands for housework more than any other factor. In fact, the more children that are in the home and the younger the children are, the less time couples will have together (Mattingly & Bianchi, 2003, p. 1003). In a recent study, "spouses with children at home reported spending nearly two hours less per day together than did those without children at home" (Wilcox & Dew, 2012, p. 9). Compared to their predecessors, both mothers and fathers are expected to spend more time with their children in nurturing roles (Stearns, 2003).

Latter-day Saint families are often larger than other families; thus LDS parents generally have more people and activities to manage. Often, fathers and mothers divide the family several nights a week, load the children into different cars, and attempt to cover all the stops: soccer practice, a piano recital, and a baseball tournament—all at the same time. Sometimes, in order to cover all of the activities, parents are left to divide and conquer. William J. Doherty (2003) has explained:

> The biggest threat to good marriages is everyday living. That may sound strange to you. What I mean is getting lost in the logistics of everyday life. We spend most of our time at home managing a household, taking care of children, and pursuing solitary activities like watching television or working. The coming of children especially seems to doom personal time for conversation between spouses, and even the time we do have is dominated by logistical talk about schedules and household tasks. At best, we feel like effective co-managers of a family business. At worst, we feel like ships passing in the night. By the time the kids leave home, we may not remember how to be different with each other. (p. 125)

Obviously, it's not 1960 anymore, when the family can gather around the fireplace every evening and sing songs while drinking Tang. The world has changed dramatically since those days. For Latter-day Saints with multiple children, to get a free night at home with nothing on the schedule calls for a celebration! Often, when parents are not driving their children to and from activities, children still "need" their parents. Studies confirm that children have first claim on their parents' non-working time, which isn't necessarily a bad thing. However, when husbands and wives neglect each other in the name of "the children," they may become frustrated with each other. Moreover, couples who never spend time together because they are constantly tending to the needs of their children will also be discouraged in the marriage. Couples who spend significant and meaningful time together will have their emotional cups filled and consequently will be able to give their children much more—not less.

Moreover, couples who work with their children as a team will be much happier in their marriage relationships. Nevertheless, too many contemporary parents spend much of their parenting time shuttling their children to fun activities, parties, and to friends' houses. Once again, free time isn't directed towards the marriage, but towards the children.

A Latter-day Saint bishop (interview notes in author's possession) recently shared the following:

> Our children's time demands and commitments is the single reason we don't spend enough time together as a couple. This causes trouble in our marriage because when we don't spend adequate time together, our marriage slips. We probably tend to let our children be too involved. We've talked about limiting their activities, but we always come back to the fact that we want them to develop their talents and do things they want to do. Because of my work and church schedule, and our children's activities, there is never time for myself or my spouse. We both face the same challenges so finding time for each other is difficult. Even if we wanted to have a special night every week for a date, it is almost impossible because our children will have a game or activity.

This busy bishop isn't much different from most Latter-day Saint parents. There is a constant desire to spend more time together as a couple, but how? What would need to be sacrificed? What would need to be changed in the family structure? Sometimes adults and children are simply too busy, and some things need to be dropped from the schedule. At other times, couples must choose to forge ahead until the season is over. Nevertheless, couples will need to seek the Lord's direction for viable solutions.

I recommend that married couples keep the "big picture" in mind as they raise their children. The "big picture" is the perspective that, ultimately, their children will grow up and have families of their own. As children begin to leave the nest, husbands and wives will have more time for each other. If they haven't discovered ways to enrich their marriage along the way, what kind of relationship will they have when they are empty nesters (Stahmann, 2007)? Too many older couples look at each other after the children are gone and realize that they no longer have much of a marriage relationship. Do not let this happen to you!

While your children are still in the home, learn to serve each other, share with one another, sacrifice for each other, and love each other. If you do so, you will experience a high degree of happiness and marital satisfaction. However, no one can have a happy marriage without the investment of time.

The Role of Rituals in Strengthening Marriage

Elder F. Burton Howard (2003) stated:

> *If you want something to last forever, you treat it differently.* You shield it and protect it. You never abuse it. You don't expose it to the elements. You don't make it common or ordinary. If it ever becomes tarnished, you lovingly polish it until it gleams like new. It becomes special because you have made it so, and it grows more beautiful and precious as time goes by. Eternal marriage is just like that. We need to treat it that way. (p. 94)

If couples want their marriages to last, they must demonstrate that they value their spouses; they must view their marriages as sacred and place them as one of their highest priorities. Therefore, couples who value their marriages will find ways to make time for each other. In the Survey of Marital Generosity, researchers reported that spouses who experience high levels of couple time were significantly less likely to report that they are prone to divorce. In fact, wives who reported having couple time less than once a week were 4 times more likely to report above-average levels of divorce proneness when compared to wives who enjoyed couple time at least once a week with their husbands. Meanwhile, husbands who reported spending less than once per week in couple time with their wives were 2.5 times more likely to be divorce prone when compared to husbands who had couple time with their wife at least once a week (Wilcox & Dew, 2012, p. 6)

The bottom line is that the more time husbands and wives spend together, the less likely they will be unsatisfied in the marriage or file for divorce. Researchers Wilcox and Dew (2012) have concluded that couple time leads to higher quality marital relationships because communication is strengthened, sexual satisfaction increases, and commitment is fortified.

One way to ensure couple time together is to employ rituals in the marriage. Rituals are social interactions that are repeated, coordinated, and significant to both parties in the relationship. It does not matter how often rituals are repeated—it could be nightly, weekly, monthly, or annually. But they are repeated. Rituals also must be coordinated. There must be a time and place for the ritual to occur, and, of course, both parties must know when to engage in the ritual. Importantly, rituals must also be significant to both husband and wife (Doherty, 2003). For example, a husband could tell a friend, "My wife and I have a great ritual. Every Monday evening after we put the children in bed, we watch Monday night football together." However, if that event is not emotionally significant to the wife, then watching football together isn't a ritual. Instead, it's probably a marriage problem.

Other couples may believe that they have rituals in their relationship, but oftentimes these rituals are actually routines. Like rituals, routines are repeated and coordinated. However, routines lack emotional significance. Therefore, if a couple eats dinner each night in front of the television—while the wife views the program and the husband reads the newspaper—this couple has established merely a routine that does very little to strengthen the marriage. However, another couple may watch the exact same television program each week—together. As they view the program, they may scratch each other's back, hold hands, and discuss the program in detail. Since this activity is repeated, coordinated, and significant to both parties, it is a ritual.

The purpose of marriage rituals is to help couples strengthen emotional bonds. Individuals fall in love with each other through rituals of intimacy and connection. When most couples commenced dating each other seriously, their time together most likely consisted of romantic dinners, long talks, bike rides, skiing, dancing, going for walks, exchanging gifts, and talking on the phone for hours (Doherty, 2000, para. 2). Most often, the very rituals that bring couples together are discontinued shortly after the marriage. Since a large proportion of Latter-day Saint couples marry while they are still in college, or even while working full-time, it doesn't take long for school and work to invade their couple time and negate their romantic rituals. Before long, babies come, along with work and church demands. Within a few short years, some good, otherwise emotionally healthy Latter-day Saint couples begin to feel that their marriage quality has fallen far below their expectations. Many husbands and wives feel that their marital needs are not being met and that marriage is less fulfilling than they had expected.

Some couples become overwhelmed with time demands, responsibilities, and perhaps even guilt. Soon, their marriages become stale and stagnant. If busy Latter-day Saint couples desire to spend more time together as husbands and wives, they must "ritualize" their time together. Happy marriages are not created by accident, and couples who spend time together must carve their time out from other worthwhile activities. Rituals can restore meaning to marriages; in fact, rituals help couples to connect and stay connected.

Connection rituals in marriage create opportunities for couples to share time and attention together. Examples of connection rituals in marriage include good-byes in the morning, greetings in the evening, phone conversations during the day, texting each other, eating together, verbal expressions of love and affection, working in the yard together, doing home improvements together, or eating at a favorite restaurant. William J. Doherty (2003) argued that "connection rituals are at the base of the pyramid of marriage, right above commitment" (p. 126). For marriages to thrive, connection rituals must be employed. The most significant connection rituals to heal and strengthen a marriage include greeting rituals, talk rituals, and dating rituals.

Greeting and Good-bye Rituals

Healthy greeting rituals occur in a marriage when the couple meets for the first time in the morning, when one spouse has been away on a trip, or when a spouse walks through the front door after a long day at work. Believe it or not, many spouses can walk through the front door of their homes without anyone in their family noticing. One husband reported that he would walk into his home each evening and no one acknowledging his presence. He would then go into his bedroom, change his clothes, and then read the newspaper before his wife even realized he was home.

Some couples get into bad habits of coordinating when they see each other for the first time. A wife may say to her husband who has just walked into the house, "Hurry and change clothes so we can get to the choir recital," or a husband could say to a wife after a long day, "Your pizza is in the fridge. Eat it quick so we can get to the game." One man reported that once when he walked into his home at the end of the long day, his wife said, "Did you close the garage door?" (Doherty, 2000, "Examples of Marriage Rituals," para. 1). Another man explained that when he entered his home, his wife would often say, "What's that smell?" Wow, isn't it great to be home? Instead of these poor greeting responses, couples should discuss the way that they greet each other after a long day apart. Examples would include a hug, a kiss, or a verbal expression. I know one couple who, when the husband would walk in the front door, they would walk, hand in hand, to an isolated room in the house where they would sit and talk to each other for ten or fifteen minutes just to catch up on the day.

Your children should have no doubt that you and your spouse are happily married—don't hide your marital happiness under a bushel! If you and your spouse do not have a strong, noticeable greeting ritual, you need to create one. Establish a ritual that will mark the moment and remind

Establish a ritual that will mark the moment and remind everyone how much you love each other—including yourselves! And don't worry if your children catch you in the act. Every child needs to see his or her parents display some public affection, even if it grosses the child out to some degree. Let there be no question in the lives of Latter-day Saint children that their parents are madly in love. © Hongqi Zhang.

everyone how much you love each other—including yourselves! And don't worry if your children catch you in the act. Every child needs to see his or her parents display some public affection, even if it grosses the child out to some degree. Let there be no question in the lives of Latter-day Saint children that their parents are madly in love. Greeting rituals could include a hug, a kiss, or a verbal expression of love, a family phrase, or anything else that is significant to both spouses.

One couple confessed that that their greeting rituals were pathetic. It was typical for Jennifer or Ron (names have been changed) to walk into their home and not even notice each other for the first half hour. What they did notice, however, was that their golden retriever, "Rex," had more passion for greeting family members than they did. For example, when Ron walked into his home after a long day, "Rex" would bark in happiness for several minutes and run circles around him. It was obvious that at least "Rex" was happy that Ron was home. Therefore, Jennifer and Ron decided that they would create a greeting ritual that could top the dog. Today, when Ron walks into their home after a long day, Jennifer goes berserk, and Ron loves it! Both husband and wife benefit from this ritual.

Indeed, husbands and wives need to be more excited than the family dog when a spouse walks into the home after a long day away. I would recommend that you choose a greeting ritual that you can both get excited about. Practice the ritual until it becomes a habit. Don't be afraid to ask your children if they know what your greeting ritual is.

Good-bye rituals are just as important as greeting rituals. A ritual that marks the parting moment for a couple demonstrates that you will miss each other and look forward to being together again. I remember as a young boy, observing a couple at the end of our street. Every morning as I walked down the street to school, this middle-aged husband and wife would be in their driveway, hugging and kissing as if he was going off to war for several years. Of course, he was just heading off to his sales job and would return home before dinner. As a young boy, there was no doubt in my mind that this couple really loved each other. Every couple needs to establish a ritual when you are leaving each other. Find a way to tell each other good-bye that is unique, that demonstrates you will miss each other, and that validates your love for each other.

And while you are at it, find a way to improve your "good-night" ritual as well! Too many couples doze off to sleep with the television blaring, while reading a book, or as they listen to the "enchanted sounds of the forest" from a CD they purchased at a drug store. Lying next to each other at the end of a long day, touching each other, and expressing love and appreciation is a perfect opportunity for prime-time connection.

Talk Rituals

Many Latter-day Saint couples understand the importance of communication; after all, that is most likely how they fell in love in the first place. Several years ago, I interviewed fifteen newly married couples on the campus of Brigham Young University. Practically every couple related to me that they fell in love by talking to each other. In fact, these couples discovered that they could talk to each other about anything, that their communication came with ease, and that they often talked into the late hours of the night about almost everything. Healthy communication is one of the most important ingredients in a successful marriage. Unfortunately, as couples become busier, their depth of communication often wanes. Marriage scholar Judith Wallerstein (1995) explained the need for deep communication and talk rituals in marriage:

> Our needs for comforting and encouragement are deep and lasting. A main task of every marriage from the early days of the relationship to its end is for each partner to nurture the other. The loneliness of life in the cities, the long commutes, the absence of meaningful contact with people have sharpened our emotional hungers. We feel tired, driven, and needy. More than ever before we need someone special who understands how we feel and responds with tenderness.

Love begins with paying attention. . . . A marriage that does not provide nurturance and restorative comfort can die of emotional malnutrition. . . . [The] task of marriage . . . is to give comfort and encouragement in a relationship that is safe for dependency, failure, disappointment, mourning, illness, and aging—in short, for being a vulnerable human being. (pp. 239–240)

One way couples can nurture each other and renew their love is through talk rituals. Or in other words, couples need to do more than just talk; instead, they need to create moments where talking can occur without interruption. Moreover, couples must not merely look for ways to find more "free time" to be together—they must make time, and create opportunities to be together. I would invite you to find a way to talk for fifteen minutes each day. Remember; don't look for fifteen free minutes on your schedule—they probably are not there. Your task will be to create those fifteen minutes. For busy Latter-day Saint couples, creating more time to be together, even if it is just fifteen minutes, can be challenging and often difficult. Dr. William J. Doherty (2003) argued that if "a married couple with children has fifteen minutes of uninterrupted, nonlogistical, nonproblem-solving talk every day, I would put them in the top five percent of married couples in the land. It's an extraordinary achievement" (p. 130).

When couples are dating, especially when they are engaged, it is common practice to talk to each other until late into the night. However, after marriage, the time compression is activated. The same spouse who was quoting poetry to you and singing love songs until 2:00 a.m. could be snoring like a lumberjack at 10:15 p.m. every evening. However, talking about deep and significant marital issues at 11:30 p.m. when both parties are exhausted is not an effective practice either. One couple recently reported to me that when they both jump into bed at the end of a busy day, they grab their smartphones and surf the Internet, read e-mail, or view their Twitter account until they fall asleep. This is not exactly the way to build a strong marriage.

Talking rituals can help couples stay on track and connect with each other. You task will be to create rituals that will work for you as a couple. One husband and wife shared a significant talk ritual in their marriage. After dinner each night, their children would clean up the kitchen while the husband and wife slipped off to the family living room. There, they would drink their favorite beverage together and discuss their day (Doherty, 2003). Superficial talk was not allowed! They disciplined themselves to talk on a more personal level, sharing their opinions, beliefs, and ideas about a myriad of topics. It was also a time to validate each other and share compliments and praise.

Dr. William J. Doherty (2003) reported that one of his finest investments was his hot tub. Fourteen years ago, he and his wife purchased a Jacuzzi and placed it out on their deck, underneath the stars. At about 10:00 p.m. each evening, they venture out to their tub, listen to jazz music, and talk about anything other than bills, report cards, and soccer tournaments (p. 130). In order for couples to fortify their marriages, they must find the time to talk to renew and strengthen their emotional bonds. If a Jacuzzi can enrich a marriage, then I recommend one for every couple! However, there are other ways that couples can connect, and you and your spouse should discuss a communication ritual that will be custom-fit to your present circumstances.

There are a myriad of talk rituals couples can practice that will strengthen their marriages. Couples can go on walks together and talk about practically anything. Many husbands and wives often call each other at certain times during the day and text love messages to each other regularly. One couple shared the following ritual that strengthens their marriage:

Here's a ritual that my husband and I have been sharing for the 22 years of our marriage. We have kept a diary of our anniversaries every year. After the kids are in bed on our anniversary, we pull out the diary, light the wedding candle that was on the altar of the church when we married, and reread the diary together. In it, we've recorded what we did to celebrate the day, any highlights of the previous year, changes that have come to our family (like the birth of our kids, moves, and so forth). It's a nice way for us to see the ebbs and flows of our relationship, and to remember how we've been blessed in all of it. It takes us a little longer each year to read the diary (by the 50th, we figure we'll need to start at about 2:00 in the afternoon), but I can't imagine doing the anniversary without it. (Doherty, 2000, "Sawing the Log," para. 9)

President Harold B. Lee (1970) once emphasized the perils of indifference. President Lee spoke pointedly to the priesthood holders when he said, "the most dangerous thing that can happen between you and your wife or between me and my wife is apathy—not hate, but for them to feel that we are not interested in their affairs, that we are not expressing our love and showing our affection in countless ways. Women, to be happy, have to be loved and so do men" (p. 241). Husbands and wives must nurture each other through talk rituals. Men cannot become apathetic in this endeavor! Find a talk ritual that you are both comfortable with and practice it often.

I would encourage husbands to take the lead on this ritual. Do not wait for your wife to "kick this practice off." Sit down with her and ask her how you can improve the communication in the marriage. After she recovers from fainting, towel her off, sit her down, offer her a cool drink, and then discuss with her several realistic options and talk rituals you would like to implement in your marriage. However, don't stop here. Continue to do this weekly, ensure that the ritual happens, and solicit your wife's valuable feedback.

Wives, if your husband isn't prone to take the lead in this area, feel free to initiate the ritual and use it as a time to bond, not bash. If you build him up and give him some confidence, he will come to enjoy your time together and desire that this ritual continue.

Dating Rituals

President Brigham Young (1930) said, "Life is best enjoyed when time periods are evenly divided between labour, sleep and recreation. . . . All people should spend one-third of their time in recreation which is rebuilding, voluntary activity—never idleness" (Gates & Widtsoe, p. 251). Couples would do well to follow President Young's counsel and spend more time in wholesome recreation. Dating is a form of recreation that renews emotional bonds and can heal the time-starved marriage. Dating is what brings couples together initially, and steady dating can advance the relationship to engagement and marriage. Dating provides women and men with an opportunity to talk and do something fun together as a couple.

It is unfortunate that so many couples discontinue dating after they are married. This is a surefire way to snuff out the flame of intimacy in any marriage. Some couples argue that they would like to date, but with several small children, babysitters are too expensive. To those couples, consider that babysitting is not an expense, but an investment. Besides, babysitters are much cheaper than divorces.

Too often, husbands make the mistake of assuming that dates must be elaborate and expensive. Many women have told me that they would be happy to get out of their homes for a few hours—regardless of where they go. What women—especially young mothers—need is the opportunity to step away from the chaos and be renewed. Sometimes, walking around the block or spending some casual time at a park will provide the same benefit as an expensive restaurant.

Husbands should initiate dating in the marriage relationship. This isn't to say that wives cannot plan dates, but the husband is responsible to make certain that this part of the marriage remains strong and consistent. Husbands and wives should hold a couple's meeting each week to coordinate schedules, talk about finances, solve problems, plan gospel training in the home, and discuss their weekly date.

I also believe that couples should also try to break out of the mold of going to dinner and a movie on each date. Elder Richard G. Scott (2012) recently spoke to students on the Brigham Young University campus regarding their dating relationships. He mentioned that attending movies on dates is a "stupid" idea for couples who are trying to get to know each other (p. 170). The same could be said about married couples who are trying to strengthen their marriage relationship. What good is it for couples to sit for two hours in a movie theater where they cannot talk or even see each other? One of the most significant purposes for a "date night" would be to open communication channels and restore emotional connection.

Couples who are trying to renew their relationships would do well to engage in some of the activities they once did when they were dating. Go putt-putt golfing, bowling, or go-kwart riding. Perhaps there are more cultural activities that both spouses enjoy, such as visiting an art museum or attending a musical concert. The point is that there are many activities couples can engage in besides dinner and a movie. Recent research documents that "couples who engage in novel activities that are fun, active or otherwise arousing—from hiking to dancing to travel to . . . games—enjoy higher levels of relationship quality" (Wilcox & Dew, 2012, p. 4).

Couples who often date each other are able to restore romance in their relationships. Thus, effective dating can lead to high levels of sexual satisfaction in the marriage. Moreover, frequent dating restores commitment in the relationship. Family scholars Bradford Wilcox and Jeffrey Dew (2012) report that "partners who put one another first, who steer clear of other romantic opportunities, and who cultivate a strong sense of 'we-ness' or togetherness are markedly happier than are less-committed couples" (p. 4). Couples who regularly date each other are able to "de-stress" their lives and escape the concerns that real life presents.

Several years ago, in speaking to Church educators, Elder Jeffrey R. Holland (1999) related how difficult and stressful life was for him and his wife, Patricia, while he was a graduate student at Yale. At the time, Elder Holland was a member of the stake presidency, a director in the institute

Continually dating your spouse will help to restore the romance in your relationship.
Matt Reier, © 2007 Intellectual Reserve, Inc.

program, a full-time student, a husband, and a father of a couple of children. Meanwhile, Patricia was the ward Relief Society president, a wife, a mother, and a part-time babysitter to make ends meet. However, this powerful couple decided that no matter what, every Friday night would be their night together. Elder Holland (1999) reflected:

> But on that one night for a few hours we would be together. We would step off the merry-go-round. We would take a deep breath or two and remind ourselves how much we loved each other, why we were doing all of this in the first place, and that surely there must be a light at the end of the tunnel somewhere.
>
> I do not remember those dates ever amounting to much. I literally cannot remember ever going to dinner, but we must have. We certainly must have at least gotten a pizza occasionally. I just don't remember it. What I do remember is walking in the Yale-New Haven Arboretum, which was just across the street from our student housing. I remember long walks there holding hands and dreaming dreams of what life might be like when things were less demanding. Down at the end of the street was a Dairy Queen where we would occasionally end up for a cone or, on really good nights, a root beer float. (pp. 2–3)

Elder Holland further stated that both he and Patricia needed those nights just to give them a sense of sanity and direction. It was a time to reconnect and celebrate what mattered most in their marriage. Those Friday night dates were something the Holland's both looked forward to, and the time they spent together was renewing and healing. Elder Holland concluded, "A drugstore psychologist once said that people need three things to be emotionally healthy: someone to love, significant things to do, and something pleasant to look forward to." He then challenged the men, "Brethren, make sure your wife has something pleasant, something genuinely fun, to look forward to regularly" (pp. 2–3).

Elder Joe J. Christensen (1995) urged couples to keep their courtships alive by doing things together—just husband and wife. "As important as it is to be with the children as a family, you need regular weekly time alone together. Scheduling it will let your children know that you feel that your marriage is so important that you need to nurture it" (p. 65).

Renowned marriage scholar John Gottman (1999) discovered that couples who devoted five extra hours per week to their marriage gleaned tremendous benefits—especially when compared to couples who did not spend extra time to strengthen their marriage. During these "Magic Five Hours," as Gottman labeled them, couples concentrated on five things: first, before leaving for the day, learning one thing that will happen in the other spouse's life that day; second, engaging in a stress-reducing conversation at the close of the day; third, doing something daily to communicate genuine affection and appreciation to each other; fourth, demonstrating physical affection throughout the day; and fifth, having a weekly date together. Although these activities require a minimum time investment, the dividends will make a significant difference in each spouse's life.

There are other rituals to consider, such as love rituals, special occasion rituals, and even community rituals that can strengthen a marriage. There are several other rituals that will help couples take their marriages back and set a course in place that will strengthen their marriage:

- If you no longer go to bed together on a regular basis, then start again.
- If there is a television in your bedroom, get rid of it.
- Express a kind word of compliment to your spouse. Be specific.
- Have a couples' meeting each week where you can discuss ways to strengthen your marriage.
- Make your spouse a booklet, expressing in it all of the things you love about him or her.
- Have a romantic dinner together.

Dating your spouse is an important way to enhance your marriage. John Luke,
© Intellectual Reserve, Inc.

- Go for a 24-hour retreat, even if you stay in hotel just down the street from your home.
- Find a way that your entire family can celebrate your wedding anniversary this year.
- Do something special for Valentine's Day this year, especially if you did nothing last year!

Conclusion

Our busy culture is not necessarily "marriage-friendly," and there are many distractions than can pull husbands and wives apart from each other. If couples do not find ways to prioritize their time, their marriages could become hollow, frustrating, and unfulfilling. If contemporary LDS couples want to strengthen their marriage relationships, they will need to insert rituals in their marriage to ensure quality time together.

Establishing rituals in marriage demonstrates to each spouse that their marriage is a priority and that they are willing to invest time and energy into the marriage because it is the most important thing in their lives. I would encourage you to have a couples meeting together and establish several rituals that will set your marriage on a course for continued happiness and fulfillment. Practice these rituals until they become habits.

President Spencer W. Kimball (1977) taught, "While marriage is difficult, and discordant and frustrated marriages are common, yet real, lasting happiness is possible, and marriage can be more an exultant ecstasy than the human mind can conceive. This is within the reach of every couple, every person" (p. 4). Rituals in marriage can help couples reach this promise of ecstasy—or joy and fulfillment—that can be found in any marriage when couples are willing to invest time, attention, and love towards each other.

Years ago, Elder Hugh B. Brown served in the First Presidency, was an Apostle, and served in many other Church capacities. Perhaps, however, it was his service to his wife that was most impressive. In his first address after being called to the Quorum of the Twelve Apostles, Elder Brown paid this tribute to his wife: "I would be ungrateful if I did not acknowledge that Zina Card Brown, my beloved wife, is more responsible for my being here today than I" (Kimball, 1999, p. ix).

Elder Brown's daughter, Mary Firmage, spoke of a ritual that she observed between her parents for years. Mary related that every day of their marriage, Elder Brown would kiss his wife, Zina, good-bye before he would leave for work. The couple would then walk to the front porch together, and Elder Brown would walk down about three steps, turn back towards Zina, and ask, "Did I kiss you goodbye?" Zina would respond with, "Why, no, you didn't." Then Elder Brown would kiss her again.

Then, as he would walk to the car, Zina would run into the dining room where she would blow kisses to her husband through the window. Next, as Elder Brown was backing the car out of the driveway, Zina would run back to the front porch where their ritual began, and she would wave a handkerchief until Elder Brown drove out of sight. However, just before the car turned the corner at the end of the street, Elder Brown would blink the brake lights three times, his code for "I love you" (Avant, 1974).

President Brown taught a powerful lesson to each of us in this ritual. The relationship between he and his wife, Zina, is a reminder to each one of us of the power of love, and the ability to heal the time-starved marriage. I would encourage every couple to create a similar ritual to President and Sister Brown. Regarding love and affection in marriage, President Brown (1960) taught:

When the husband and wife tell each other of their affection and demonstrate it by their conduct by both what they do and refrain from doing, then their marriage, like the tides of the ocean, will not be seriously disturbed by surface storms. . . .

While deep feelings of affection are too sacred for flaunting, each person in love, especially after marriage, should seek every opportunity to display affections in the home. Love is the key that unlocks the inner feeling of the heart, and it must not be lost or allowed to rust through disuse. Any key that rests will rust. . . .

Daily investments in mutual compliments pay wonderful dividends in family solidarity, understanding, and success. . . . Little acts of tenderness, kindness, and consideration continued through life, will make the tree of love ever bearing, like orange trees, with buds, blossoms, and ripened fruit the year round. Love in December can and should be as warm as it was in June—and even sweeter. (pp. 95–98)

Time management can be a challenge for most Latter-day Saint couples. However, ignoring the time challenges and hoping that life will magically get better is not the solution. Couples must be purposeful in employing rituals that will help them prioritize their marriage relationships. As they engage in discovering rituals that will enhance their marriage, peace and happiness will be their reward.

References

Ardern, I. S. (2011, November). A time to prepare. *Ensign, 41*(11), 31–32.

Aron, A., Aron, E. N., Norman, C. C., McKenna, C., & Heyman, R. E. (2000). "Couples' shared participation in novel and arousing activities and experienced relationship quality." *Journal of Personality and Social Psychology, 78*(2), 273–284.

Avant, G. (1974, October 26). Sister Hugh B. Brown: Creative mother brightens home. *Church News,* 43–45.

Baird, R. B. (1985). Improve the shining moments. *Hymns of The Church of Jesus Christ of Latter-day Saints.* Salt Lake City: The Church of Jesus Christ of Latter-day Saints, no. 226.

Ballard, M. R. (1989). The effects of television. *Ensign, 19*(5).

Bennett, W. J. (2011). *The book of man: Readings on the path to manhood.* Nashville: Thomas Nelson.

Benson, E. T. (1987, November). To the fathers of Israel. *Ensign, 17*(11), 50.

Brandt, B. (2003). An issue for everybody. In J. de Graaf (Ed.). *Take back your time: Fighting overwork and time poverty in America.* San Francisco: Berrett-Koehler.

Brown, H. B. (1960). *You and your marriage.* Salt Lake City: Bookcraft.

Christensen, J. J. (1995, May). Marriage and the great plan of happiness. *Ensign, 25*(5), 65.

Daly, K. J. (2001, May). Deconstructing family time: From ideology to lived experience. *Journal of Marriage and Family, 63,* 283–294.

Dew, J. (2009). Has the marital time cost of parenting changed over time? *Social Forces, 88*(2), 519–542.

Doherty, W. J. (2000). Intentional marriage: Your rituals will set you free. Keynote Address, Fourth Annual Smart Marriage Conference, Denver, CO, July 1, 2000, 4. Retrieved from http://www.smartmarriages.com/intentionalmarriage.html

Doherty, W. J. (2003). *Take back your marriage: Sticking together in a world that pulls us apart.* New York: Guilford Press.

Fisher, K., & Robinson, J. (2009). Average weekly time spent in 30 basic activities across 17 countries. *Social Indicators Research, 93*(1), 249–254.

Gager, C. T., & Sanchez, L. (2003, January). Two as one? Couples' perceptions of time spent together, marital quality, and the risk of divorce. *Journal of Family Issues, 24*(1), 21–50.

Gates, S. Y., & Widtsoe, L. D. (1930). *The life story of Brigham Young.* New York: Macmillan Books.

Gerson, K., & Jacobs, J. A. (2004). "The work-home crunch." *Contexts, 3*(4), 29–37.

Glorieux, I., Minnen, J., & Tienoven, T. (2010). Spouse 'together time': Quality time within the household. *Social Indicators Research, 101*(2), 281–287.

Gottman, J. M. (1999). *The seven principles for making marriage work.* New York: Three Rivers Press.

Gottman, J. M., Gottman, J. S., & DeClaire, J. (2006). *10 lessons to transform your marriage.* New York: Three Rivers.

Holland, J. R. (1999, February 5). "Our consuming mission." *An evening with Elder Jeffrey R. Holland, 5 February 1999.* Retrieved from http://www.lds.org/manual

/teaching-seminary-preservice-readings-religion-370-471-and-475/our-consuming-mission?lang=eng

Holland, J. R. (2000, February 15). How do I love thee? *Brigham Young University speeches, 1999–2000.* Provo, UT: Brigham Young University.

Howard, F. B. (2003, May). Eternal marriage. *Ensign, 33*(5), 94.

Jabr, F. (2012, February 14). The perils and pleasures of online gaming for married life. *Scientific American.* Retrieved from http://blogs.scientificamerican.com/observations/2012/02/14/the-perils-and-pleasure-of-online-gaming-for-married-life/?print=true

Johnson, S. M. (2005). Dispelling the myths of Mormon womanhood. In C. G. Hart, L. D. Newell, E. Walton, & D. C. Dollahite, (Eds.). *Helping and Healing Our Families* (p. 205). Salt Lake City: Deseret Book.

Kimball, S. W. (1999). Forward. In E. B. Firmage (Ed.), *An abundant life: The memoirs of Hugh B. Brown* (vii–x). Salt Lake City: Signature Books.

Kimball, S. W. (1976, September 7). Marriage and divorce. *Brigham Young University 1976 speeches.* Provo, UT: Brigham Young University.

Kimball, S. W. (1977). First Presidency message: "Oneness in marriage." *Ensign, (7)*3, 4.

Kingston, P. W., & Nock, S. L. (1987, June). Time together among dual earner couples. *American Sociological Review, 52*(3) 391–400.

Larsen, D. L. (1985, March) Enriching marriage. *Ensign, 15*(3), 20.

Lee, H. B. (1970). *Teachings of Harold B. Lee.* Salt Lake City: Bookcraft.

Mattingly, M. J., & Bianchi, S. M. (2003, March). Gender differences in the quantity and quality of free time: The U.S. experience. *Social Forces, 81*(3), 999–1029.

National Fatherhood Initiative. (2007). *Father Facts.* Gaithersburg, MD: National Fatherhood Initiative.

Nelson, R. M. (1991, May). Listen to learn. *Ensign, 21*(5), 23.

Nelson, R. M. (2006, May). Nurturing marriage. *Ensign, 36*(5), 36.

Nelson, R. M. (2008, November). Celestial marriage. *Ensign, 38*(11).

Olson, D. H. (1980). National survey of marital strengths: Executive summary. https://www.prepare-enrich.com/pe_main_site_content/pdf/research/national_survey.pdf

Online Education. Videogame statistics. *Education Database Online.* Retrieved from http://www.onlineeducation.net/videogame

Parkman, A. M. (2004, July). The importance of gifts in marriage *Economic Inquiry, 42*(3), 483–495.

Parrott, L. & Parrott, L. (2006). *Your time-starved marriage.* Grand Rapids: Zondervan.

Robinson. J. P., & Godbey, G. (2000). *Time for life: The surprising ways Americans use their time.* University Park, PA: The Pennsylvania University Press.

Rosin, H. (2010, July/August). The end of men. *The Atlantic.*

Sayer, L. C. (2005, September). Gender, time and inequality: Trends in women's and men's paid work, unpaid work and free time. *Social Forces, 84*(1), 285–303.

Scott, R. G. (2012, September 12). To have peace and happiness. *Brigham Young University 2010–2011 speeches.* Provo, UT: Brigham Young University.

Sifferlin, A. (2012, February 16). Is online gaming messing up your marriage? *TIME Healthland.* Retrieved from http://healthland.time.com/2012/02/16/is-online-gaming-messing-up-your-marriage/

Stahmann, R. F., & Wood, N. D. (2007). *25 keys to a great marriage.* Sandy, UT: Silverleaf Press.

Stearns, P. M. (2003). *Anxious parents: A history of modern childrearing in America.* New York: New York University Press.

Stone, B. (2005, April 11). Hi-tech's new day. *Newsweek, 74.*

Teachings of presidents of the Church: Brigham Young. (1997). Salt Lake City: The Church of Jesus Christ of Latter-day Saints.

US Bureau of Labor Statistics. (2012, October). Highlights of women's earnings in 2011. (Report No.1038). Retrieved from http://www.bls.gov/cps/cpswom2011.pdf

US Census Bureau (2005, October). Computer and Internet use in the United States: 2003. Retrieved from http://www.census.gov/prod/2005pubs/p23-208.pdf

Uchtdorf, D. F. (2010, November). Of things that matter most. *Ensign, 40*(11), 22.

Stinnett, N., & DeFrain, J. (1985). *Secrets of strong families.* Boston: Little, Brown, & Company.

Umberson, D., Williams, K., Powers, D., Liu, H., & Needham, B. (2005, December). Stress in childhood and adulthood: Effects on marital quality over time. *Journal of Marriage and Family, 67*(5), 1332–1347.

Wallerstein, J. S., & Blakeslee, S. (1995). *The good marriage: How and why love lasts* (p. 239). Boston: Houghton Mifflin; see also Fowers, B. J. (2000). *Beyond the myth of marital happiness* (p. 38). San Francisco: Jossey-Bass.

Weiner-Davis, M. (1992). *Divorce busting: A revolutionary and rapid program for staying together.* New York: Simon & Schuster.

Weiner-Davis, M. (2009). Time together. *Divorce Busting.* Retrieved from http://www.divorcebusting.com/a_time_together.htm

Wilcox, W. B., & Dew, J. (2012). The date night opportunity: What does couple time tell us about the potential value of date nights. The National Marriage Project. Charlottesville: University of Virginia.

RICHARD J. McCLENDON &
DEBRA THEOBALD McCLENDON

4

Commitment to the Covenant:
LDS Marriage and Divorce

THE Church of Jesus Christ of Latter-day Saints has long stressed the eternal value and nature of marriage while warning against the tragic and ill effects of divorce. Prophets, past and present, have counseled Church members to make their marriage a top priority in their lives and to avoid attitudes and behaviors that contribute to divorce. This prophetic counsel has more recently been confirmed by social science research showing that entering into and keeping the marriage covenant produces a happier and healthier life.

In spite of religious and scientific evidence, marriage is on the decline in America. There appears to be an even more alarming concern—that divorce has become the "default" solution to marriages that struggle even at rather modest levels. Rather than seeking resolutions to marital challenges within the marriage covenant itself, many couples are disregarding their vows and divorcing as an attempt to avoid even modest levels of marital discomfort. Although we recognize there are a number of social forces driving this trend, we believe one factor in particular has had a significant role: society has adopted a more casual regard for promises, vows, and contracts in general. This diminished commitment toward keeping promises has eroded the institute of marriage; driving significant numbers to postpone marriage, enticing many to abandon marriage for cohabitation, and for those who are married, weakening their will to endure modest challenges and tempting them to see their marriage as a temporary obligation rather than a long-term one.

Unfortunately, members of The Church of Jesus of Christ of Latter-day Saints have also been influenced by this cultural trend. We will further explore this issue and discuss ways that Latter-day Saints can inoculate themselves against adopting such attitudes toward their marital vows and realign themselves with the words of the prophets, scripture, and sound scientific research.

The Problem: The Loss of Commitment and the Divorce Culture

Social change commonly occurs in slow and steady doses. Trends that produce new ideas and beliefs eventually establish new values and norms. Because it takes time, shifts in values usually come in subtle transitions of which society may be largely unaware. Although some of these values may be good for society, many are harmful. In these cases, unless a person becomes conscientious of and alerted to their dangers, he or she can easily slip into believing that such values and behaviors are acceptable in God's eyes. As a protection against this, the Lord has warned Latter-day Saints to "beware concerning [them]selves" (D&C 84:43). He has also cautioned that even the "humble followers of Christ" in the latter days will be "led, that in many instances they do err because they are taught by the precepts of men" (2 Nephi 28:14). This counsel provides a striking reminder that we must be vigilant when encountering social change.

One of the subtle, yet harmful, value shifts that has occurred over that past several decades has been a drift toward casualness in our commitments, agreements, and promises. Such a trend can be found in business, law, and politics, where making promises and contracts is a natural aspect of the operation of business. Unfortunately, today parties to agreements no longer have high expectations that their contracts will be honored. Perhaps, however, no other aspect of society has been affected as significantly by this trend than has the institution of marriage. What was once a promise "until death do you part" has now shifted to "until debt do you part." The holy binding of husband and wife is no longer seen as a firm promise "through sickness and in health" but has largely been reduced to the level of a flimsy high school promise of "going steady," where the relationship is easily dissolved for any number of insignificant reasons.

Historically, marriage was largely viewed by both individuals and society at large with a deep level of commitment and satisfaction. From a social science perspective, this level of commitment is not misplaced. In their widely acclaimed book *The Case for Marriage*, Waite and Gallagher (2000) reported that married individuals have, on average, significantly higher levels of happiness, physical and emotional health, and financial well-being when compared to singles, cohabiters, or divorcees. In addition they found that the large majority (86%) of unhappily married people who stayed married had happier marriages five years later. In other words, "permanent marital unhappiness is surprisingly rare among the couples who stick it out" (pp. 148–149). Further analysis by Waite and colleagues (2002) found that unhappily married adults who divorced or separated were no happier, on average, than unhappily married adults who stayed married. They also reported that even unhappy spouses who had divorced and *remarried* were no happier, on average, than unhappy spouses who stayed married. Thus, if people choose divorce because they think it will bring them a sense of greater happiness that has eluded them within the marriage, existing research shows little if any evidence that their assumption is true (p. 4).

In spite of these compelling findings, the past several decades of American culture have weakened public support for the marriage vow. Marriage rates are down, and divorce is now often advocated as a solution to marital difficulties culturally, politically, and legally. According to Waite and Gallagher (2000), much of this shift in attitude can be attributed to the "privatization of marriage" in which marriage is regarded as a private and individual decision (p. 176). When struggling with marital difficulty and considering whether to divorce, the central question often asked by individuals today is, "What would make me happy?" This question is often promoted by lawyers, educators, counselors, and even clergy, reinforcing "the idea that emotional gratification is the main purpose and benefit of marriage" (p. 176). Elder Dallin H. Oaks (2012) recently quoted a Harvard law professor in his description of the current law and attitude toward marriage and divorce: "The [current] American story about marriage, as told in the law and in much popular literature, goes something like this: marriage is a relationship that exists primarily for the fulfillment of the individual spouses. If it ceases to perform this function, no one is to blame and either spouse may terminate it at will" (p. 44). This self-focused perspective is contributing to our culture's anti-commitment attitudes. It underlies what is driving an unprecedented increase in marital postponement and cohabitation in the United States, and is eroding the barrier that once protected society against a casual acceptance of divorce.

In the late 1960s through the lobbying efforts of lawyers, no-fault divorce came on the American scene to make divorce a faster and less judgmental legal process. It has created a legal culture regarding marriage and divorce that has spilled over into societal attitudes toward marriage in general. Being married has little distinction from that of cohabitation. "Thanks to no-fault, the marriage contract is no longer enforceable. It takes two to marry but only one to divorce at any time, for any reason, as fast as the courts can sort out property and custody issues" (Waite & Gallagher, 2000, p. 178).

How have these social and legal trends affected marriage and divorce among Latter-day Saints? McClendon and Chadwick (2005) found that most marriages in the Church continue to be strong and vibrant. When compared to the national percentages, Latter-day Saints are significantly different than their national peers showing lower age at first marriage, lower numbers of single-parent families, and larger family size. Like the national average, Latter-day Saints also rank extremely high in marital happiness. Many scholars believe that the current lifetime divorce rate in the United States is between 40% and 50%. In their examination of the divorce rate within The Church of Jesus Christ of Latter-day Saints, using both civil and temple marriages combined, McClendon and Chadwick (2005) estimated that the current lifetime divorce rate for returned-missionary men to be approximately 12% and for returned-missionary women around 16%. They estimated that the lifetime rate for non-returned missionary men to be approximately 38% and about 22% for non-returned-missionary women (p. 39). These data show that although divorce rates among Latter-day Saints are lower than they are in the general American public, divorce has definitively found its way into mainstream Latter-day Saint culture. Church leaders are mindful of this trend and of the ever-present attacks that Satan places on the family in general. Elder L. Tom Perry (2012) recently warned, "As we know, [Satan] is attempting to erode and destroy the very foundation of our society—the family. In clever and carefully camouflaged ways, he is attacking commitment to family life throughout the world and undermining the culture and covenants of faithful Latter-day Saints" (p. 27).

In a bold statement to members of the Church about marriage and divorce, President Gordon B. Hinckley (1991) declared:

> Of course, all in marriage is not bliss. . . . The remedy for most marriage stress is not in divorce. It is in repentance. It is not in separation. It is in simple integrity that leads a man to square up his shoulders and meet his obligations. It is found in the Golden Rule. . . .
>
> There must be a willingness to overlook small faults, to forgive, and then to forget.
>
> There must be a holding of one's tongue. Temper is a vicious and corrosive thing that destroys affection and casts out love. . . .
>
> There may be now and again a legitimate cause for divorce. I am not one to say that it is never justified. But I say without hesitation that this plague among us, which seems to be growing everywhere,

Presdient Hinckley taught: "The remedy for most marriage stress is not in divorce. It is in repentance. It is not in separation. It is in simple integrity that leads a man to square up his shoulders and meet his obligations. It is found in the Golden Rule." © Auremar.

is not of God, but rather is the work of the adversary of righteousness and peace and truth. (pp. 72–74)

This prophetic warning voice helps us as Latter-day Saints to recognize that a thorough and complete commitment to the marriage vow and to God is at the center of a successful marriage. Our purpose now is to discuss more specifically this counsel and to find ways to apply it. Before we do so however, we want to note that we are discussing ideas and solutions that can aid us in attaining the *ideal*. We are well aware that in mortality attaining the ideal is not always possible, but seeking after it is. As the authors, we ourselves would be defined by the current societal standard as a "blended family." We have personal understanding of the heartache of divorce, the trauma of chronic problems that seem to have no solution no matter how hard one tries to have faith and behave well, and the sensitivity that is required to raise children whose lives are splintered between two households. This personal perspective has supported and even strengthened our religious and scientific convictions about commitment in marriage and has contributed to our strong position about the responsibility each of us has to hold tenaciously to the ideal. Certainly, the manner in which the ideal is implemented in families will vary based on individual circumstances (see The Family: A Proclamation to the World, 1995), but some core principles can help guide and sustain us as we make decisions regarding that implementation.

The Solution: Fierce Loyalty to the Covenant of Marriage and to God

In light of the current societal and cultural trends regarding marriage, what can be done to stem the tide of casual marital commitments? We discuss three solutions that will revitalize marriage and reenthrone commitment at the forefront of marriage. The first is to "mean what you say" in regards to entering into and keeping the marital promise. Fierce loyalty to one's vow will produce greater trust between spouses which in turn builds greater loyalty and investment in the marriage. Second is to "do" marriage. A marital commitment is more than just saying "yes" or "I do" during the marriage ceremony. It requires daily actions of love and service to fully honor the promise. Finally, "look to God" as a partner in the marriage covenant. His influence will provide assurances and peace for spouses that will give them greater courage and determination to work together through marital differences and challenges.

Mean What You Say

Fierce loyalty to one's word is the foundation of trust in all relationships, especially marriage. It has been said that

> commitment is what transforms a promise into a reality. It is the words that speak boldly of your intentions, and the actions that

speak louder than words. It is making time when there is none; coming through time after time after time, year after year after year. Commitment is the stuff character is made of—the power to change the face of things. It is the daily triumph of integrity over skepticism. (Commonly attributed to Abraham Lincoln or Shearson Lehman Brothers)

When we truly mean what we say and are willing to defend our word at all costs and in all situations, we create a special bond of trust that elevates the marital relationship and protects it during tests and challenges. If we truly love our spouse, we will clearly express to them our deep loyalty to our marital commitment. Elder Jeffrey R. Holland (2012) recently said that "the crowning characteristic of love is always loyalty."

Waite and Gallagher (2000) found an interesting correlation between marital loyalty and marital investment: "The more uncertain people are that any partnership will last, the more they act as individuals and the less they act as permanent partners. But the more spouses act as separate individuals, the less they get from the marriage partnership, and the more likely the marriage will fail" (p. 180). Of course, this type of self-fulfilling prophecy also works conversely. When spouses clearly communicate to each other that they are fully committed to honoring their marital vows and that divorce is not an option, they will invest in their marriage with greater confidence, which in turn naturally promotes greater loyalty and commitment.

The Book of Mormon's strong emphasis on covenant-making can teach us how to "mean what we say" when it comes to keeping our covenants, especially in marriage. The Nephite/Lamanite culture, like the Hebrew culture, viewed the making of an oath or covenant as a final vow, never to be broken. When problems arose or were anticipated, they either didn't enter into the covenant in the first place or they worked within the covenant to resolve problems. They never considered that they would break the covenant. The story of Nephi and Zoram illustrates this principle. After Zoram discovered that Nephi was not Laban, as he had presumed, Nephi made an

As spouses act like and treat their partnership as a permanent relationship, they will act more like permanent partners and less like individuals. David Stoker, © Intellectual Reserve, Inc.

oath wherein he promised Zoram that he would spare his life and make him a free man if he went with him and his brothers into the wilderness. We are told that "Zoram did take courage" upon hearing Nephi's oath and reassurances that he need not fear for his life. To this, Zoram then responded with his own oath that he would "tarry with [them] from that time forth" (1 Nephi 4:35). Nephi then stated, "When Zoram had made an oath unto us, our fears did cease concerning him" (v. 37).

Surprisingly, this commitment to keeping one's promise was also the belief and practice among the more wicked Nephites and Lamanites. Although they allowed themselves to commit serious sins, they were strongly socialized against violating a promise. For example, in Alma 44, Captain Moroni commanded the Lamanite army to make a covenant of peace or they would be destroyed. Zerahemnah, the captain of the Lamanites, rejected the offer by saying, "We will not suffer ourselves to take an oath unto you, which we know that we shall break" (v. 8). Although his private goal was to deceive and murder in order to gain power, because of the cultural norms of the day, Zerahemnah was not willing to make an oath that he knew he would likely break. Later, when Zerahemnah and his army were at the brink of being destroyed, he did choose to make an oath of peace and—to the modern-day reader's surprise—he kept it. There is no record that Zerahemnah himself ever returned.

The Book of Mormon also illustrates for us the power that keeping oaths and covenants has in unifying and building trust and loyalty. When Amalickiah conspires to be king, Captain Moroni rallies the people to defend their lands, liberty, and religion. Moroni does this by establishing a covenant and raising the title of liberty, explaining:

> Whosoever will maintain this title upon the land, let them come forth in the strength of the Lord, and enter into a covenant that they will maintain their rights, and their religion, that the Lord God may bless them.
>
> And it came to pass that when Moroni had proclaimed these words, behold, the people came running together with their armor girded about their loins, rending their garments in token, or as a covenant, that they would not forsake the Lord their God; or, in other words, if they should transgress the commandments of God, or fall into transgression, and be ashamed to take upon them the name of Christ, the Lord should rend them even as they had rent their garments. (Alma 46:20–21)

Those who entered into a covenant of liberty centered their commitment in Christ and were true to the promises they made, even at the peril of their lives. This level of commitment allowed the Nephites to synergize their trust in each other and to build the type of loyal community necessary for Moroni to lead and eventually win the war against the Lamanites.

Another Book of Mormon example that illustrates the unifying, strengthening power of keeping covenants is that of the two thousand stripling warriors. Their special preservation through several battles can be traced back to the covenant that both they and their parents made with the Lord. Their parents made an oath with God that they would never again take up their swords to battle, but rather, if necessary, give their lives as a token of their commitment. Later, so their parents could continue to honor their covenant, their sons covenanted to give their lives if necessary for the defense of their freedom, family, and country. Although they fought and many were injured, their lives were preserved through their faith in God and their belief that as they kept their commitment to him, he would deliver them (see Alma 57:26–27).

Keeping our commitments, then, is one of the most important values we can embrace. A discussion about values is not limited to a religious discussion or a recitation by the young women during our Sunday block of church meetings. Values are at the core of our daily living. We espouse values in many realms, such as spiritual/religious, health/fitness, educational/professional, family/child-rearing, civic/political, relationships with others, etc. Psychological models have begun to understand the mental health benefits of living our lives in a manner consistent with our values. Acceptance and Commitment Therapy (ACT) is a therapy model in which helping clients pursue a life consistent with their values plays a prominent role in the therapeutic process. When values are sacrificed in the service of fears, doubts, frustrations, anxieties, disappointments, and the like, life is put into a state of paralysis. The belief that one "can only be happy when . . ." becomes a self-fulfilling prophecy as the "when" often doesn't come in the manner or in the timing that might be preferred. Instead, ACT maintains that people can experience difficulties, even chronic problems, and still move forward in their lives in pursuit of their deeply held values. "Willingness to experience difficult thoughts, feelings, and experiences is put in the service of our values. This is what makes willingness different from wallowing" (Luoma, Hayes, & Walser, 2007, p. 41). Thus, when values are sustained and pursued, mental health and life satisfaction improves, even when external circumstances do not necessarily improve. Lorde (1997) has said: "When I dare to be powerful, to use my strength in the service of my vision, then it becomes less important whether or not I am unafraid" (p. 13). Thus, if we mean what we say when we commit to our marital covenants, we demonstrate to our spouse, our God, and others in our personal life a deep sense of integrity regarding one of our most important values.

"Do" Marriage

A second solution to strengthen commitment to the covenant is to "do" marriage in God's way. We learn in Doctrine and Covenants 19:11 that "eternal" is another name for God. Within Latter-day Saint circles, the term "eternal marriage" is sometimes used casually, spoken with an apparent assumption that once a man and woman are sealed in the temple they have an eternal marriage. However, the phrase "eternal marriage" represents God's marriage, or in other words, the quality of marriage that God enjoys. A temple sealing ceremony is only the beginning step necessary to achieve this type of marriage. The marriage, as an entity of its own, requires daily work from both partners if it is to attain the same quality as is enjoyed in the heavenly realms.

Elder Oaks (2007) has said, "The kind of marriage required for exaltation—eternal in duration and godlike in quality—does not contemplate divorce" (p. 70). Along this vein, however, some people claim commitment to the covenant as a reason for staying in a difficult marriage, yet treat their spouse with disrespect and even contempt, or suffer passively with resignation to an unhappy lot. Allow us to be bold and assert that physically staying in the marriage is only one of many steps that are required in order to fully honor the marital covenant—one must remain emotionally and spiritually present and do all that is possible to create the type of relationship worthy of the title "eternal marriage." Elder Oaks further said: "Under the law of the Lord, a marriage, like a human life, is a precious, living thing. If our bodies are sick, we seek to heal them. We do not give up. While there is any

A temple sealing ceremony is only the beginning of an eternal marriage. Marriage requires daily work from both partners to attain the quality of God's marriage. Rezolution Films, © Intellectual Reserve, Inc.

prospect of life, we seek healing again and again. The same should be true of our marriages, and if we seek Him, the Lord will help us and heal us" (pp. 71–73).

We are, therefore, advocating a higher law which encourages prioritizing the building and strengthening of the marriage relationship until it can grow and flourish into one that is God-like in quality. "In the strongest marriages, husband and wife share a deep sense of meaning. They don't just 'get along'— they also support each other's hopes and aspirations and build a sense of purpose into their lives together" (Gottman & Silver, 1999, p. 23). The following story, told by Elder Spencer J. Condie (1993) illustrates how a couple can elevate their relationship by working within the covenant:

> A few years ago my wife, Dorothea, and I were walking across the grounds of a temple in a foreign land when we met a very radiant, cheerful, silver-haired sister. Her cheerful, Christlike countenance

seemed to set her apart from those around her, and I felt inclined to ask her to explain why she looked so happy and content with life.

Well, . . . several years ago I was in a hurry to get married, and quite frankly, after a few months I realized I had married the wrong man. . . . He had no interest in the Church as he had initially led me to believe, and he began to treat me very unkindly for several years. One day I reached the point where I felt I could go on no longer in this situation, and so in desperation I knelt down to pray, to ask Heavenly Father if He would approve of my divorcing my husband.

I had a very remarkable experience. . . . After I prayed fervently, the Spirit revealed a number of insights to me of which I had been previously unaware. For the first time in my life, I realized that, just like my husband, I am not perfect either. I began to work on my intolerance and my impatience with his lack of spirituality.

I began to strive to become more compassionate and loving and understanding. And do you know what happened? As I started to change, my husband started to change. Instead of my nagging him about going to church, he gradually decided to come with me on his own initiative.

Recently we were sealed in the temple, and now we spend one day each week in the temple together. Oh, he's still not perfect, but I am so happy that the Lord loves us enough to help us resolve our problems. (p. 15)

In addition to religious and scriptural insights, there are many interventions for "doing" marriage advocated within the field of psychology. A commonly cited finding in the field of Positive Psychology indicates that people tend to flourish when their ratio for positive and negative affect is 3:1 or higher (Fredrickson & Losada, 2005). In this context, to flourish means "to live within an optimal range of human functioning, one that connotes goodness, generativity, growth, and resilience" (p. 678). Three instances of positive emotion for each instance of negative emotion promotes flourishing, whereas ratios that fall below this level represent a state of languishing in which people describe their lives as empty and hollow. In the context of marriage, however, the standards to achieve a sense of flourishing or thriving are higher than the ratios needed to thrive as individuals. Gottman (1994), a leading marital/relationship researcher, has found that, for those couples who would rate themselves as happily married, the positivity to negativity ratio is 5:1. Although this standard of five instances of positivity for each instance of negativity may appear daunting, there is good news here—couples are not expected to be perfect in their relationships in order to feel happy, satisfied, or fulfilled with each other. In fact, there is evidence that some conflict engagement is healthy. Mistakes can and will be made, disagreements will occur, and frustrations will sometimes rise. The key to building a flourishing marriage is to increase the overall positivity in the relationship. A kind word, an expression of gratitude, or a gentle touch may be small things, but they work together to offset difficulties and can be very powerful. We read in Alma 37:7, "And the Lord God doth work by means to bring about his great and eternal purposes; and by *very small means* the Lord doth confound the wise and bringeth about the salvation of many souls" (emphasis added).

In addition to increasing positivity in our relationships by generating new behaviors we can also increase positivity by becoming more aware of efforts toward positivity that are already present. In one study in which couples were observed in their own homes, those in happy marriages noticed almost all of the positive things their partners did for them, while those in unhappy marriages failed to recognize 50% of the positive acts their spouses performed (Gottman & Silver, 1999, pp. 83–84).

Overhauling some of our more dysfunctional relationship patterns may also be necessary in order to build an eternal marriage that will be resistant to divorce. Gottman and Silver (1999) report certain types of negativity so "lethal" to marriage that they categorized them as the Four Horsemen of the Apocalypse—criticism, contempt, defensiveness, and stonewalling (p. 27). Those caught in such destructive patterns within the marital relationship need

If dysfunctional patterns continue to be manifest in spite of consistent efforts to overcome, working with a trusted mental health professional may be useful. © Wavebreak Media Ltd.

to focus on elevating their own contributions to the partnership, rather than focusing on what they believe their spouse should be doing, but isn't (p. 83).

If dysfunctional patterns continue to be manifest in spite of consistent efforts to overcome, working with a trusted mental health professional may be useful. In recent years, Church leaders have discussed the importance of utilizing mental health professionals. Elder Alexander B. Morrison (2005) has discussed the differing roles of priesthood leaders and mental health professionals to help Church members understand how each may be of service to them:

> No mental health professional, regardless of his or her skill, can ever replace the role of a faithful bishop as he is guided by the Holy Ghost in assisting Church members to work through the pain, remorse, and depression associated with sin. . . . We must understand, however . . . that ecclesiastical leaders are spiritual leaders and not mental health professionals. Most of them lack the professional

skills and training to deal effectively with deep-seated mental illnesses. . . . Remember that God has given us wondrous knowledge and technology that can help us overcome grievous problems such as mental illness. (pp. 31–35)

As we examine our relationships, we can come to understand the best way to implement the idea of "doing" marriage in God's way. Whether it be by strengthening our resolve to make our relationship more Godlike, investing emotionally and spiritually in the process, or by addressing problematic or dysfunctional behavior patterns with or without the assistance of a bishop or mental health professional, a purposeful approach to marriage will undoubtedly produce a greater commitment to the covenant.

Look to God

Look to God within the covenant for solutions when faced with challenges or obstacles, rather than looking for a solution outside of the covenant. By remaining together and prayerfully working the problem with the Lord's help, couples will not only save the marriage but the process will provide newfound strength, trust, and love that will provide a foundation for even greater loyalty for one another.

The Book of Mormon provides a powerful example of how looking to God can help overcome challenges in marriage. In Alma 58, Helaman explains that he and his army of stripling warriors were in dire circumstances, receiving very little assistance from the government in order to maintain the lands for which they had fought so valiantly. This created a tremendous fear in their hearts. In writing to Captain Moroni about this problem, Helaman explains:

We were grieved and also filled with fear, lest by any means the judgments of God should come upon our land, to our overthrow and utter destruction.

Therefore we did pour out our souls in prayer to God, that he would strengthen us and deliver us out of the hands of our enemies, yea, and also give us strength that we might retain our cities, and our lands, and our possessions, for the support of our people.

Yea, and it came to pass that the Lord our God did visit us with assurances that he would deliver us; yea, insomuch that he did speak peace to our souls, and did grant unto us great faith, and did cause us that we should hope for our deliverance in him.

And we did take courage with our small force which we had received, and were fixed with a determination to conquer our enemies, and to maintain our lands, and our possessions, and our wives, and our children, and the cause of our liberty.

And thus we did go forth with all our might against the Lamanites. (Alma 58:9–13)

When Helaman and his army felt fear and grief, they first looked to God for help by seeking him in mighty prayer. Although the Lord didn't immediately remove or remedy the problem, he did send them "assurances" that he "would" deliver them. This set off a chain reaction of feelings and events that changed their course. With assurances from God, Helaman and his young army felt peace and great faith, which in turn increased their courage and gave them a "fixed determination" to "go forth" with all their might in conquering their enemy and to "hope for a deliverance in [God]." This they did and were successful.

There is much to be learned from this story about how to work through marital conflicts and challenges. Feelings such as fear, grief, anger, doubt, and heartache surround everyone involved in marital conflict. However, like Helaman and his army, the first step a couple must take is to look to God in fervent, mighty prayer; they must "pour out [their] souls" (Alma 58:10) to God that he will strengthen and deliver them from the enemy of pride, hurt feelings, anger, misunderstandings, and the like. As couples sincerely petition Heavenly Father's help in their marriage, there may be special times

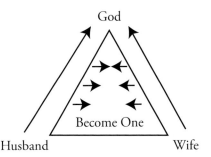

When we look to God, he draws us toward him, and in so doing, we become partners with him in our quest for an eternal-quality marriage.

when he helps eliminate a problem immediately and in a miraculous way; however, most likely, as in Helaman's situation, God will first send assurances which can lead to peace and great faith. Greater courage and determination will then be born in order to work together in resolving disagreements and misunderstanding and in finding a way to forgive each other.

This "look to God" principle can provide direction in psychological treatment as well. Psychologists have noted that religious convictions provide valuable tools that can be used therapeutically (Propst, 1988). One such religious concept used as an intervention in treating religious marital couples puts God at the head of a triangle with the wife and husband residing at the other two points. In this simple chart, a powerful religious and interpersonal concept is taught. When spouses are far from God, they are far from each other. The converse is also true: when they are far from each other, they are typically far from God. However, if both wife and husband as individuals and as a couple are looking to God and seeking to develop their relationship with him and grow closer to him, then as they move toward him narrowing the distance between them and making the triangle smaller, the distance between the spouses also narrows (that is, wife and husband grow closer together). Thus, when we look to God, he draws us toward him, and in so doing, we become partners with him in our quest for an eternal-quality marriage.

Additional Considerations for Marriages with Ongoing Difficulties

Elder Oaks (2007) has said, "For most marriage problems, the remedy is not divorce but repentance. . . . The first step is not separation but reformation" (p. 71). There are those who humbly seek to follow this counsel and are committed to their marriage and committed to building within it a relationship of eternal quality, yet continually find themselves struggling with ongoing marital difficulties and disappointments. To these couples Presdient Brigham Young (1862) offered this comforting insight:

> I think it has been taught by some . . . that if a wife does not love her husband in this state she cannot love him in the next. This is not so. Those who attain to the blessing of the first resurrection will be pure and holy, and perfect in body. Every man and woman that reaches to this unspeakable attainment will be as beautiful as the angels that surround the throne of God. If you can, by faithfulness in this life, obtain the right to come up in the morning of the resurrection, you need entertain no fears that the wife will be dissatisfied with her husband, or the husband with the wife; for those of the first resurrection will be free from sin and from the consequences and power of sin. (p. 24)

There is hope in this declaration.

With this being said, however, we do acknowledge that there may be circumstances when it could be appropriate to "stop trying" to find a marital solution within the context of the covenant. In such circumstances the utmost care, spiritual sensitivity, and consideration must be given through fasting, humble prayer, and counsel with priesthood leaders. Elder James E. Faust (1993) provided some guidance in this area:

Many problems within the covenant of marriage can be worked out together in prayer.
Craig Dimond, © Intellectual Reserve, Inc.

What, then, might be "just cause" for breaking the covenants of marriage? . . . In my opinion, "just cause" should be nothing less serious than a prolonged and apparently irredeemable relationship which is destructive of a person's dignity as a human being.

At the same time, I have strong feelings about what is not provocation for breaking the sacred covenants of marriage. Surely it is not simply "mental distress," nor "personality differences," nor having "grown apart," nor having "fallen out of love." This is especially so where there are children. (p. 35)

Conclusion

A marriage ceremony is a brief event that starts a couple onto the very lengthy journey of marriage—two imperfect people working toward building a relationship of eternal quality. The marriage requires work and constant effort to build and maintain. It requires the commitment to remain together while the imperfections of each partner are being purged. Elder Oaks (2007) observed that "a good marriage does not require a perfect man or a perfect woman. It only requires a man and a woman committed to strive together toward perfection" (p. 73).

Current American societal standards regarding commitment to the marital covenant are low. Latter-day Saints would be well-advised to avoid following the trends toward postponing marriage or favoring divorce over tolerating imperfections in the marital relationship. The solution for Latter-day Saints is to establish and maintain fierce loyalty to the covenant of marriage and to God. When we "mean what we say" in honoring our covenants and promises, "do" marriage mindfully and purposefully, and "look to God" as a partner in our marriage, we can preserve and strengthen our relationships. President Spencer W. Kimball (1976) said: "Real, lasting happiness is possible, and marriage can be more an exultant ecstasy than the human mind can conceive. This is within the reach of every couple, every person. . . . It is certain that almost any good man and any good woman can have happiness and a successful marriage if both are willing to pay the price."

References

Condie, S. J. (1993, November). A mighty change of heart. *Ensign, 23(11)*, 15.

Faust, J. E. (1993, May). Father, come home. *Ensign, 23*(5), 35.

First Presidency and Council of the Twelve (1995, November). The family: A proclamation to the world. *Ensign, 25*(11), 102.

Fredrickson, B. L., & Losada, M. F. (2005). Positive affect and the complex dynamics of human flourishing. *American Psychologist, 60*(7), 678–686.

Gottman, J. M. (1994). *What predicts divorce: The relationship between marital processes and marital outcomes.* New York: Lawrence Erlbaum.

Gottman, J. M., & Silver, N. (1999). *The seven principles for making marriage work.* New York: Three Rivers Press.

Hinckley, G. B. (1991, May). What God hath joined together. *Ensign, 21*(5), 72–74.

Holland, J. R. (2012, November). The first great commandment. *Ensign, 42*(11), 83–85.

Kimball, S. W. (1976, September 7). Marriage and divorce. BYU Devotional Address: http://speeches.byu.edu/?act=viewitem&id=706.

Lorde, A. G. (1997). *The cancer journals.* San Francisco: Aunt Lute Books.

Luoma, J. B., Hayes, S. C., & Walser, R. D. (2007). *Learning ACT: An acceptance & commitment therapy skills-training manual for therapists.* Oakland, CA: New Harbinger Publications.

McClendon, R. J., & Chadwick, B. A. (2005). Latter-day Saint families at the dawn of the twenty-first century. In Hart, C., Newell, L.D., Walton, E., & Dollahite, D. C. (Eds.). *Helping and healing families: Principles and practices inspired by "The family: A proclamation to the world"* (pp. 32–43). Salt Lake City: Deseret Book.

Morrison, A. B. (2005, October). Myths about mental illness. *Ensign, 35*(10), 31–35.

Oaks, D. H. (2007, May). Divorce. *Ensign, 37*(5), 70–73.

Oaks, D. H. (2012, November). Protect the children. *Ensign, 42*(11), 43–46.

Perry, L. T. (2012, November). Becoming goodly parents. *Ensign, 42*(11), 26–28.

Propst, L. R. (1988). *Psychotherapy in a religious framework: Spirituality in the emotional healing process.* New York: Human Sciences Press.

Waite, L. J., & Gallagher, M. (2000). *The case for marriage.* New York: Doubleday.

Waite, L. J., Browning, D., Doherty, W. J., Gallagher, M., Luo, Y., & Stanley, S. M. (2002). Does divorce make people happy? Findings from a study of unhappy marriages. *Institute for American Values.* New York, NY: www.americanvalues.org.

Young, B., (1862). Future state of existence. In *Journal of Discourses, 10,* 24.

LLOYD D. NEWELL,
JULIE H. HAUPT, & CRAIG H. HART

5

Rearing Children in Love & Righteousness: Latitude, Limits, & Love

THE First Presidency (1999) counsels parents to "devote their best efforts to the teaching and rearing of their children in gospel principles which will keep them close to the Church," and further states that "no other instrumentality can take [the home's] place or fulfill its essential functions in carrying forward this God-given responsibility." The proclamation on the family supports parents in magnifying their divinely designed responsibilities in the Father's great plan of happiness (see Alma 42:8) by specifically identifying the principles that ultimately will make the most difference in their efforts.

In this chapter, we discuss three parenting principles rooted in the doctrines of the proclamation and substantiated by social science research. The first principle is based on the fundamental doctrine that "each is a beloved spirit son or daughter of heavenly parents, and as such, each has a divine nature and destiny" (First Presidency, para. 2), and that through this mortal experience each will have an opportunity to use agency "to progress toward perfection and ultimately realize their divine destiny as heirs of eternal life" (para. 3). A parent can take the primary role in helping children and teens learn to make wise choices through *granting appropriate levels of latitude* based on an understanding of their individual differences and developmental levels.

The second principle is related to this teaching process. Parents instruct children in the ways of the Lord by *setting reasonable limits* and appropriately enforcing them. The proclamation describes this function by stating that "parents have a sacred duty . . . to teach [children] to . . . observe the commandments of God, and be law-abiding citizens wherever they live." Granting latitude and setting limits always works best in the context of the third principle, the development of a *strong parent-child bond* expressed in loving relationships that helps children be more disposed to positive parental influence. As stated in the proclamation, parents "have a sacred duty to rear their children in love and righteousness" (First Presidency, para. 6).

Parenting scholarship and research confirm that latitude (or autonomy granting), limits (or regulation), and love (or connection) are the chief characteristics of what scholars refer to as the *authoritative parenting* style. A parenting style reflects the emotional and interactional climate created in the home by the behavioral practices parents typically use in relating to their children. Decades of research comparing the authoritative parenting style to other common styles, such as the coercive (or authoritarian) style, the permissive (or *laissez-faire*) style, or the neglectful style, demonstrate clearly that children and adolescents reared by authoritative parents tend to be better adjusted to school, less aggressive and delinquent, less likely to abuse drugs, more friendly and accepted by peers, and more communicative, self-motivated, academically inclined, and willing to abide by laws. They are also more capable of moral reasoning and are more self-controlled (Hart, Newell, & Olson, 2003). Additionally, research demonstrates these positive child outcomes to be associated with authoritative parenting across gender, socioeconomic status, and culture. Nonformulaic by nature, authoritative parenting principles can be adapted to gender, personalities, and individual needs of children and teens in families with various heritage and cultural backgrounds.

As parents seek to learn their duties and apply correct principles in their parenting responsibilities within their own families, they will find their efforts resulting in a closer association with the Holy Spirit, increased sanctification in their own souls, and a greater measure of happiness in their own lives. President Gordon B. Hinckley (1997) said, "Of all the joys of life, none other equals that of happy parenthood. Of all the responsibilities with which we struggle, none other is so serious. To rear children in an atmosphere of love, security, and faith is the most rewarding of all challenges. The good result from such efforts becomes life's most satisfying compensation" (p. 421).

In examining latitude, limits, and love, this chapter will provide a discussion of the doctrinal foundation, scholarly support, and practical application of each of these three foundational parenting principles. In practice, these three elements often seamlessly overlap, though each makes a separate positive contribution to childrearing, especially when applied in a balanced manner appropriate to circumstances and child temperamental characteristics.

Certainly, the best example of the application of these principles is found in the manner in which our Heavenly Father parents each of us as his children. As taught by the proclamation, our Eternal Father has demonstrated his deep interest in our possibilities by allowing his children to exercise the God-given gift of agency, allowing us *latitude* in this mortal existence to gain a mortal body and learn through our own experiences. To keep us directed back to our heavenly home, God has introduced *limits* or commandments, along with "sacred ordinances and covenants available in holy temples [that] make it possible for individuals to return to the presence of God and for families to be united eternally" (First Presidency, para. 3). Finally, the entire gospel plan is based upon our Father's *love*, with its central feature of the Atonement of Jesus Christ standing as a powerful reminder of God's belief in each individual's potential to inherit his greatest gift—eternal life (see D&C 14:7). Each of these principles—latitude, limits, and love—will be discussed in turn.

Latitude

Fundamental to granting latitude in authoritative parenting is an understanding of the divine principle of agency and an appreciation of the unique personality and individualized needs of children. When children are taught true doctrine, internalize correct principles, and have opportunities to make choices within an environment of unfailing love and concern and with sensitivity to their developmental level, they are more likely to learn to choose wisely (Ballard, 2006; Wilson, 2012). Whatever the nature and disposition of a given child, wise parents work to adjust, relate to, and rear each child in a manner that is attuned to individual needs. As President James E. Faust (1990) observed, "Child rearing is so individualistic. Every child is different and unique. What works with one may not work with another" (p. 34). Individualizing the amount of latitude granted to each child in matters of both behavior and thinking should be based upon their dispositions, needs, age, and temperament. Children, in turn, will be more open to parental input and direction in the positive emotional climate that is created as needs are better met with more individualized approaches. President Brigham Young encouraged parents to "study their [children's] dispositions and temperaments, and deal with them accordingly" (Widtsoe, 1978, p. 207). In making important decisions about granting latitude, both spiritual perspectives and scholarly findings can be helpful as parents understand more about how agency interacts with individual personalities, genetic traits, and environmental influences.

Respecting Agency and Spiritual Personality

Latter-day Saint theology includes a remarkable wealth of information about the influence of the premortal life. For example, the First Presidency stated, "All people who come to this earth and are born in mortality, had a preexistent, spiritual personality, as the sons and daughters of the Eternal Father" (Smith, Lund, & Penrose, 1912, p. 417). President Joseph F. Smith (1916) noted, "Notwithstanding this fact that our recollection of former things was taken away, the character of our lives in the spirit world has much to do with our disposition, desires and mentality here in mortal life" (p. 426). Regarding the cultivation of spiritual gifts, Elder Bruce R. McConkie (1979) stated, "Being subject to law, and having their agency, all the spirits of men, while yet in the Eternal Presence, developed aptitudes, talents, capacities, and abilities of every sort, kind, and degree. During the long expanse of life which

Each individual displays different interests, personalities, and behaviors through unique biological blueprints provided by parents coupled with the child's own spiritual predispositions, talents, and desires. © Benis Arapovic.

then was, an infinite variety of talents and abilities came into being" (p. 23). Certainly, the way individual children respond to their earthly environments is greatly influenced by their spiritual identity and the spiritual gifts cultivated as an expression of their agency in the premortal realm (see D&C 46; Alma 13:3–5; Abraham 3:22–23; Moroni 10; Moses 5:24; 1 Corinthians 12–14).

Indeed, each individual displays different interests, personalities, and behavior through unique biological blueprints provided by parents coupled with the child's own spiritual predispositions, talents, and desires. These spiritual traits interact with genetic individuality in ways that are often observed in daily interactions in the home (Hart, 2008). Without a doubt, an individual's characteristics are further refined by environmental factors in and out of the home (such as, parents, peers, siblings, school, and culture) and by the ways that children respond to them (Hart, Newell, & Olson, 2003). In fact, even among children in the same family, some children may be more difficult or easy to rear due, in part, to inherent personality characteristics that stem from spiritual, biological, or social-emotional predispositions.

As President David O. McKay (1953) noted, "Man has a dual nature: one, related to the earthly or animal life; the other, akin to the Divine" (p. 347). Some biological or genetic tendencies may make up part of the "natural man" that must be overcome throughout life. Children come from the heavenly realm and are born into a world beset with temptations for the "natural man," but also full of spiritual opportunities for growth towards the "divine" (Mosiah 3:19). Helping children learn to use their agency wisely in cultivating divine attributes happens in a bidirectional parent-child interaction process that plays out across development.

We now turn our attention to overviewing bodies of research literature that offer social science support for fundamental doctrines that shed light on principles for raising children and teens in optimal ways. Since this chapter is not designed to overview individual studies and associated methodologies, readers are encouraged to examine endnote academic sources that synthesize multitudes of scientific findings supporting the points that follow (see Bornstein & Lamb, 2011; Hart, Newell, & Olson, 2003; Eisenberg, 2006; Kuczynski, 2003; Smith & Hart, 2011; Hart, Newell, & Haupt, 2008; Hart, Newell, & Sine, 2000; Hart, Newell, & Haupt, 2012).

Understanding Genetics and Environmental Influences

In addition to our understanding of the influence of spiritual personality, a growing body of evidence suggests that biological characteristics play a role in children's dispositions and temperaments in ways that interact with environmental influences. These include biologically driven tendencies toward inhibition or shyness, sociability, impulsiveness and "thrill seeking," activity level (degree of lively energetic behavior and perpetual motion), aggression, cognition and language acuity, behavior problems stemming from psychiatric disorders, emotionality (for example, intensity of arousal related to fear, anger, or elation), and religiosity. Evidence also exists to show that different genetically based characteristics can turn on or turn off at different points in development in ways that may be partially influenced by environmental factors. Thus, it may well be that some children cycle in and out of more easy and difficult developmental periods as they grow.

All this can influence how parents and children respond to each other. For example, some children with more spirited dispositions (such as aggressive, highly emotional, or thrill-seeking tendencies) may raise concerns and evoke more formal intervention by parents in terms of rules, redirection, punishment, and monitoring than children who are "easier" to rear. This can be particularly true when child behavior falls outside cultural norms and family expectations. Thus, even though there are shared parenting influences, children by their very natures can foster different parenting behaviors for different siblings in the same family. Or they may respond to similar parenting practices in different ways depending on how experiences are filtered through their perceptions and past experiences. Even children understand that parents adjust their practices to the different needs and personality characteristics of their siblings.

Research exploring genetic contributions to children's development suggests that as an expression of their individual personalities and agency, children select, modify, and even create their own environments influenced by these biological predispositions (Plomin, Reiss, Hetherington, & Howe, 1994). For example, a more sociable child may by nature seek out opportunities to interact with peers, but may be less academically motivated. Alternatively, a more socially passive child in the same family may actively avoid social gatherings and prefer to spend time in solitary activities (such as reading or drawing) and be more academically inclined. Sensitive parents watch carefully and recognize ways to help children constructively build talents and abilities, learn to make wise choices, and provide as much latitude as they can responsibly manage.

By contrast, minimizing latitude can have serious consequences for children, as in the case of overprotective parents. For example, recent studies show that temperamentally shy and inhibited children are more likely to

Children's development is influenced by their individual personalities, agency, and genetic make-up. Sensitive parents watch carefully and recognize ways to help children constructively build their talents and abilities. Christina Smith, © Intellectual Reserve, Inc.

withdraw from peer group interaction when their parents are overprotective (Nelson et al., 2006b). It is often a natural tendency for parents to "protect" their children from failure in social relationships when they perceive their child is having difficulty engaging in ongoing peer group activities. However, this usually has the opposite effect in that it does not allow children opportunities to develop critical social skills that can only be developed through interactions with peers.

Granting Latitude

Many practical applications may be suggested to parents for ways they can respect individuality, guide behavior, and assist children to make wise choices in behavior and attitude. Granting latitude refers not only to behavioral dimensions (such as deciding whether to study for a test or to attend a basketball game), but also to psychological autonomy (exploring their own thoughts and opinions that may be different from their parents). Elder Larry Y. Wilson (2012) stated, "Wise parents prepare their children to get along without them. They provide opportunities for growth as children acquire the spiritual maturity to exercise their agency properly" (p. 104). While many examples could be given that would be considered clearly authoritative, the following are a few suggestions of practical ways to apply the concept of latitude to parenting:

Giving choices and respecting individuality. Children benefit from being given many choices and appropriate levels of latitude to make their own decisions in a variety of domains whenever possible (for example, a teen is allowed to choose whether to complete chores in the morning or afternoon; a young child chooses a jacket or sweater on a fall afternoon). Elaborating upon this practice, Elder M. Russell Ballard (2006) stated, "Parents need to give children choices and should be prepared to appropriately adjust some rules, thus preparing children for real-world situations" (p. 32).

In the behavioral realm, supporting children's autonomy in this manner whenever possible helps them view adults as providers of information and guidance rather than as deliverers of messages of control. Parental communication

Children need opportunities during their formative years to begin taking ownership and solving problems, with the assistance of their parents. © Racorn.

is open and nonjudgmental, with more emphasis on listening and completely understanding before talking. In the psychological realm, respect for authority and independent thinking are valued and not viewed as being mutually exclusive. Research has shown that children are more likely to be respectful to parents and others when there is reciprocity and a degree of power sharing, negotiation, and compromise in their relationships with parents (Dumas, LaFreniere, & Serketich, 1995; Pettit & Lollis, 1997; Siqueland, Kendall, & Steinberg, 1996). Conversations that demonstrate a genuine regard and respect for others' opinions can send the message that individuals are valued, despite differences that may exist in opinions and beliefs.

Saying yes more often than no. Sister Marjorie Hinckley said, "I tried hard never to say 'no' if I could possibly say 'yes.' I think that worked well because it gave my children the feeling that I trusted them and they were responsible to do the best they could" (Pearce, 1999, p. 55). A daughter of President Heber J. Grant shared the following insights: "In matters of small importance, father seldom said 'no' to us. Consequently, when he did say 'no,' we knew he meant it. His training allowed us to make our own decisions

Overprotective parenting does not prepare children and teens adequately to learn from their own experiences and gain the skills needed to face challenges and effectively solve personal problems. © Larisa Lofitskaya.

whenever possible. He always explained very patiently just why he thought a certain procedure was unwise and then he would say, 'That's the way I feel about it; but of course, you must decide for yourself.' As a result, our decision was usually the same as his. He was able somehow to motivate us to want to do the right thing rather than to be forced to do it" (*Teachings . . . Heber J. Grant*, 2002, p. 200).

Allowing children to take responsibility. Children need opportunities during their formative years to begin taking ownership and solving problems, with the assistance of their parents. However, too much assistance by parents who hover or try too hard to protect children and teens from facing problems and consequences of their decisions can interrupt this process. While this type of overprotective parenting (what some have called "helicopter parenting") may cushion life's difficult experiences, it does not prepare children and teens adequately to learn from their own experiences and to gain needed skills in facing challenges and effectively solving personal problems.

Likewise, continually forcing parental points of view usually does not result in children and teens being able to learn how to make good choices and take responsibility for their decisions. What are parents to do when a child adopts an attitude, behavior, or opinion that is unacceptable? Balancing the provision of appropriate psychological autonomy (that is willingness to respect and encourage autonomous thinking, attitudes, opinions, and perceptions) with appropriate behavioral control (active monitoring and regulation of activities and associations) is a delicate and challenging area for parents. It requires discernment, inspiration, and action that usually play out in different ways depending on the individual nature and disposition of each child and teen.

Elder Robert D. Hales (1999) gave wise counsel to parents who are dealing with these situations: "Act with faith; don't react with fear. When our teenagers begin testing family values, parents need to go to the Lord for guidance on the specific needs of each family member. This is the time for added love and support and to reinforce your teachings on how to make choices. It is frightening to allow our children to learn from the mistakes they may make, but their willingness to choose the Lord's way and family values is greater when the choice comes from within than when we attempt to force those values upon them. The Lord's way of love and acceptance is better than Satan's way of force and coercion, especially in rearing teenagers" (p. 34).

Unfortunately, some children, despite gospel-centered teaching in the home, will use their agency to make decisions that take them far from parental values. In these cases, good judgment is needed to strike the right balance between love and law. Elder Dallin H. Oaks (2009) said:

> If parents have a wayward child—such as a teenager indulging in alcohol or drugs—they face a serious question. Does parental love require that these substances or their consumption be allowed in the home, or do the requirements of civil law or the seriousness of the conduct or the interests of other children in the home require that this be forbidden?

To pose an even more serious question, if an adult child is living in cohabitation, does the seriousness of sexual relations outside the bonds of marriage require that this child feel the full weight of family disapproval by being excluded from any family contacts, or does parental love require that the fact of cohabitation be ignored? I have seen both of these extremes, and I believe that both are inappropriate.

Where do parents draw the line? That is a matter for parental wisdom, guided by the inspiration of the Lord. There is no area of parental action that is more needful of heavenly guidance or more likely to receive it than the decisions of parents in raising their children and governing their families. (p. 28)

Because authoritative parenting implies flexibility in dealing with the unique disposition of each child, this style is more effective than the others in dealing with children who use their agency unwisely. Judiciously keeping doors open for children who stray and experience ensuing negative consequences often results in eventual reawakenings to earlier parental teachings, helping them take responsibility for their actions and take the steps that are needed to get on course. In addition to family and loved ones, friends and ward members who have provided earlier positive influence can often be instrumental in assisting individuals who are making their way back into the fold.

Assist children and teens to adopt religious faith. One of the most powerful tools that parents have in teaching their children positive values and helping them build a foundation for making good moral choices is their religious faith (Smith, 2005; Dean, 2010). Providing opportunities for children and teens to have spiritual awakenings in the home through religious practices and traditions (which are elaborated later in this chapter) increases the likelihood that they will actively seek to be engaged in a religious community. Research demonstrates that youth activities and religious education provide opportunities for moral discussion and civic engagement in ways that help youth think beyond themselves and consider the needs of others (King &

Furrow, 2004). In addition, adolescents who embrace a religious community are more likely to exhibit behavior that is consistent with positive moral values. They are more involved in activities that help the less fortunate and in community service that reflects a concern for others, compared to non-affiliated youth (Kerestes, Youniss, & Metz, 2004).

Religious involvement fosters better academic performance and prosocial behavior (acting out of a desire to put the needs of others before self) and discourages misconduct as well (Dowling et al., 2004). It is also associated with less delinquent behavior, including lower levels of sexual activity and drug and alcohol use (Bahr & Hoffman, 2010; Smith, 2005; Regnerus, Smith, & Fritsch, 2003). Religious activity provides young people with expanded networks of exemplary, religiously oriented adults and peers—conditions that also provide opportunities for internalizing important values that help children and teens override temptations that stem from biological urges or negative peer group pressure (Bridges & Moore, 2002; Jang & Johnson, 2001). In actuality, the quality of the parent-child relationship more often determines the type of peers that teenagers choose and whether they accept and adhere to parental values (Furman, Simon, Shaffer, & Bouchey, 2002; Laird, Pettit, Bates, & Dodge, 2003; Zhou, et al., 2002). In short, religious practices and traditions create conditions that engender greater moral maturity and help to provide a foundation for making good choices.

Limits

While providing latitude that can enhance the probability that children become independent and learn to use their agency wisely, parents also need to set limits around their children's and teens' exposure and access to influences that could bring them emotional, physical, and spiritual harm (such as early dating, inappropriate media, and immodest dress). These limits, accompanying reasons, and expectations for abiding by them are best taught in the home and can provide a foundation for children and teens to make good decisions when they are away from home (Walker, Fraser, & Harper, 2012).

The quality of the parent-child relationship more often determines the type of peers that teenagers choose and whether they accept and adhere to parental values. © *Goodluz.*

Responsibility for decision making is usually granted within acceptable parameters set by parents, and parental oversight might be relaxed as children mature and consistently make good choices (such as allowing decisions among appropriate media and peer group activities with continued monitoring but less direct parental involvement over time). However, these limits may sometimes need to be retightened in a spirit of love and concern in order to provide reminders of parental expectations when trust and confidence need to be re-earned, such as in situations where decisions leading to potential harm have been made (for example, friends talking a teen into trying an alcoholic drink at a late-night party) (Kerr, Stattin, & Ozdemir, 2012; Baumrind, Larzelere, & Owens, 2010). How far to go with what researchers refer to as *confrontive discipline* that is firm, direct, clear, and consistent in these kinds of situations requires careful discernment as noted earlier in the counsel from Elder Hales about acting with faith rather than reacting with fear (Baumrind, 2012).

Clearly, children need limits as well as frequent reassurance of their parents' love and confidence in them so that they are more open to parental teaching, guidance, and correction when necessary. President Brigham Young (1864) counseled, "Kind looks, kind actions, kind words, and a lovely, holy deportment towards them will bind our children to us with bands that cannot be easily broken; while abuse and unkindness will drive them from us." In fact, research underscores the sensitive nature of the parent-child relationship in findings demonstrating that whether children feel acceptance or rejection by parents has an impact on their psychological adjustment and desire to adhere to parental expectations and limits (Khaleque & Rohner, 2002). President Spencer W. Kimball (1982) taught, "Setting limits to what [children] can do means to th[ose] child[ren] that you love . . . and respect [them]" (p. 341). Warm and responsive parenting tends to promote lasting bonds with parents and "felt security" within children (Hart, Newell, & Olson, 2003), especially as parents have important conversations with their children and follow through with needed consequences in an appropriate manner. This, in turn, has a greater possibility of producing long-term change and has been linked to better behavior at the time and in the future.

While love is surely foundational to all successful approaches to human relationships, our Heavenly Father's example demonstrates not the dichotomy but the harmony that exists in an approach that emphasizes both high standards of conduct and high support. Indeed, this kind of warm and responsive child rearing mitigates hostility, resentment, feelings of rejection, and anger in children, all of which have been admonished in holy writ through the ages. "Provoke not your children to wrath: but bring them up in the nurture and admonition of the Lord" (Ephesians 6:4). In order to achieve such ends, parents require wisdom greater than their own by obtaining the Lord's help in making decisions about correcting misbehavior in a spirit of love. This loving context helps the children or teens achieve greater maturity and increase their ability to conform their lives to socially acceptable standards and to the commandments of God.

Seeking Guidance from the Spirit

Seeking guidance from the Spirit will assist parents in finding ways to discipline children and adolescents in a context of love, respect, consistency, fairness, and sensitivity. When the child has been corrected in a calm, controlled manner, that same Spirit which prompted the response can create a sense of compassion, charity, and forgiveness towards the child. Parents can remember that power and influence is righteously used when it is characterized by "persuasion, by long-suffering, by gentleness and meekness, . . . by love unfeigned[,] by kindness, and pure knowledge" (D&C 121:41–42). President Hinckley (1999) stated: "Rear [your children] in love. You don't have to kick them around. You don't have to get angry with them. You just have to love them. If they make mistakes, forgive them and help them to avoid a repetition" (p. 4). In order to properly affirm a righteous course of action under the stress and anxiety that often accompany a child's misbehavior, several considerations are helpful.

First, maintain composure and perspective. President Young observed, "I have seen more parents who were unable to control themselves than I

Confrontive discipline requires careful discernment. Act with faith instead of reacting with fear. Welden C. Andersen, © Intellectual Reserve, Inc.

ever saw who were unable to control their children" (*Teachings . . . Brigham Young*, 1997, p. 338). Often, sincere prayer and pondering are important ways to seek the support of the Spirit in controlling one's emotions in order to address the offense without giving offense. Children depend upon their parents to provide an example of emotional control and to be reasonable and responsive at all times—in other words, parents need to be at their best, even when children are at their worst. As President David O. McKay (1955) observed, "Children are more influenced by sermons you act than by sermons you preach" (p. 26).

Second, take a moment to evaluate the situation and what is at stake. What is causing the misbehavior? Is there an opportunity to teach? Is this a mountain or a molehill? Addressing the core problem and avoiding the temptation to react irritably to difficult or annoying behavior can bring parents more quickly to an effective intervention. For example, poor behavior may be tied to an *unfulfilled need* (being tired, hungry, or bored), *a stage of growth* (teething or the natural striving for autonomy during the toddler stage and again during the teenage years), *the present environment* (friends being mean; fear of the dark at bedtime; academic or peer-group struggles), or *a lack of information* (not yet understanding that friends are not happy when one refuses to share). In each of these cases, a quick, fix-it-all strategy, such as time-out or physical punishment may not be appropriate. Deliberate, repeated misbehavior is a better candidate for invoking a negative consequence. Meanwhile, misguided or immature behaviors may be better remedied in a more common sense manner that matches the need; that is, through teaching and listening and reasoning, meeting needs, or helping a child cope with a challenging situation.

Third, when punishment is warranted, use the mildest form of punishment likely to be effective. Speaking of the Savior, President J. Reuben Clark Jr. said, "I feel that [the Savior] will give that punishment which is the very least that our transgression will justify. . . . I believe that when it comes to making the rewards for our good conduct, he will give us the maximum that it is possible to give" (cited in Faust, 2001, p. 19). For example, depending on their nature, some children might respond quickly to a reminder for better behavior, while others might need a more serious consequence as incentive to change or increase their awareness of the seriousness of the infraction.

Fourth, and finally, as the scripture admonishes, let love follow the punishment, "showing forth afterwards an increase of love toward him whom thou hast reproved" (D&C 121:43). Although it can be very difficult at times, sincerely striving to keep the Spirit during disciplinary encounters will elevate the peace and security in the home while providing an environment more conducive to improved behavior. Parenting with the Spirit will help families avoid the coercive or permissive practices that often destroy peace, strain relationships, and ultimately create negative outcomes for the child.

Avoiding Coercion or Permissiveness

Compared to the authoritative style of parenting, frequent use of coercive parenting practices, including physical punishment and psychological control, invite a host of difficulties to child adjustment. This style is characterized by homes where there is a climate of hostility manifested by frequent spanking, yelling, criticizing, and forcing in ways that are dictatorial and arbitrarily imposed. This style of parenting has been linked to many forms of antisocial, withdrawn, and delinquent behaviors in children and adolescents (Hart, Newell, & Olson, 2003). Prophets have particularly discouraged the overuse of physical punishment. For example, President Young stated, "I will here say to parents, that kind words and loving actions toward children will subdue their uneducated nature a great deal better than the rod, or, in other words, than physical punishment" (*Teachings . . . Brigham Young*, 1997, p. 337). "Let the child have a mild training until it has judgment and sense to guide it. I differ with Solomon's recorded saying as to spoiling the child by sparing the rod" (Young, 1956, p. 196).

President Hinckley (1994) echoed this sentiment when he said, "I have never accepted the principle of 'spare the rod and spoil the child.' . . . Children don't need beating. They need love and encouragement" (p. 53). Some research shows that coercive tactics may result in immediate or short-term compliance. For example, one or two non abusive, mild slaps on the buttocks in limited situations, such as out-of-control children that pose danger to themselves or others, can be beneficial as a last resort, but only for younger children. However, other research indicates that even though limited spanking may immediately stop a child from misbehaving and willfully defying in the short term, it actually increases the likelihood of greater disobedience and antisocial behavior later on and is more likely to be done in parental anger. This approach also models physical aggression and could come at a steep cost to the parent-child relationship and children's self-regulation (Baumrind et al., 2010; Gershoff & Bitensky, 2007; MacKenzie, Nicklas, Waldfogel, and Brooks-Gunn, 2013).

In support of the view that sparing the rod is a better approach, the scriptural metaphor of a good shepherd and the importance of his rod reminds us that he guides his sheep by gathering the lambs in his arms, carrying them in his bosom, and gently leading them along (see Isaiah 40:11). The shepherd's rod is never used for beating sheep, else the passage "thy rod and thy staff . . . comfort me" (Psalm 23:4) makes little sense. It is used instead to ward off intruders; to count sheep as they "pass under the rod" (see Ezekiel 20:37; Leviticus 27:32); to part the wool to examine for defects, disease, or wounds; and to nudge sheep gently from going in the wrong direction. The rod is viewed as a protection and is also translated from the Hebrew in other places as "the word of God" or "the rod of his mouth" or "the voice of his mouth" (see Micah 6:9; Isaiah 11:4; 1 Nephi 15:23–24; Psalm 23:4).

Accordingly, there are alternate ways one can choose to read the scriptures that appear to support the view that "sparing the rod will spoil the child." For example, Proverbs 13:24 states, "He that spareth his rod hateth his son: but he that loveth him chasteneth him betimes." One might choose to read this as, "They who withhold the word of God hateth their children: They who loveth their children, correct (or teach) them early on (when they are young)." And Proverbs 23:13–14, "Withhold not correction from the child: for if thou beatest him with the rod, he shall not die. Thou shalt beat him with the rod, and shalt deliver his soul from hell," one might choose to read as, "Withhold not correction from children; for if you regulate them with the word of God, they will not die. Regulate your children with the word of God, and you will deliver their souls from hell."

Psychological control is a coercive approach designed to manipulate children's psychological and emotional experience and expression, and it has been associated with children's "externalizing" (that is, aggressive, disruptive, or delinquent behavior) and "internalizing" (anxiety or depression) disorders in childhood and adolescence (Barber & Olsen, 1997; Barber, Mingzhu, Olsen, McNeely, & Bose, 2012). Parents who use psychologically controlling behaviors may communicate disrespect to a child or teen. This can be done by conveying a lack of interest in what a child is saying, invalidating or discounting a child's feelings, or attacking the child in a condescending or patronizing way. They may also seek to control or manipulate the child through love withdrawal, through shaming, through erratic emotional behavior, or by creating unwarranted guilt ("If you do this, you will make me feel like I'm a bad parent and embarrass me in front of the neighbors"). In particular, love withdrawal (angrily refusing to talk to or look at a child after he or she misbehaves) is especially damaging to the delicate nature of the parent-child relationship (Nelson, Hart, Yang, Olsen, & Jin, 2006a; Nelson, Yang, Coyne, Olsen, & Hart, 2013). Wise parents follow the Lord's example of continuous love by assuring their children that "[their] hand[s are] stretched out still" (Isaiah 5:25).

Commonly in our day, by contrast, the permissive style of parenting focuses on high warmth combined with low expectations for mature child behavior. As a result, parents may overindulge children, neglect them by leaving them to their own devices, or provide inconsistent and confusing messages about what behavior is acceptable and unacceptable. Accordingly, President Ezra Taft Benson (1970) stated, "Permissive parents are part of the problem" (p. 22). Although permissive parents exert a degree of control over their children, they do so to a lesser degree than coercive and authoritative parents (Baumrind, 1996). For example, permissive parents tend to avoid using their authority to control their children's behavior, are tolerant of children's impulses (including aggression), encourage children to make their own decisions without providing necessary limits, refrain from imposing structure on children's time (that is, bedtime, mealtime, TV watching), and keep consequences for misbehavior at a minimum.

Social science research suggests that children raised by permissive parents may have greater difficulty respecting others, coping with frustration, delaying their gratification for a greater goal, and following through with their plans. Children of permissive parents have been found to be often quite social and to have a low rate of internalized problems (for example, depression and anxiety), but they tend to do poorly in academics, are more defiant of authority figures, and have a higher rate of adolescent sexual activity and drug and alcohol use. In sum, research has shown that authoritative parenting, in contrast to coercive parenting and permissive parenting, increases the probability of positive child developmental outcomes (Larzelere, Morris, & Harrist, 2013; Barber & Olsen, 1997; Hart, Newell, & Olsen, 2003; Eisenberg, 2006; Kuczynski, 2003; Smith & Hart, 2011).

Because authoritative parenting implies flexibility, this style is more effective than the others in dealing with children, since each child has unique characteristics and varying temperamental dispositions. For example, some teenagers are self-motivated to engage in appropriate activities, do not require curfews, and are home at reasonable hours. Other teens, without restrictions, lose control of their lives and wander onto dangerous paths. When authoritative practices are consistently used, each child and teen is guided in a balanced style of latitude, limits, and love that best matches his or her unique set of strengths and weaknesses.

Setting and Enforcing Appropriate Limits

Actively and skillfully employing authoritative parenting practices requires parents to work diligently in managing the many day-to-day decisions that are required to help children meet high expectations in a loving environment. While it may be quick and easy to select a particular consequence

Occasional extra privileges can encourage good performance and build strong relationships between parents and children. © Intellectual Reserve, Inc.

that applies to almost every wrongdoing, authoritative parents recognize that with each disciplinary encounter, they have an opportunity to teach, train, and socialize the child towards more socially acceptable standards. They also recognize that this process takes time and that choosing a strategy that fits the situation requires considering and selecting from a variety of approaches to find a good fit. The following are some examples of ways to apply authoritative, limit-setting practices in the home setting.

Rewarding good behavior. Rewarding good behavior and framing expectations in a positive manner can go far in inviting children to regulate their behavior in desirable ways (see entry "reward," pp. 430–431 in the Topical Guide of the LDS scriptures). Periodically surprising a child with extra privileges or providing ways to "earn benefits" associated with desirable behavior can also encourage good performance (such as, providing a sincere compliment or taking a child out for ice cream to celebrate consistent piano practice). Positive interactions build strong relationships. For example, research demonstrates that parents who maintain at least a 5- or 6-to-1 ratio of positive to negative interactions with their children and teens have more stable and adaptive relationships with them (Cavell & Strand, 2003).

Reasoning or induction. President Joseph F. Smith (1977) counseled, "Use no lash and no violence, but . . . approach them with reason, with persuasion and love unfeigned. . . . The man that will be angry at his boy, and try to correct him while he is in anger, is in the greatest fault. . . . You can only correct your children by love, in kindness, by love unfeigned, by persuasion, and reason" (pp. 316–317). Reasoning or induction in concert with enforcing limits is effective because it does more than simply correct behavior. It potentially teaches the child the reasons for socially acceptable behavior, communicates clear limits, acknowledges the emotions being felt, emphasizes consequences to others for hurtful behavior, and presents more acceptable strategies for dealing with conflict. Although not required for every situation, research shows that consistent efforts to provide simple rationales that are often repeated eventually sink in and can win voluntary obedience even in two- to three-year-old children. Numerous studies have documented positive ways that reasoning with children (especially in advance of a problem) can help them willingly regulate their own behavior, resulting in more confident, empathetic, helpful, and happy children (Hart, Newell, & Olsen, 2003).

Elder Ballard (2003) encouraged parents to "help children understand the reasons for rules, and always follow through with appropriate discipline when rules are broken. It is important as well to praise appropriate behavior. It will challenge all of your creativity and patience to maintain this balance, but the rewards will be great. Children who understand their boundaries through the consistent application of important rules are more likely to do well at school, to be more self-controlled, and to be more willing to abide by the laws of the land" (p. 7). He continues, "Helping children learn how to make decisions requires that parents give them a measure of autonomy, dependent on the age and maturity of the child and the situation at hand" (p. 8). Discussing reasons for rules can happen throughout the day as parents share expectations and suggest possible solutions. For example, in helping young children learn to share, a parent might say: "I know you are eager to play with the toy first, but Lisa can only stay ten more minutes. Please share your toy with her and you can play with it after she goes home." In helping an elementary school child deal with a child who frequently demeans him on the playground, a parent might say: "I understand how hard it is to have people say mean things about you. The situation won't be solved by calling him names or by seeking revenge. Let's talk about what we can do to resolve this situation in a way that is kind."

Communicate effectively with teens. The teenage years can be a challenge for both parents and teens. With his characteristic positive outlook and clear counsel, President Thomas S. Monson (2012) has exhorted teenagers:

> You entered that period some have labeled "the terrible teens." I prefer "the terrific teens." What a time of opportunity, a season of growth, a semester of development—marked by the acquisition of knowledge and the quest for truth.
>
> No one has described the teenage years as being easy. They are often years of insecurity, of feeling as though you just don't measure up, of trying to find your place with your peers, of trying to fit in. This is a time when you are becoming more independent—and perhaps desire more freedom than your parents are willing to give you right now. They are also prime years when Satan will tempt you and will do his utmost to entice you from the path which will lead you back to that heavenly home from which you came and back to your loved ones there and back to your Heavenly Father. (p. 126)

Our children are being tempted and buffeted like never before in the world's history, and so parents who are patient and loving, strong and effective, and wise and inspired are needed more than ever.

Wise parents remember that a warm tone of voice, a loving touch, and the sincere feeling behind the words they use often communicate much more than the words themselves. For example, in reasoning with teens, if not carefully worded, induction can come across as preachments and may provoke some opposition and testiness with older children and teens. Playing a "consultant role" often works better than attempting to lecture to teens (Cline & Fay, 1990; Cline & Fay, 1992). This involves reflective listening (for example, saying something like, "So you feel your teacher doesn't explain math very well and you are suffering for it"), using less directive "I" rather than more intrusive "you" statements ("Since you are excited about a career in medicine, I am confused about your decision to drop advanced biology"), musing and wondering aloud about potential consequences and alternatives ("Think how our home would look if none of us did our part to keep it clean"), and leaving more ownership for problem solving to the teen as a way of validating the teen's ability to work out a solution ("As long as it's done this week, I'll leave it up to you to decide when you'll mow the lawn").

Use subtle approaches when viable. Limit-setting strategies can also include subtle approaches that maintain a positive tone and do not require imposing penalties. For example, young children sometimes respond better to simply being redirected to more acceptable behaviors (such as, being shown how to gently pet a cat rather than being punished for inadvertently mishandling it). Planning ahead can also eliminate problems before they occur (putting safety latches on cupboards for curious toddlers, modeling sensitivity to an elderly grandparent's physical limitations). A technique called *predisposing* consists of sharing standards in advance of a situation that could potentially be a problem by forestalling it before it can occur ("Since dinner will be ready soon after we return home, I'm not planning to buy you candy during our visit to the store right now; perhaps next time").

Be clear and firm about rules and expectations. In authoritative homes, parents are clear and firm about rules and expectations. They take corrective action when children or teens do not respond. Children quickly learn whether their parents are likely to follow through and adjust their reactions accordingly. Firm and friendly reminders are better than the coercive methods that simply administer harsh, domineering, or arbitrary punishments. Authoritative parents patiently and proactively explain reasons for setting rules and then administer needed corrective measures promptly when children do not abide by them (Baumrind, 2012). Research has shown that when firm habits of good behavior are established early in life through parental regulatory practices that include ingredients of limit-setting, judicious use of appropriate punishment, much positive reinforcement, and frequent reasoning, parents are better able to relax control as their children grow older (Baumrind, 1996).

Monitor behavior. Monitoring the behaviors of children and teens will allow vigilant parents to be aware of safety hazards, media choices, frayed emotions, and children's needs in order to catch and resolve small issues before they turn serious. During the adolescent years, monitoring the adolescents' whereabouts and behaviors has been demonstrated to be crucial in reducing delinquent activity (Laird, Pettit, Bates, & Dodge, 2003). In this age of cell phones and texting, parents can establish with their adolescents clear guidelines for checking in and reporting on activities, who they are with, when they will return, and ways to communicate a need for rescue in case of a compromising situation (Kerr, Stattin, & Ozdemir, 2012). A warm, nurturing parent-child relationship that is cultivated early in life can go far in establishing positive and open parent-child communication habits that can continue into the teen years.

Following through with consequences. Setting limits and calmly following through with pre-established consequences when rules are violated is one way that parents can help children learn to be self-regulating. Examples could include temporarily suspending teen driving privileges for traffic violations, withholding a privilege until chores or homework are completed, or enforcing a time-out when a child hurts others out of anger, then discussing alternative methods for dealing with the contentious situation. In particular, setting limits around potentially harmful influences (for example, inappropriate media, early dating, or late nights out) helps children feel more safe and secure. Authoritative parents take responsibility for setting an appropriate number of rules for regulating children's behavior that can be realistically remembered and enforced. Some children may require more rules or more varied types of rules and punishments than others, depending on their individual natures. A strong family culture built around gospel principles helps children and teens recognize that standards such as those found in the Church's pamphlet, *For the Strength of Youth*, are not just good ideas, but represent the teachings of the prophets and the counsel of the Lord to youth in navigating the dangerous waters of today's culture.

In summary, many authoritative approaches to limit setting are possible. The foregoing suggestions are not intended to be an exhaustive list but are simply meant to illustrate appropriate responses consistent with maintaining the presence of the Spirit during disciplinary encounters. As parents show sensitivity to the situation and needs of the child, wisdom and inspiration can prevail. President Faust (1990) stated: "I do not know who is wise enough to say what discipline is too harsh or what is too lenient except the parents of the children themselves, who love them most. It is a matter of prayerful discernment for the parents. Certainly the overarching and undergirding principle is that the discipline of children must be motivated more by love than by punishment" (p. 32).

Love

As parents strive to help children and youth stay close to the Church, become morally grounded, adopt socially acceptable behaviors, and develop into young men and women who are fully prepared to accept adult roles, nothing will be more powerful in this process than the quality of the parent-child relationship. Nothing is more powerful in parenting than love. President Hinckley (1997) stated, "Every child is entitled to grow up in a home where there is warm and secure companionship, where there is love in the family relationship, where appreciation one for another is taught and exemplified, and where God is acknowledged and His peace and blessings invoked before the family altar" (416).

Children are less likely to push limits and seek attention through misbehavior when they feel that they are a high priority in their parents' lives.

Children are less likely to push limits and seek attention through misbehavior when they feel that they are a high priority in their parents' lives. © *Nagy-Bagoly Ilona.*

President Joseph F. Smith (1977) counseled, "If you wish your children to be taught in the principles of the gospel, if you wish them to love the truth and understand it, if you wish them to be obedient to and united with you, love them! And prove to them that you do love them by your every word or act to them" (p. 316). Certainly, as parents reason with their children and guide them to more appropriate behavior, it is important to remember that ultimately love and the parents' relationship to their children will be the best vehicle for helping children learn to love, live, and appreciate the simple truths of the gospel embodied in the family proclamation, such as love, respect, repentance, forgiveness, and compassion.

Following Our Heavenly Father's Example

Our Father in Heaven has given us a perfect example of how we should parent through the ways that he parents us. He gives us commandments, outlining the limits and boundaries within which we should conduct our

Parents should take time to be real friends with their children. © *Konrad Bak.*

lives. When we fail to meet his expectations, we face consequences and punishments according to his eternal laws that are consistent with our transgressions, and his rebukes are accompanied and motivated by his unfailing love. He will not withdraw his perfect and constant love from us, although we may withdraw from him at times (Eyring, 2012). He is always there for us when we earnestly seek him in humility and righteousness (see D&C 88:63, 83). He loves us perfectly. Elder D. Todd Christofferson (2011) stated, "If we sincerely desire and strive to measure up to the high expectations of our Heavenly Father, He will ensure that we receive all the help we need, whether it be comforting, strengthening, or chastening" (p. 99).

Parents become more like him as they learn to love unconditionally as he does and as they invest time in building relationships. President Ezra Taft Benson (1974) counseled: "Be a real friend. Mothers, take time to be a real friend to your children. Listen to your children, really listen, talk with them, laugh and joke with them, sing with them, play with them, cry with them, hug them, honestly praise them. Yes, regularly spend unrushed one-on-one time with each child. Be a real friend to your children" (p. 32). Wise parents love not as their children become more lovable, since some days are certainly challenging. Rather, parents seek the gift of charity to experience a divine expanding of their capability to love through the good times and the bad—and thus are increasingly filled with his love (see Moroni 7:48). As parents unfailingly love each other and each child with fullness of heart, relationships can change, miracles of forgiveness and understanding can take place, and family solidarity and closeness can result.

Realizing the Benefits of Emotional Connection

Over the course of many decades, research has confirmed the significance of a strong parent-child bond and has demonstrated remarkably positive results in child outcome. For example, children are less aggressive and more sociable and empathetic if they have parents (particularly fathers) who are more loving, patient, playful, responsive, and sympathetic to children's feelings and needs. Similarly, mothers who take the time to engage in mutually enjoyable activities with their children more effectively convey values and rules to them (Kochanska, 1997). Within the encircling arms of a warm, strong relationship, limits are much easier to explain and enforce, and latitude is given with greater trust.

In a study of Latter-day Saint families, research demonstrated that parents who take the time to become emotionally connected with their teens, to set regulatory limits, and to foster autonomy are far more likely to have adolescents who are more careful in their selection of peers, regardless of what part of the country they live in. Children reared in these types of family environments—where prayer, scripture study, and religious values are stressed—were also more likely to internalize religiosity. Personal prayer and scripture study as well as private spiritual experiences were found to be a strong deterrent to delinquent behavior (Top & Chadwick, 1998).

Though they love their children and may have good relationships with them, parents may still wonder how they might maintain a strong and righteous influence on their children in a world where there are many other

Mothers who take the time to engage in mutually enjoyable activities with their children more effectively convey values and rules to them. John Luke, © 2010 Intellectual Reserve, Inc.

influences seeking for their time, attention, and loyalty. Within the context of a warm, loving relationship, research suggests that it is in the moral and spiritual domains where parents can have the most influence (Leman, 2005), even though schools, culture, the media and peer interaction can play major roles as well (Comunian & Gielen, 2006; Gibbs, Basinger, Grime, & Snarey, 2007; Speicher, 1994). For example, studies have shown that while peers have influence, they seem to matter more in superficial aspects of behavior like hair and clothing styles, the use of slang, and transient day-to-day behaviors, all of which can shift frequently with changes in friendships. Parents are more likely to have influence on core values that are reflected in religiosity, political persuasion, and educational plans, to name a few (Collins, Maccoby, Steinberg, Hetherington, & Bornstein, 2000; Sebald, 1986).

This recognition can help parents stay encouraged in their continuing efforts to love, train, encourage and pass virtuous values to their family through planned and spontaneous teaching of gospel principles in the

Quality time does not replace quantity time. Quality is a direct function of quantity—and mothers, to nurture their children properly, must provide both. © Igor Yaruta.

home, while demonstrating a high level of love and support. In speaking to mothers, though this principle can also apply to fathers, Elder Ballard (2006) stated: "Mothers must not fall into the trap of believing that 'quality' time can replace 'quantity' time. Quality is a direct function of quantity—and mothers, to nurture their children properly, must provide both. To do so requires constant vigilance and a constant juggling of competing demands. It is hard work, no doubt about it" (p. 31).

Showing Love and Support

Demonstrating love and support to children and teens includes maintaining a consistent presence in the child's life and a strong commitment to their well-being. In addition, authoritative parents are generous in their verbal expressions of love and their willingness to provide the support needed for children and youth to thrive (such as attending the teen's extra-curricular events or meeting with a child's teachers at a parent-teacher conference). The following suggestions provide practical applications and counsel for building a loving parent-child relationship.

Be companionable and invest time. President Gordon B. Hinckley (1997) stated, "Fathers, be kind to your children. Be companionable with them" (p. 52). President Dieter F. Uchtdorf (2010) added, "In family relationships *love* is really spelled t-i-m-e, time. Taking time for each other is the key for harmony at home" (p. 22). Whether taking time to play ball with a young son in the park or being available and sympathetic in reassuring a teen struggling with homework, the consistent, loving presence of an interested parent makes a difference.

Safeguard relationships. Sister Marjorie Hinckley was an excellent example of the importance of safeguarding relationships with children. Speaking of her mother-in-law, Kathleen H. Hinckley writes, "When I called her for advice, she verbalized something I would say over and over to myself for many years to come, 'Just save the relationship.' I believe those words are the most simple and powerful parenting principle I have ever learned" (cited in Pearce, 1999, p. 56). All this takes significant time and energy.

Don't be afraid to apologize. Even the most wonderful, responsive parents will, from time to time and under difficult circumstances, lose patience with demanding children. Just as there are no perfect children, there also are no perfect parents. Parents who admit mistakes and say they are sorry model sincere efforts to change and overcome human weaknesses. At one moment, parents may be more permissive because of various external and internal factors, at another moment more coercive. However, authoritative parents recognize their errors and make adjustments along the way. President Dieter F. Uchtdorf (2011) stated: "God wants to help us to eventually turn all of our weaknesses into strengths, but He knows that this is a long-term goal. . . . Many of you are endlessly compassionate and patient with the weaknesses of others. Please remember also to be compassionate and patient with yourself" (p. 120).

Reassure after reproof. After imposing a reasonable consequence for an action, such as being removed from an activity or experiencing the natural consequence of a poor choice, children may need added reassurance. Physical affection may assist a young child with a quivering lip to restore a sense of inner security. A carefully chosen affirming statement at a time of reproof is generally important at all ages to keep relationships strong. At times, humor about the situation can be also be appropriately used to break the tension ("Okay, enough of this serious stuff, time for a group hug!"). Perhaps a change of activity may help, particularly when it gives children a chance to resume positively interacting with their parent. Finally, expressing confidence in the child can help alleviate their concerns ("I know it's been a hard day. We all make mistakes. Let's start over and try again").

Focus more on effort than outcome. President Hinckley (1997) reminded parents: "Never forget that these little ones are the sons and daughters of God and that yours is a custodial relationship to them. . . . They may do, in the years that come, some things you would not want them to do, but be patient, be patient. You have not failed as long as you have tried. Never forget that" (p. 422). No matter the outcome of our sincere efforts, the Lord blesses us for our efforts. He is aware of our offerings of time and energy in behalf of our families. However, sometimes, despite the best efforts of parents, children exercise their agency in irresponsible ways and wander onto forbidden paths. Parents would do well not to berate themselves for what they think could have been. Just as surely as parents should not take all the blame for unrighteous and rebellious offspring, parents cannot take all the credit for faithful offspring. Maintaining an eye towards our Savior can help us recognize through all the uncertainties and disappointments of life that the Redeemer of the world can help repair our world when everything seems to fray apart. His Atonement heals all wounds and can comfort every heart pierced through with sorrow. The sweet reassurance of the gospel and the enabling power of the Atonement enlarge our hearts with love, understanding, patience, and hope—for ourselves and our loved ones.

Conclusion

Sister Cheryl A. Esplin (2012) stated, "Raising our children is a much greater responsibility than we can do alone, without the Lord's help. He knows exactly what our children need to know, what they need to do, and what they need to be to come back into His presence" (p. 10). We have ready access to the surest source of knowledge about parenting. As we learn through study, experience, and revelation, we can strengthen our capacities to apply these principles, live according to the truths of the proclamation, and approach the opportunities and challenges of parenting with greater confidence.

References

Bahr, S. J., & Hoffman, J. P. (2010). Parenting style, religiosity, peers, and adolescent heavy drinking. *Journal of Studies on Alcohol and Drugs, 71*, 539–543.

Ballard, M. R. (2003). The sacred responsibilities of parenthood. *2003–2004 Speeches*, Provo, UT: Brigham Young University.

Ballard, M. R. (2006, March). The sacred responsibilities of parenthood. *Ensign, 36*(3), 26–33.

Barber, B. K., & Olsen, J. A. (1997). Socialization in context: Connection, regulation, and autonomy in the family, school, and neighborhood, and with peers. *Journal of Adolescent Research, 12*(2), 287–315.

Barber, B. K., Mingzhu, X., Olsen, J. A., McNeely, C. A., & Bose, K. (2012). Feeling disrespected by parents: Refining the measurement and understanding of psychological control. *Journal of Adolescence, 35*(2), 273–287.

Baumrind, D. (1996). The discipline controversy revisited. *Family Relations, 45*(4), 405–414.

Baumrind, D. (2012). Differentiating between confrontive and coercive kinds of parental power-assertive disciplinary practices. *Human Development, 55*, 35–51.

Baumrind, D., Larzelere, R. E., & Owens, E. B. (2010). Effects of preschool parents' power assertive patterns and practices on adolescent development. *Parenting: Science and Practice, 10*, 157–201.

Benson, E. T. (1970, October). "Strengthening the Family." In Conference Report, 21–25.

Benson, E. T. (1974). *God, family, country: Our three great loyalties*. Salt Lake City: Deseret Book.

Bornstein, M., H. & Lamb, M. E. (2011). *Developmental science: An advanced textbook*. New York, NY: Psychology Press.

Bridges, L. J., & Moore, K. A. (2002, September). Religious involvement and children's well-being: What research tells us (and what it doesn't). Retrieved from http://www.childtrends.org/wp-content/uploads/2002/01/Child_Trends-2002_01_01_FR_ReligionSpiritAdol.pdf

Cavell, T. A., & Strand, P. S. (2003). Parent-based interventions for aggressive children. In L. Kuczynski (Ed.), *Handbook of dynamics in parent-child relations* (pp. 395–420). Thousand Oaks, CA: Sage Publications.

Christofferson, D. T. (2011, April). "As many as I love, I rebuke and chasten." *Ensign, 41*(4), 99.

Clark, J. R., Jr. (1955). As ye sow. *Brigham Young University Speeches of the Year* (p. 7). Provo, UT: Brigham Young University.

Cline, F. W., & Fay, J. (1992). *Parenting with love and logic: Teaching children responsibility*. Colorado Springs, CO: Pinon Press.

Collins, W. A., Maccoby, E. E., Steinberg, L., Hetherington, E. M., & Bornstein, M. H. (2000). Contemporary research on parenting: The case for nature and nurture. *American Psychologist, 55*(2), 218–232.

Comunian, A. L., & Gielen, U. P. (2006). Promotion of moral judgment maturity through stimulation of social role-taking and social reflection: An Italian intervention study. *Journal of Moral Education, 35*(1), 51–69.

Dean, K. C. (2010). *Almost Christian: What the faith of our teenagers is telling the American church*. Oxford, UK: Oxford University Press.

Dowling, E. M., Gestsdottir, S., Anderson P. M., von Eye, A., Almerigi, J., & Lerner, R. M. (2004). Structural relations among spirituality, religiosity, and thriving in adolescence. *Applied Developmental Psychology, 8*(1), 7–16.

Dumas, J. D., LaFreniere, P. J., & Serketich, W. J. (1995). "'Balance of power'": A transactional analysis of control in mother-child dyads involving socially competent, aggressive, and anxious children. *Journal of Abnormal Psychology, 104*(1), 104–113.

Eisenberg, N. (Ed.). (2006). *Handbook of child psychology: Social, emotional, and personality development*, vol. 3, Hoboken, NJ: John Wiley & Sons.

Esplin, C. A. (2012, May). Teaching our children to understand. *Ensign, 42*(5), 10.

Eyring, H. B. (2012, November). Where is the pavilion? *Ensign, 42*(11), 72.

Faust, J. E. (1990, November). The greatest challenge in the world—Good parenting. *Ensign, 20*(11), 34.

Faust, J. E. (2001, November). The Atonement: Our greatest hope. *Ensign, 31*(11), 19.

First Presidency and Council of the Twelve Apostles. (1995, November). The family: A proclamation to the world. *Ensign, 25*(11), 102.

Furman, W., Simon, V. A., Shaffer, L., & Bouchey, H. A. (2002). Adolescents' working models and styles for relationships with parents, friends, and romantic partners. *Child Development, 73*(1), 241–255.

Gershoff, E. T., & Bitensky, S. H. (2007). The case against corporal punishment of children: Converging evidence from social science research and international human rights law and implications for U.S. public policy. *Psychology, Public Policy, and Law, 13*(4), 231–272.

Gibbs, J. C., Basinger, K. S., Grime, R. L., & Snarey, J. R. (2007). Moral judgment development across cultures: Revisiting Kohlberg's universality claims. *Developmental Review, 27*, 443–500.

Hales, R. D. (1999, May). Strengthening families: Our sacred duty. *Ensign, 29*(5), 34.

Hart, C. H., Newell, L. D., & Haupt, J. H. (2008, August). Love, limits, and latitude. *Ensign, 38*(8), 60–65.

Hart, C. H., Newell, L. D., & Haupt, J. H. (2012). Parenting with love, limits, and latitude: Proclamation principles and supportive scholarship. In A. J. Hawkins, D. C. Dollahite, & T. W. Draper (Eds.), *Successful marriages and families: Proclamation principles and research perspectives* (pp. 103–117). Provo, UT: Brigham Young University.

Hart, C. H., Newell, L. D., & Olsen, S. F. (2003). Parenting skills and social-communicative competence in childhood. In J. O. Greene & B. R. Burleson (Eds.), *Handbook of communication and social interaction skills* (pp. 753–797). Mahwah, NJ: Lawrence Erlbaum.

Hart, C. H., Newell, L.D., & Sine, L. L. (2000). Proclamation-based principles of parenting and supportive scholarship. In D. C. Dollahite (Ed.), *Strengthening our families: An in-depth look at the proclamation on the family* (pp. 100–123). Salt Lake City: Deseret Book.

Hart, C. H. (2008). Our divine nature and life decisions. *2008–2009 Speeches.* Provo, UT: Brigham Young University.

Hinckley, G. B. (1994, November). Save the children. *Ensign, 24*(11), 53.

Hinckley, G. B. (1997, November). Some thoughts on temples, retention of converts and missionary service. *Ensign, 27*(11), 52.

Hinckley, G. B. (1997). *Teachings of Gordon B. Hinckley.* Salt Lake City: Deseret Book.

Hinckley, G. B. (1999, February). Life's obligations. *Ensign, 29*(2), 4.

Hinckley, G. B., Monson, T. S., & Faust, J. E. (1999, December). First Presidency letter. *Liahona, 23*(12), 1.

Holden, G. W. (1995). Parental attitudes toward childrearing. In M. H. Bornstein (Ed.), *Handbook of parenting, vol. 3: Status and social conditions of parenting* (pp. 359–392). Mahwah, NJ: Lawrence Erlbaum.

Jang, S. J., & Johnson, B. R. (2001). Neighborhood disorder, individual religiosity, and adolescent use of illicit drugs: A test of multilevel hypotheses. *Criminology, 39*(1), 109–143.

Kerestes, M., Youniss, J., & Metz, E. (2004). Longitudinal patterns of religious perspective and civic integration. *Applied Developmental Science, 8*(1), 39–46.

Kerr, M., Stattin, H., & Ozdemir, M. (2012). Perceived parenting style and adolescent adjustment: Revisiting directions of effects and the role of parental knowledge. *Developmental Psychology, 48*(6), 1540–1553.

Khaleque, A., & Rohner, R. P. (2002). Perceived parental acceptance-rejection and psychological adjustment: A meta-analysis of cross-cultural and intracultural studies. *Journal of Marriage and Family, 64*, 54–64.

King, P. E., & Furrow, J. L. (2004). Religion as a resource for positive youth development: Religion, social capital, and moral outcomes. *Developmental Psychology, 40*(5), 703–713.

Kimball, E. L. (Ed.). (1982). *The teachings of Spencer W. Kimball.* Salt Lake City: Bookcraft, 341.

Kochanska, G. (1997). Mutually responsive orientation between mothers and their children: Implications for early socialization. *Child Development, 68*(1), 94–112.

Kuczynski, L. (Ed.). (2003). *Handbook of dynamics in parent-child relations.* Thousand Oaks, CA: Sage Publications.

Laird, R. D., Pettit, G. S., Bates, J. E., & Dodge, K. A. (2003). Parents' monitoring-relevant knowledge and adolescents' delinquent behavior: Evidence of correlated developmental changes and reciprocal influences. *Child Development, 74*(3), 752–768.

Larzelere, R. E., Morris, A. S., & Harrist, A. W. (Eds.). (2013). *Authoritative parenting: Synthesizing nurturance and discipline for optimal child development.* Washington, DC: American Psychological Association.

Leman, P. J. (2005). Authority and moral reasons: Parenting style and children's perceptions of adult rule justifications. *International Journal of Behavioral Development, 29*(4), 265–270.

MacKenzie, M. J., Nicklas, E., Waldfogel, J., & Brooks-Gunn, J. (2013). *Pediatrics.* Retrieved from http://pediatrics.aappublications.org/content/early/2013/10/16/peds.2013-1227

McConkie, B.R. (1979). *The mortal Messiah: From Bethlehem to Calvary.* Salt Lake City: Deseret Book.

McKay, D. O. (1953). *Gospel ideals.* Salt Lake City: Improvement Era Publication, 347.

McKay, D. O. (1955, April). In Conference Report, 26.

Monson, T. S. (2012, May). Believe, obey, and endure. *Ensign, 42*(5), 126.

Nelson, D. A., Hart, C. H., Yang, C., Olsen, J. A., & Jin, S. (2006a). Aversive parenting in China: Associations with child physical and relational aggression. *Child Development, 77* (3), 554–572.

Nelson, D. A., Yang, C., Coyne, S. M., Olsen, J. A., & Hart, C. H. (2013). Parental psychological control dimensions: Connections with Russian preschoolers' physical and relational aggression. *Journal of Applied Developmental Psychology, 34*(1), 1–8.

Nelson, L. J., Hart, C. H., Wu, B., Yang, C., Roper, S. O., & Jin, S. (2006b). Relations between Chinese mothers' parenting practices and social withdrawal in early childhood. *International Journal of Behavioral Development, 30*(3), 261–271.

Oaks, D. H. (2009, November). Love and law. *Ensign, 39*(11), 22–23.

Pearce, V. H. (Ed.). (1999). *Glimpses into the life and heart of Marjorie Pay Hinckley.* Salt Lake City: Deseret Book.

Pettit, G. S., & Lollis, S. (1997). Introduction to special issue: Reciprocity and bidirectionality in parent-child relationships: New approaches to the study of enduring issues. *Journal of Social and Personal Relationships, 14(4),* 435–440.

Plomin, R., Reiss, D., Hetherington, E. M., & Howe, G. W. (1994). Nature and nurture: Genetic contributions to measures of the family environment. *Developmental Psychology, 30*, 32–43.

Regnerus, M., Smith, C., & Fritsch, M. (2003). *Religion in the lives of American adolescents: A review of the literature: A research report of the national study of youth and religion.* Chapel Hill, NC: National Study of Youth and Religion.

Sebald, H. (1986). Adolescents' shifting orientation toward parents and peers: A curvilinear trend over recent decades. *Journal of Marriage and the Family, 48*, 5–13.

Siqueland, L., Kendall, P. C., & Steinberg, L. (1996). Anxiety in children: Perceived family environments and observed family interaction. *Journal of Clinical Child Psychology, 25*(2), 225–237.

Smith, C. (2005). *Soul searching: The religious and spiritual lives of American teenagers.* New York, NY: Oxford University Press.

Smith, J. F. (1977). *Gospel doctrine* (3rd ed.). Salt Lake City: Deseret Book.

Smith, J. F., Jr. (1916). Is man immortal? *Improvement Era*, 426.

Smith, J. F., Lund, A. H., & Penrose, C. W. (1912). Pre-existent states. *Improvement Era*, 417.

Smith, P. K., & Hart, C. H. (Eds.). (2011). *The Wiley-Blackwell handbook of childhood social development* (2nd ed.). Oxford, UK: Wiley-Blackwell Publishers.

Speicher, B. (1994). Family patterns of moral judgment during adolescence and early adulthood. *Developmental Psychology, 30*, 624–632.

Teachings of presidents of the Church: Brigham Young. (1997). Salt Lake City: The Church of Jesus Christ of Latter-day Saints, 337–338.

Teachings of presidents of the Church: Heber J. Grant. (2002). Salt Lake City: The Church of Jesus Christ of Latter-day Saints.

Top. B. L., & Chadwick, B. A. (1998). Raising righteous children in a wicked world. *Brigham Young Magazine, 52*(2), 26–34.

Uchtdorf, D. F. (2010, November). Of things that matter most. *Ensign, 40*(11), 22.

Uchtdorf, D. F. (2011, November). Forget me not. *Ensign, 41*(11), 120.

Walker, L. M., Fraser, A. M., & Harper, J. M. (2012). Walking the walk: The moderating role of proactive parenting on adolescents' value-congruent behaviors. *Journal of Adolescence, 35*, 1141–1152.

Widtsoe, J. A. (Ed.). (1978). *Discourses of Brigham Young. 1.* Salt Lake City: Deseret Book.

Wilson, L. Y. (2012, May). Only on the principles of righteousness. *Liahona, 36*(5), 103–105.

Young, B. (1864, December 7). *Deseret News,* 2.

Young, B. (1956). *Journal of discourses.* Los Angeles, CA: Gartner Printing & Litho., 196.

Zhou, Q., Eisenberg, N., Lousoya, S. H., Fabes, R. A., Reiser, M., Guthrie, I. K., . . . Shepard, S. A. (2002). The relations of parental warmth and positive expressiveness to children's empathy-related responding and social functioning: A longitudinal study. *Child Development, 73,* 893–915.

JENET JACOB ERICKSON

6

Motherhood:
Restoring Clarity and Vision in a World of Confusing Messages

IN 2010, the authors of a premier family science journal article made a statement that culminated a 50-year period of questioning the meaning of motherhood (Biblarz & Stacey, 2010). Arguing that research does not indicate children's need for a mother and a father, they concluded that "the gender of parents only matters in ways that don't matter" (National Council on Family Relations, 2010). The statement suggests a question we may not have ever expected could be asked. That is, "Does having a mother really matter to children and family life?"

Current arguments for "genderless parenting"—parenting that is not defined by the inherent importance of both a father and a mother—are built on a progression of cultural shifts in attitudes about women and motherhood. Arguably, these ideas developed in reaction to traditions that did not recognize women's capacities and competence outside of traditional roles. In an effort to advocate for women as individuals equal in capacity and competence to their male counterparts, traditional roles that rested upon assumptions of gender differences were questioned and critiqued. Underlying the push for equality was a relentless demand for "sameness." The need for men and women to be "the same" in order to establish their equality led to a notion of interchangeability—that one could do what the other could do, and just as well, given the chance. While "equality" may have been the perceived goal of this effort, a less desirable outcome seems to have come with it. That is, if gender itself is not essential, then mothers—or fathers, for that matter—are also not essential. Ironically, the effort to build equality led to the conclusion that the unique contributions of mothers (and fathers) are unnecessary. All that is needed are committed caregivers.

Since the dawn of the Restoration, prophets and apostles have revealed truths regarding the significance and divinity of motherhood and taught eternal patterns that protect the sacred relationship of equality and interdependence between mothers and fathers. These truths are unparalleled in their ability to dispel confusion and rectify distortions inherited by a culture filled with arguments questioning the place of womanhood and the meaning of motherhood. By drawing on the eternal perspective of motherhood, this chapter will address some of the specific issues and dilemmas that have contributed to this confusion. Scientific theories and research that explore the unique significance of motherhood are clarified by revealed truths of the restored gospel.

How Did We Get to This Place?

In 1963, Betty Friedan released *The Feminine Mystique*, her report from the "trenches" of marriage and motherhood. In some ways, Friedan's book was an expansion of efforts to bring awareness to the invisible experiences of women dealing with challenges of unequal power and opportunity, where men had greater privilege. In the developed world, these unequal privileges were reflected in political, educational, and employment opportunities, economic benefits, and occurrences of domestic violence.

Friedan's work reacted to the problems of these inequities in the modern world by advocating for the expansion of women's opportunities in educational and professional work. But it also seriously questioned the meaning and contribution of a woman's life when she is mainly engaged in child-rearing. The demands of caring for children full-time meant that women would be dependent on men economically, and hence have less access to the economic, political, and societal power Friedan perceived to matter most. From this point of view, the family—including motherhood and marriage—was a "risky proposition" because it "ranked lowest in terms of prestige" and obligated women "to subordinate their personal objectives . . . devoting themselves to the day-to-day well-being of other family members," which "may be deemed virtuous," but was not "a path to power and success" (Polatnik, 1973, pp. 70, 76).

In some ways, these dilemmas were a predictable response to dramatic changes with industrialization and urbanization in the nineteenth century. Prior to industrialization, mothers and fathers worked side by side to build their household economy, represented in the family farm or small artisan shop. With industrialization, the work of production moved outside the home, creating a split between work and home. Fathers were moved to the periphery of family life as they went out into "the world" to establish themselves as earners, while mothers became the primary socializers, educators, and caregivers of their children (Blankenhorn, 1995). Work that had once been shared by family members was now assigned to women, resulting in more burdensome and isolating tasks.

At the same time, an entire code of conduct emerged for women, inflexibly defining their roles and reinforcing the division between men and women in household labor. Because their property and earnings belonged to their husbands, married women could not pursue personal economic interests. Lacking "the means and motive for self-seeking," cultural ideals prescribed women's appropriate attitude to be selfless—to absorb and even redeem the home from the strains that resulted from the "evils" of the business world. Women were "to live for others" by giving up all self-interest—and in that way to save the home (Cott, 1977, pp. 70–71). Perhaps predictably, caregiving labor became identified with women's oppression. Children came to be viewed as a liability—expensive, inconvenient, and an encroachment on personal fulfillment. A simple desire for fairness seemed to demand her liberation from such work and the family responsibilities associated with it.

But rather than challenging the attitudes that had devalued women, the new woman advocated for by radical feminists ironically looked more like "the old man" they had criticized (Elshtain, 1982). By crossing the line into contempt for motherhood, feminist ideas that had intended to elevate women became self-defeating, because they required that women embrace a view of the meaning of life that "had rejected or devalued the world of the traditionally 'feminine'" (p. 447). An honest evaluation of what has followed since this time would have to acknowledge significant benefits for women in terms of educational, professional, and political opportunities. But it would also have to acknowledge significant challenges for women and mothers— many of which reflect the dismantling of the protections of the institution of marriage and family that had been identified as "the enemy."

Stevenson and Wolfers' (2009) recent analysis of changes in women's reported happiness over time indicates an important paradox. By most objective measures, including a decreased gender wage gap, educational attainment that now surpasses men, unprecedented control over fertility, technology that has freed women from domestic drudgery, and increased freedoms within the family and the market sphere, women's lives have dramatically improved over the last 35 years. But during that same period, there has been a significant decline in reported happiness among US women and women internationally, especially when compared with men's reported happiness. This decrease in reported happiness appears across all educational levels, age groups, marital categories, and employment statuses. Further, decreased happiness has been reported across multiple life domains, including marital satisfaction, job satisfaction, family financial situation, and life as a whole.

While it is impossible to definitively explain the causes for this reported decrease in happiness, it is likely that the challenges faced by women today, far less likely for women in the past, could be part of the reported decline. In the year 1970, out of 1,000 unmarried women ages 15 and older, there were 76.5 marriages. By the year 2008, that rate dropped to 37.4 marriages per 1,000 unmarried women. At the same time, the rate of divorce increased. In the year 1960, out of every 1,000 married women ages 15 and older, there were 9.2 divorces. In 1980, the divorce rate rose to 22.6 per 1,000 married women and then decreased to a current rate of 16.9, which has been a consistent average since 2005.

Ironically, no-fault divorce legislation, first passed in 1968, purportedly sought to benefit women by enabling them to leave destructive marriages without the challenge of establishing fault in their spouse. But by enabling one spouse to dissolve a marriage without establishing any cause, no-fault divorce inadvertently made marriage contractual and allowed one spouse to opportunistically exploit the family. In the decades since, no-fault divorce has arguably contributed to a host of problems for women, including dramatic increases in poverty within female-headed households, greater likelihood of unstable and abusive couple relationships, reduced incentives to marry, and increased marriage age (Allen, 2006).

Partly in response to increases in the likelihood of divorce, rates of cohabitation have also dramatically increased, a change that has also not benefited women. Relative to marriage, cohabiting unions tend to be much less stable, and to have less commitment, trust, and sexual fidelity, as well as more violence. Where 15% of married families may have broken up by the time a child is five years old, 50% of cohabiting families will have broken up (University of Virginia, 2011). At the same time, there have been dramatic increases in the number of women bearing children outside of the stability and support of marriage. In 1960, only 5.3% of births were to unmarried women. But by 2007, that percentage had increased to 40%, bringing with it the attending challenges of poverty, instability, and dramatically increased risks for children born in this situation (University of Virginia, 2011, p. 92).

These changes have contributed to significantly greater reliance on women's participation in the workforce in order to provide essential family income. As a positive outcome of feminist advocacy, women today have increased opportunities for diverse and fulfilling employment opportunities. But perhaps unexpectedly, many women today are employed for far

Many women today are employed for far more hours than they would like. © *Iakov Filimonov.*

more hours than they would like to be. Consistent with numerous other surveys, the 2005 nationally representative Motherhood Study found that although 47% of mothers were working full-time, only 15% wanted to be. Those who were working their preferred work hours felt less depressed and stressed, and more appreciated, confident, and content than those working more than they wanted to be (Jacob, 2008, 217).

These outcomes provide evidence for the significant challenges women and mothers face as the institution of marriage and family—identified by some as "the enemy"—has been dismantled. Perhaps ironically, research results garnered over the last 35 years of experimentation with new family structures consistently indicate that the safest and most facilitative structure of healthy thriving for women (as well as men and children) is within the structure of marriage and family. This is not to suggest that traditional patterns of family life adhered to in the past did not need changing. But it does clearly suggest that the dismantling and replacing of traditional structures of marriage and motherhood is not the path to better outcomes and satisfaction for women.

Prophetic Teachings about the Eternal Significance of Motherhood

Teachings of the restored gospel provide further clarity in resolving the complexity of these issues and establishing the significance and blessings of motherhood. A First Presidency statement in 1942 declared, "Motherhood is near to divinity. It is the highest, holiest service to be assumed by mankind. It places her who honors its holy calling and service next to the angels" (Clark, 1946, p. 178). The calling of motherhood has been identified as the most ennobling endowment God could give his daughters, "as divinely called, as eternally important in its place as the Priesthood itself" (p. 801).

This endowment of motherhood enables women to be a uniquely profound influence in the lives of those around them, particularly their children. By giving birth to and nurturing the souls of the children of God, women perform an incomparably sacred role in which they become partners with God (Kimball, 1976). As President Thomas S. Monson (1998) eloquently explained, "May each of us treasure this truth: . . . One cannot remember mother and forget God. Why? Because these two sacred persons, God and mother, partners in creation, in love, in sacrifice, in service, are as one" (p. 6).

These statements give motherhood—and hence, womanhood—an unparalleled position of significance in Heavenly Father's plan of happiness. The divine nature of women is defined by motherhood, the eternally appointed identity of all women. Thus, the significant identity of mother is not restricted to those who bear children in mortality. Some women may not experience motherhood in this life, but the premortal, mortal, and eternal identity of women as mothers with the call to nurture life has been established. As clarified by General Relief Society Presidency member Sheri Dew (2001): "Of all the words they could have chosen to define her role and her essence, both God the Father and Adam called Eve

Motherhood is a divine calling, the most ennobling endowment God could give his daughters. Mothers are of utmost significance in Heavenly Father's plan of happiness. Matt Reier, © Intellectual Reserve, Inc.

'the mother of all living' and they did so *before* she ever bore a child. . . . Motherhood is more than bearing children. . . . It is the essence of who we are as women. It defines our very identity, our divine stature and nature, and the unique traits our Father gave us" (pp. 96–97).

In their divine identity as mothers, all women have been called to partner with God in providing mortal bodies to his children and doing all they can to help guide those children home to him. As Sister Dew (2001) continues, "Every one of us can show by word and by deed that the work of women in the Lord's kingdom is magnificent and holy. I repeat: *We are all mothers in Israel*, and our calling is to love and help lead the rising generation through the dangerous streets of mortality" (p. 97). In light of the divine identity of all women as mothers, the First Presidency declared in 1935, "The true spirit of the Church of Jesus Christ of Latter-day Saints gives to woman the highest place of honor in human life" (Grant, p. 276).

Demeaning this divine identity of motherhood has been identified as a diabolical tactic that takes from women and men the true sources of happiness. Elder Richard G. Scott (2000) explained, "Satan has unleashed a seductive campaign to undermine the sanctity of womanhood, to deceive the daughters of God and divert them from their divine destiny. He well knows women are the compassionate, self-sacrificing, loving power that binds together the human family. . . . He has convinced many of the lie that they are third-class citizens in the kingdom of God. That falsehood has led some to trade their divinely given femininity for male coarseness" (p. 36).

These prophetic statements establish the foundational truth that fulfilling the eternally divine calling of motherhood provides unparalleled opportunity for joy and meaning in both this life and eternity. They also clarify why rejecting, distorting, or demeaning the eternally significant calling of motherhood has contributed to decreased happiness among women, men, and children. Of course that does not mean that motherhood will always be a blissful experience. Indeed, the stated significance of this calling underscores its potential to facilitate growth by developing a more divine nature—which is inherently a stretching and humbling process.

Prophetic Teachings about the Eternal Significance of Nurturing Work

Prophets of the restored gospel have also consistently affirmed and elevated the work of nurturing inherent to motherhood. The countless acts of self-less service mothers perform are recognized as expressions of the highest love and noblest of womanly feelings (Faust, 1986). The work of nurturing, including the temporal caregiving of feeding, tending, bathing, clothing, wiping, and cleaning, is viewed as a holy work. Through the sacrificing love of nurturing life—physically, emotionally, and spiritually—a mother creates a foundation from which self-confidence and integrity are woven into the fabric of her children's character (Scott, 1996). As Elder Bruce C. Hafen and Sister Marie K. Hafen (1993) explained, "Just as a mother's body may be permanently marked with the signs of pregnancy and childbirth, [the Savior] said, 'I have graven thee upon the palms of my hands' (1 Nephi 21:15–16). For both a mother and the Savior, those marks memorialize a wrenching sacrifice—the sacrifice of begetting life—for her, physical birth; for him, spiritual rebirth" (p. 29).

These truths provide the foundation for understanding why investing her life in nurturing work does not inhibit a woman's individual development. Rather, it enlarges it. Elder Robert D. Hales (2008) clarified, "The world would state that a woman is in a form of servitude that does not allow her to develop her gifts and talents. Nothing, absolutely nothing, could be further from the truth. Do not let the world define, denigrate, or limit your feelings of lifelong learning and the values of motherhood in the home" (pp. 8–9). He added, "Motherhood is the ideal opportunity for lifelong learning. A mother's learning grows as she nurtures the child in his or her development years. They are both learning and maturing together at a remarkable pace. It's exponential, not linear. . . . In the process of rearing her children, a mother studies such topics as child development; nutrition; health care; physiology; psychology; nursing with medical research and care; and educational tutoring in many diverse fields such as math, science, geography,

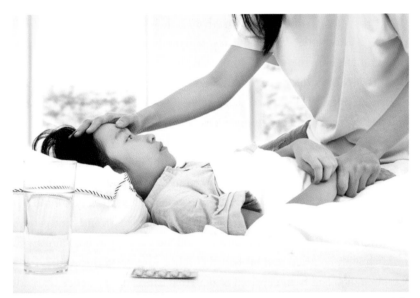

The countless acts of selfless service mothers perform are recognized as expressions of the highest love and noblest of womanly feelings. The work of nurturing, including the temporal caregiving of feeding, tending, bathing, clothing, wiping, and cleaning, is viewed as a holy work. © Tomwang.

literature, English, and foreign languages. She develops gifts such as music, athletics, dance, and public speaking. The learning examples could continue endlessly" (p. 8).

Thus, where voices questioning the significance of caregiving work have tied it to the diminishment and even "death" of the self, prophets have clarified how motherhood enables the birth of a new and fuller self. By participating in the sacred work of nurturing mothers open the door to unparalleled growth and learning.

Scientific Research Confirming the Importance of Motherhood

The unique significance of motherhood and nurturing work bears out in research studies exploring influences on children's development. Findings from these studies seem to confirm what President David O. McKay (2003) declared: "Motherhood is the greatest potential influence either for good or ill in human life. The mother's image is the first that stamps itself on the unwritten page of the young child's mind. It is her caress that first awakens a sense of security, her kiss, the first realization of affection; her sympathy and tenderness, the first assurance that there is love in the world" (*Teachings . . . David O. McKay*, p. 156).

John Bowlby's (1944) attachment theory provides some of the first theoretical underpinnings for evidence of the significant influence of the relationship between mother and child from infancy. Bowlby's exploration of the importance of this bond started after he observed a consistent pattern of disrupted mother-child relationships and later adult psychopathology in research with homeless and orphaned children after WWII (pp. 107–127). Children who had been deprived of maternal care during extended periods in their early lives seemed to develop into individuals who "lacked feeling, had superficial relationships, and exhibited hostile or antisocial tendencies" (Kobak, 1999, p. 25). This led Bowlby to conclude that the attachment between mother and child is critical for a child's healthy social-emotional development.

Mary Ainsworth (1978) expanded on Bowlby's ideas by exploring how the quality of the attachment between mother and child influenced the child's development. She found that children seemed to thrive when they had an emotionally secure attachment with their mothers. Using Bowlby's early formulation, she conducted numerous observational studies on infant-parent pairs during the child's first year for hundreds of children in Scotland and Uganda. In order to evaluate the quality of the attachment she devised a laboratory procedure known as the Strange Situation Protocol to evaluate how infants and toddlers experienced separation and reuniting with their parents after a brief period. The infants' and toddlers' responses during this procedure provided the basis for identifying the security of the parent-child attachment. The security of the attachment was related to how mothers interacted with their children, which Ainsworth labeled *maternal sensitivity*.

The attachment between mother and child is critical for a child's healthy social-emotional development. Christina Smith, © Intellectual Reserve, Inc.

According to Ainsworth, maternal sensitivity is a measure of how a mother detects, interprets, and responds appropriately to her child's needs, how positive and kind she is in her interactions, and how much she respects her child's autonomy in exploring and growing (Ainsworth, Blehar, Waters, & Wall, 1978). When a mother is consistently available and supportive, the child receives the physical and psychological security necessary to foster play, exploration, and appropriate social behaviors (Bretherton & Munholland, 1999). If this security is threatened, fear activates the attachment system to help restore access to the attachment figure. Fear that is not appropriately addressed seems to lead to feelings of depression, anxiety, aggression, and defensive distortions of vulnerable feelings (Kobak, 1999). In contrast, a secure attachment enables an infant to develop feelings that he or she deserves love, feelings that help the infant learn to appreciate, understand, and empathize with the feelings of others and appropriately regulate relationship closeness and conflict resolution (Bretherton & Munholland, 1999). These findings did not suggest that every child with an insecure attachment necessarily experienced problems. But the insecure attachment seemed to initiate pathways associated with later pathology (Sroufe, Carlson, & Shulman, 1993).

Further studies led researchers to conclude that the way a mother interacts with her child, her maternal sensitivity, is the strongest, most consistent predictor of her child's cognitive, social, and emotional development (National Institute of Child Health and Human Development, 2003, p. 994). Neuropsychological studies of infant brain development provided additional evidence supporting the importance of mothers' interactions. Mothers seem to have a unique ability to sensitively modify the stimulation they give to their infants. Through finely tuned perceptions, they match their infants' intellectual and emotional state and provide the optimal "chunking" of bits of positive interaction needed for the child's developing brain (Schore, 1994). In speaking of this finely tuned process, three scholars from the University of California at Berkeley concluded, "Whether they realize it or not, mothers use the universal signs of emotion to teach their babies about the world. . . . Emotionality [love] gives the two of them a common language years before the infant will acquire speech. . . . It isn't just his mother's beaming countenance but her *synchrony* that he requires—their mutually responsive interaction" (Lewis, Amini, & Lannon, 2000, pp. 61–62).

Such attentive, loving interactions are not only important during infancy. Numerous studies have demonstrated that the quality of a mother's relationship with her child is associated with her child's social interactions and behaviors across development (Buehler, 2006; Gilamo-Ramos, Jaccard, Dittus, & Bouris, 2006). Children seem to do best when mothers show love by communicating about and being aware of their activities and behaviors. Expressing love through listening, communicating, and monitoring enables a mother to be warm and supportive while setting and enforcing appropriate limits. Studies consistently indicate that adolescents who report telling their mothers where they are going and what they will be doing after school and on weekends also report lower rates of alcohol misuse, drug use, sexual activity, and delinquency (Barnes, Hoffman, & Welte, 2006). Children's academic success and healthy behaviors have also been tied to their mothers' involvement in talking with them, listening to them, and answering their questions (Luster, Bates, Vandenbelt, & Nievar, 2004).

Scientific Research Exploring the Unique Contributions of Motherhood

The relationship formed through a mothers' attentive love provides the foundation for all of the other unique contributions of motherhood. Mothering scholar Sara Ruddick (1983) has identified these unique contributions as reflections of three central tasks for which attentive love provides the foundation. These mothering tasks include: (a) Preserve children's lives and well-being, (b) foster children's growth and development, and (c) enable children to become acceptable contributors in their societies (pp. 213–231).

The quality of a mother's relationhip with her child is associated with her child's social interactions and behaviors across development. Children seem to do best when mothers show love by communicating about and being aware of their activites and behaviors. © Vitaly Valua.

Preserving Life

From the moment of her child's birth, a mother faces the realization that a fragile life depends on her (Stern & Bruschweiler-Stern, 1998). The physical connection inherent in the biological relationship between mother and child seems to make mothers particularly sensitive to responsibility for the child's protection and well-being (Doucet, 2006). Her fear for the baby's survival and growth may also make her vigilant and attentive to finding the best food, care, and medical help and to avoiding possible dangers. These natural attunements, especially when shared with the father, serve important constructive and protective functions for a child (Stern & Bruschweiler-Stern, 1998). Studies consistently indicate that mothers have a significant role in influencing their children's health and well-being throughout their development.

Nurturing Growth and Development

The desire to sustain the life of the child is part of the second central task of mothering, that of nurturing growth and development. Research findings suggest that the ways mothers nurture their children's individual growth is the critical influence on their development. Although men can and do take on this work of nurturing, there are important and useful differences between men and women. Further, much of the day-to-day work and responsibility for this nurturing care continues to "rest with women." As a result, mothers are more often identified in research studies as central to these nurturing processes (Doucet, 2006, p. 111).

Rituals and routines. One of the primary ways mothers nurture growth and development is through helping create an environment of safety, peace, and learning. A central part of creating that environment is through organizing the home and family so that routines and rituals are carried out effectively. A range of studies indicate that having ordered and predictable routines (waking up, getting dressed, taking vitamins or medications, brushing teeth, going to school, doing homework, eating dinner, going to bed, and so on) is central to children's healthy development (Fiese, 2006). Furthermore, mothers have the primary role in carrying out family rituals and traditions (such as Christmas, Easter, the Fourth of July, family celebrations including birthdays, and distinctive family traditions such as Sunday night sing-alongs or periodic service projects).

For preschool and school-age children, routines and rituals are especially important in helping with self-regulation, skill development, problem solving, and development of good academic habits. For adolescent children, routines and rituals have been associated with a sense of identity and family belonging, warmth in relationships with parents, fewer risk behaviors, and better psychological health (Fiese, 2006). Mothers significantly influence the environment in which their children grow and develop through the routines and rituals they ensure are carried out (Ring, 2006).

Emotion work. A second critical way that mothers influence development is through the *emotion work* they perform to maintain and strengthen individual well-being and family relations. Mothers do this emotion work by facilitating conversations about feelings, listening carefully to family members' feelings, recognizing the importance of feelings and offering encouragement, expressing appreciation, and asking questions to elicit family members' sharing of feelings. For many mothers, providing this kind of emotion work is integral to their efforts to nurture the growth and development of children (Erickson, 2005). While a father may be oriented towards fixing the problem that arises, mothers often seem particularly adept at helping children to express and provide comfort regarding feelings (Doucet, 2006).

Mothers' emotion-comforting work may be especially effective if they are available when children are most willing to share their thoughts and feelings. Research findings suggest that the hours after school may be particularly important for mothers in sharing experiences and monitoring children (Aizer, 2004). During these moments at "the crossroads," children may be more inclined to share feelings experienced during the day. Children also seem to be more inclined to open up and share when working

Children seem to be more inclined to open up and share when working alongside parents in household responsibilities. Craig Dimond, © Intellectual Reserve Inc.

alongside parents in household responsibilities. Washing dishes, preparing food, folding laundry, and doing other household tasks provide opportunities for thoughts and feelings to be shared while hands are busy working.

Teaching. A third critical way in which mothers influence development is through teaching. Mothers are a critical influence on intellectual development and children's learning in part because of the relational bond they develop with their child and in part because they often spend the most time with the child. During a child's infancy, the cognitive stimulation and emotional support mothers provide lays the foundation for intellectual and linguistic functioning throughout development. As mothers talk to their infants, direct their attention to objects in the environment, and label the objects they see, they provide cognitive stimulation that enhances their infant's language skills and intellectual abilities (Tamis-LeMonda & Bornstein, 1989).

As children grow, mothers provide essential stimulation when they ask questions or give suggestions that invite the child's thinking or when they provide conceptual links among objects, activities, locations, persons, or emotions (Hubbs-Tait, A. Culp, R. Culp, & Miller, 2002). Mothers continue to provide cognitive stimulation for preschool and school-age children when they read to their children and teach them concepts; encourage them in hobbies; take them to libraries, museums, and theaters; and expose them to books and other sources of learning in the home (Votruba-Drzal, 2003). Dinnertime conversations, car rides, and shared work also provide opportunities for engaging children in important developmental processes. The significant influence of this cognitive stimulation is enhanced through the emotional support she provides by being positive, particularly when a child is trying to learn a task or solve a problem. Her expression of positive emotions without inappropriately intruding or restraining fosters a secure environment for children to learn and grow (Hubbs-Tait, A. Culp, R. Culp & Miller, 2002).

Perhaps even more significant than the cognitive stimulation a mother provides is her teaching of wisdom and truth to guide her children's development. Research findings consistently indicate that children whose mothers openly discuss the risks of behaviors such as illicit sexual activity, alcohol and substance abuse, and smoking are less likely to engage in dangerous behaviors (Guilamo-Ramos, Jaccard, Dittus, & Bouris, 2006). Further, children whose mothers pass on their religious beliefs and facilitate their children's involvement with religion report the lowest levels of delinquency among adolescents (Pearce & Haynie, 2004). These findings indicate that her teachings become a key ingredient in preparing her children to live fulfilling and contributing lives.

Mothers who pass on their religious beliefs and facilitate their children's involvement with religion report the lowest levels of delinquency among adolescents. Christina Smith, © Intellectual Reserve, Inc.

In summary, research findings have supported the truth that a mother's loving, attentive relationship with each child becomes the foundation by which all other mothering tasks become effective. From the foundation of love, mothers significantly influence children's development by creating an environment in which their growth and development can flourish. Consistent routines and rituals are important in creating this kind of environment. Mothers also significantly influence development through strengthening emotional well-being and relationships among family members. Finally, research indicates that mothers are a critical influence on children's development through the cognitive stimulation and teaching they provide.

Scientific Evidence for the Importance of Nurturing Work

In spite of widespread recognition that responsive, instructive interactions between a mother and child are the most consistent predictors of a child's cognitive, social, and emotional development, the ordinary caregiving work (feeding, clothing, bathing, etc.) through which these interactions occur has consistently been belittled. Summarizing prevailing attitudes about ordinary caregiving work, Shehan, Burg, and Rexroat (1986) concluded, "much of the existing literature concerning the impact of women's work roles . . . has assumed that the nature of *housework* is inherently isolating, restrictive, unskilled, repetitive, devalued, low in status, and consequently, not very rewarding" (p. 407).

What this orientation fails to recognize, however, is the inherent and irreplaceable value of the work being devalued—for women as well as men and children. Ahlander and Bahr's (1995) review of research exploring the role of caregiving work in family life identified some of the profound meanings and moral implications of this ordinary work for families and the wider society (pp. 54–68). The interactions associated with household work "provide an area of teaching and learning that is part of everyday life, salient to parents and children alike" (Goodnow & Warton, 1991, p. 27). In contrast to work in the marketplace, which is defined by the individualistic goals of personal recognition, wages, opportunities, and self-fulfillment, work in the family context is distinctly defined by stewardship and solemn obligations, intense loyalties, and moral imperatives (Blankenhorn, 1990).

For mothers as well as fathers, caregiving work becomes the critical medium through which children develop the trust and security on which their development and wellbeing depend. As philosopher Wendell Berry (1987) explains, the multitudinous acts of caregiving in family life "give the word love its only chance to mean, for only they can give it a history, a community, and a place." Through ordinary caregiving work, "love become[s] flesh"—made real to parents and children through its constant physical expression (p. 10). The bonds of love forged through such caregiving become the foundation for all the other tasks of parenting.

Thus, ironically, the ordinary family work that has been tied to women's oppression provides the key opportunities needed to bond parents to children and children to parents through recognizing and filling one another's needs over and over again. Precisely because it is menial work, each member of the family, regardless of age, can feel like they are making a meaningful contribution. Its relentless repetition is what creates daily invitations for each member to "enter the family circle" and experience what it means to belong to something bigger than one's self. Ordinary chores thus "become daily rituals of family love and belonging" (Bahr & Loveless, 2000, "For Our Sakes," para. 4).

The fact that it is mundane is also what allows the mind to be free to focus on sharing and learning from one another while hands are busy working for the well-being of the family. In doing so, feelings of hierarchy are dissolved, opening the way for concerns to be discussed among children and parents. Family work thus invites more intimate conversation between parents and children than other kinds of interactions that might come from physical activities such as play.

Beyond the bonding that can result, household work develops moral identity and responsibility through the emotional connections and kinship obligations that grow out of participating in the essential work of family life (Harris, 1990). Working together with those for whom they share a uniquely strong obligation fosters helpfulness and a cooperative spirit in children (Goodnow, 1988). Through shared participation in the ordinary tasks of family life, children develop the social definition of self that is core to self-control and family commitment—altruistic and prosocial behavior (Wallinga, Sweaney, & Walters, 1981; White & Brinkerhoff, 1981). The civic virtue that forms the basis for the thriving of all societal institutions depends on children's development of this kind of moral obligation and responsibility. Thus, the profound implications of ordinary caregiving work for the family as well as society at large.

Conclusion

In response to the question, "Does having a mother really matter to children and family life?" scientific studies consistently support what prophets since the Restoration have taught. That is, women have an unparalleled, profound influence as they fulfill their calling to nurture in the divine role of mother-hood. Although the Prophet Joseph F. Smith (*Teachings . . . Joseph F. Smith*, 1998) lost his mother, Mary Fielding Smith, when he was only 13 years of age, his teachings were replete with conviction of the endless influence of mothers on the eternal lives of their children. His statements reveal in pro-phetic vision what the research studies identified above can only begin to show: "Sisters, you do not know how far your influence extends. A mother that is successful in raising a good boy, or girl, to imitate her example and to follow her precepts through life, sows the seeds of virtue, honor and integrity and of righteousness in their hearts that will be felt through all their career in life; and wherever that boy or girl goes, as man or woman, in whatever society they mingle, the good effects of the example of that mother

Working together with those for whom they share a uniquely strong obligation fosters helpfulness and a cooperative spirit in children. © Iakov Filimonov.

will be felt; and it will never die, because it will extend from them to their children to generation to generation" (p. 32).

Such profound influence invites the fullest consecration of one's self. Yet it is precisely such full consecration that defines ultimate meaning and joy, for there is no more sacred purpose to which one can be consecrated. In speaking of such consecration Elder David A. Bednar (1999) affirmed: "The word consecrate means to develop and to 'dedicate to a sacred purpose.' Sacrifice is what I offer, surrender, yield, or give up. Consecration, on the other hand, is to fully develop and dedicate to a sacred purpose . . . The best application of the principle of consecration that I can think of, being developed and dedicated to a sacred purpose, is motherhood. . . . [A mother] has not given up anything; rather, she has been dedicated and consecrated to a holy purpose. She has developed herself and applied those skills as God has directed in the most important undertaking of a lifetime" ("Consecration," paras. 1, 8).

Motherhood can lead to overwhelming joy as we reflect on the blessings our children and grandchildren are in our lives. John Luke, © Intellectual Reserve, Inc.

One mother's words looking back on a lifetime of consecrated work describe the feelings of so many who feel the joy of the late harvest as they invest their lives in the nurturance of our Father's children. Her words transform worldly distortions of the work of motherhood by acknowledging the privilege God has bestowed upon his daughters in enabling them to participate in this sacred work:

> I awoke early this morning and could not go back to sleep. It must be that my 60 years is finally leading me to those days when you can't sleep in. But most of all I was awakened by a profound sense of overwhelming joy. Those feelings seem to come upon me more and more—and they are always accompanied by images and pictures of our children. As I picture them—their lives, their spouses, their children—I marvel at what has come of the union of Jim and me. What a remarkable journey! What a remarkable gift! There

have been seasons of sorrow and seasons of struggle—those too I remember. But the joy in what God has enabled through us seems to eclipse those struggles that seemed and sometimes even now seem so difficult. As I see it all in a picture before me, I can't help but simply feel gratitude—gratitude for the precious privilege of being a nurturer, a mother. (LaDawn Jacob, personal interview)

References

Ahlander, N. R., & Bahr, K. S. (1995, February). Beyond drudgery, power, and equity: Toward an expanded discourse on the moral dimensions of housework in families. *Journal of Marriage and Family, 57*(1), 54–68.

Ainsworth, M. D. S., Blehar, M. C., Waters, E., & Wall, S. (1978). *Patterns of attachment: A psychological study of the strange situation.* Hillsdale, NJ: Lawrence Erlbaum Associates.

Aizer, Anna. (2004). Home alone: Supervision after school and child behavior. *Journal of Public Economics, 88,* 1835–1848.

Allen, Douglas. (2006). An economic assessment of same-sex marriage laws. *Harvard Journal of Law and Public Policy, 29.*

Bahr, K., & Loveless, C. (2000, Spring). Family work. *Brigham Young University Magazine.* Retrieved from http://magazine.byu.edu/?act=view&a=151

Barnes, G. M., Hoffman, J. H., & Welte, J. W. (2006, November). Effects of parental monitoring and peer deviance on substance use and delinquency. *Journal of Marriage and Family, 68,* 1084–1104.

Bednar, D. A. (1999, January 5). Your whole souls as an offering unto him. Ricks College devotional, January 5, 1999. Retrieved from http://www2.byui.edu /Presentations/ transcripts/devotionals/1999_01_05_bednar.htm

Berry, Wendell. (1987, July). Men and women in search of common ground. *Sunstone, 11*(4), 10.

Biblarz, T. J., & Stacey, J. (2010). How does the gender of parents matter? *Journal of Marriage and Family, 72,* 3–22.

Blankenhorn, D. (1990). American family dilemmas. In Blankenhorn, D., Bayme, S., & Elshtain, B. J. (Eds.), *Rebuilding the nest: A new commitment to the American family.* Milwaukee, WI: Family Service America, 3–25.

Blankenhorn, David. (1995). *Fatherless America: Confronting our most urgent social problem.* New York: Basic Books.

Bowlby, John. (1944). Forty-four juvenile thieves: Their characters and home-life. *International Journal of Psychoanalysis 25,* 19–52, 107–127.

Bretherton, I. & Munholland, K. A. (1999). Internal working models in attachment relationships. In J. Cassidy & P. R. Shaver (Eds.). *Handbook of attachment.* New York: Guilford Press, 89–111.

Buehler, C. (2006, February). Parents and peers in relation to early adolescent problem behavior. *Journal of Marriage and Family, 68,* 109–124.

Clark, James R., ed. (1975). *Messages of the First Presidency of The Church of Jesus Christ of Latter-day Saints, 6.* Salt Lake City: Bookcraft, 178.

Clark, J. R. Jr. (1946, December). Our wives and our mothers in the eternal plan. *Relief Society Magazine, 33*(12), 795–804.

Cott, Nancy. (1977). *The bonds of womanhood.* New Haven, CT: Yale University Press, 70–71.

Dew, Sheri L. (2001, November). Are we not all mothers? *Ensign, 31*(11), 96–97.

Doucet, Andrea. (2006). *Do men mother?* Toronto: University of Toronto Press.

Elshtain, Jean Bethke. (1982). Feminism, family, and community. *Dissent 29,* 442–49.

Erickson, Rebecca. (2005, May). Why emotion work matters: Sex, gender, and the division of household labor. *Journal of Marriage and Family, 67,* 337–351.

Faust, James E. (1986, September). A message to my granddaughters: Becoming "great women." *Ensign, 16*(9), 16–21.

Fiese, B. H. (2006). *Family routines & rituals.* New Haven, CT: Yale University Press.

Friedan, Betty. (1997). *The feminine mystique.* New York: Norton.

Goodnow, J. J. (1988). Children's household work: Its nature and functions. *Psychological Bulletin, 103*(1), 5–26.

Goodnow, J. J., & Warton, P. M. (1991, January). The social bases of social cognition: Interactions about work and their implications. *Merrill-Palmer Quarterly, 37,* 27.

Grant, Heber J. (1935, May). First Presidency message. *Improvement Era, 38*(5), 276.

Guilamo-Ramos, V. Jaccard, J., Dittus, P., & Bouris, A. M. (2006, December). Parental expertise, trustworthiness, and accessibility: Parent-adolescent communication and adolescent risk behavior. *Journal of Marriage and Family, 68*, 1229–1246.

Hafen, Bruce C., & Hafen, Marie K. (1993). Eve heard all these things and was glad: Grace and learning by experience. In D. H. Anderson & S. F. Green (Eds.). *Women in the covenant of grace: Talks selected from the 1993 Women's Conference.* Salt Lake City: Deseret Book.

Hales, Robert D. (2008, August 19). The journey of lifelong learning. *Speeches: Brigham Young University Education Week.* Retrieved from http://speeches.byu .edu/reader/mreader.php?id=12394&x=83&y=4

Harris, C. C. (1990). *Kinship.* Minneapolis, MN: University of Minnesota Press.

Hubbs-Tait, L., Culp, A., Culp, R. E., & Miller, C. E. (2002, February). Relation of maternal cognitive stimulation, emotional support, and intrusive behavior during Head Start to children's kindergarten cognitive abilities. *Child Development, 73*(1), 110–131.

Jacob, Jenet I. (2008). Work, family, and individual factors associated with mothers attaining their preferred work situations. *Family and Consumer Sciences Research Journal, 36*(3), 208–29.

Kimball, Spencer W. (1976, March). The blessings and responsibilities of womanhood. *Ensign, 6*(3), 70–73.

Kobak, R. Rogers. (1999). The emotional dynamics of disruptions in attachment relationships: Implications for theory, research, and clinical intervention. In D. J. Cassidy, & P. R. Shaver (Eds.). *Handbook of Attachment: Theory, Research, and Clinical Applications.* New York: Guilford Press, 21–43.

Lewis, T., Amini, F., & Lannon, R. (2000). *A general theory of love.* New York: Random House.

Luster, T., Bates, L., & Vandenbelt, M., & Neivar, M. A. (2004). Family advocates' perspectives on the early academic success of children born to low-income adolescent mothers. *Family Relations, 53*(1), 68–77.

Monson, Thomas S. (1998, April). Behold thy mother. *Ensign, 28*(4), 2–6.

National Institute of Child Health and Human Development (NICHD), Early Childhood Research Development. (2003, July/August). Does amount of time spent in child care predict social-emotional adjustment during the transition to kindergarten? *Child Development 74*(4), 976–1005.

National Council on Family Relations (2010, February 1). Do children need both a mother and a father? New study examines if the gender of parents matter. *Featured Journal Articles.* Retrieved from http://www.ncfr.org/press-room/journal-news-releases/do-children-need-both-mother-and-father

Pearce, L. D., & Haynie, D. L. (2004). Intergenerational religious dynamics and adolescent delinquency. *Social Forces, 82*(4), 1553–1572.

Polatnik, M. (1973). Why men don't rear children: A power analysis. *Berkeley Journal of Sociology, 18*(1973–74), 45–80.

Ring, K. (2006). What mothers do: Everyday routines and rituals and their impact upon young children's use of drawing for meaning making. *International Journal of Early Years Education, 14*(1), 63–84.

Ruddick, S. (1983). Maternal thinking. In *Mothering: Essays in Feminist Theory.* Totowa, NJ: Roman and Allanheld, 213–231.

Schore, A. N. (1994). *Affect regulation and the origin of the self: The neurobiology of emotional development.* Hillsdale, NJ: Lawrence Erlbaum Associates.

Scott, Richard G. (1996, September). The joy of living the great plan of happiness. *Ensign, 26*(11), 73–75.

Scott, Richard G. (2000, May). The sanctity of womanhood. *Ensign, 30*(5), 36.

Shehan, C. L., Burg, M. A., & Rexroat, C. A. (1986, Autumn). Depression and the social dimensions of the full-time housewife role. *Sociological Quarterly, 27*(3), 407.

Sroufe, L. A., Carlson, E., & Shulman, S. (1993). Individuals in relationships: Development from infancy through adolescence. In D. C. Funder, R. D. Parke, C. Tomlinson-Keasey, & K. Widaman (Eds.). *Studying lives through time: Personality and development.* Washington, D. C.: American Psychological Association, 315–342.

Stern, D. N., & Bruschweiler-Stern, N. (1998). *The birth of a mother.* New York: Basic Books.

Stevenson, B., & Wolfers, J. (2009). The paradox of declining female happiness. *American Economic Journal: Economic Policy, 1*(2), 190–225.

Tamis-LeMonda, C. S., & Bornstein, M. H. (1989). Habituation and maternal encouragement of attention in infancy as predictors of toddler language, play, and representational competence. *Child Development, 60*(3), 738–751.

Teachings of Presidents of the Church: David O. McKay. (2003). Salt Lake City: The Church of Jesus Christ of Latter-day Saints.

Teachings of Presidents of the Church: Joseph F. Smith. (1998). Salt Lake City: The Church of Jesus Christ of Latter-day Saints.

University of Virginia. (2011). The state of our unions 2011: How parenthood makes life meaningful and how marriage makes parenthood bearable. *The National Marriage Project and the Institute for American Values.* Retrieved from http://nationalmarriageproject.org/wp-content/uploads/2012/05/Union_2011.pdf

Votruba-Drzal, E. (2003, May). Income changes and cognitive stimulation in young children's home learning environments. *Journal of Marriage and Family, 65,* 341–355.

Wallinga, C. R., Sweaney, A. L., & Walters, J. (1987). The development of responsibility in young children: A 25-year view. *Early Childhood Research Quarterly, 2*(2), 119–131.

White, L. K., & Brinkerhoff, D. B. (1981, November). Children's work in the family: Its significance and meaning. *Journal of Marriage and Family, 43*(4), 789–798.

7

Faithful Fathering

Becoming a faithful father is an enduring endeavor and a conse-crated calling. Of the many names by which he might have chosen to be called, God asked us to call him *Father*. Many prophets have empha-sized the preeminence of this sacred calling and have called for fathers to be faithfully involved in the home. As President Thomas S. Monson (2010) instructed priesthood brethren, "The Lord has been very explicit in talking to us fathers. . . . He has indicated that the greatest work we parents can do is performed in our homes" (p. 15). President Gordon B. Hinckley (1998a) said, "What greater thing in all this world can there be than to become the father of a precious child, a son or daughter of God, our Father in Heaven?" (p. 51). President Ezra Taft Benson (1987a) coun-seled priesthood holders, "Remember your sacred calling as a father in Israel—your most important calling in time and eternity—a calling from which you will never be released" (p. 51). In addition, many respected scholars have reported empirical evidence in academic journals that fathers serve in indispensable roles in the family as "companions, care providers, spouses, protectors, models, moral guides, teachers, and breadwinners" (Lamb, 1997, p. 3).

We believe that being a successful father is not so much about doing extraordinary things as it is about diligently doing many simple faithful things, each of which is doable by the least of us. © Jozef Polc.

Adequately fulfilling the role of faithful fathering may be daunting, but with the help of the Lord, faithful fathers can do difficult things (see Philippians 4:13). We believe that being a successful father is not so much about doing extraordinary things as it is about diligently doing many simple faithful things, each of which is doable by the least of us. As Alma taught, "By small and simple things are great things brought to pass" (Alma 37:6). Faithful fathering is also about striving to do our best even though we are prone to making mistakes. President Monson (2008a) said, "To you who are fathers of boys, . . . I say, *strive* to be the kind of example the boys need" (p. 66, emphasis added). We are convinced that being a faithful father is within the grasp of all faithful men as they persevere and strive to do small and simple, yet significant, things.

The purpose of this chapter is to examine the sacred stewardship of being a faithful father as taught in "The Family: A Proclamation to the World" and to share a hopeful vision that, with the help of the Lord, fathers can successfully perform these responsibilities. We explore the four key stewardships of faithful fathering emphasized in the seventh paragraph of the family proclamation: presiding, providing, protecting, and partnering (First Presidency, 1995). By magnifying these four sacred stewardships, fathers learn what they need to know, do what they need to do, and become who they need to become in order to bless their children and claim their blessings as rightful heirs of eternal life in the highest degree of the celestial kingdom.

Presiding

By divine design, fathers are to preside over their families in love and righteousness.
(First Presidency, 1995, p. 102)

The stewardship to preside in love and righteousness rests squarely on the shoulders of a faithful father. President Howard W. Hunter (1994) taught, "Your leadership of the family is your most important and sacred responsibility" (p. 50). Elder L. Tom Perry (2004) explained, "Fathers, by divine decree, you are to preside over your family. . . . You place the family in its proper priority. It's the part of your life that will endure beyond the grave" (p. 72). Presiding in the family is a calling from which faithful fathers will never be released. Because it is a vital, irreplaceable responsibility, it is critical that its meaning is understood through a gospel lens. In a worldly sense,

The stewardship to preside in love and righteousness rests squarely on the shoulders of a faithful father. © 1989 Intellectual Reserve, Inc.

presiding may imply having power through ambition and achievement in order to rule, coerce, or control. Faithful fathers understand that this paradigm of power and authority comes from the adversary and debilitates their wives and children. Rather, they inseparably associate presiding with attributes of Christ such as humility, selflessness, submission, service, stewardship, and charity. By understanding and magnifying their presiding role in terms of righteous principles, faithful fathers are blessed with the grace and love required to perform the lofty stewardship given them.

To preside in righteousness, faithful fathers should take the lead in family worship within the home, as well as outside the home (such as in chapels and temples). Presiding involves leading the family in prayer, scripture study, family home evening, Sabbath day activities, and other family devotional activities, as well as leading family members to attend church and go to the temple. Leading out in such worship is an opportunity for fathers to demonstrate by example what their children should prioritize as they face ever-increasing enticements. Such an example can prove more difficult to ignore than instruction alone. Additionally, a father's consistency and diligence can ensure that these crucial activities are neither forgone nor forgotten. Research done with Latter-day Saint families has shown the importance of meaningful religious practices in the home. One qualitative study of stable, active Latter-day Saint families found that spiritual growth, a happier daily life, more focus and direction, and better personal behavior were outcomes of engaging in these religious practices (Loser, Klein, Hill, & Dollahite, 2008; Loser, Hill, Klein, & Dollahite, 2009).

Research has also shown how such religious beliefs and practices can be especially helpful in promoting responsible and involved fathering and in teaching fathers how to preside in the home. For example, in-depth interviews of married fathers, many of whom were Latter-day Saints, found that these men feel a strong connection with their children when guiding them spiritually (Brotherson, Dollahite, & Hawkins, 2005; Hill et al., 2008). Narratives of personal experiences of Latter-day Saint fathers of children with special needs suggest that their religious beliefs provide them with a powerful framework that inspires and guides their fathering behaviors (Dollahite, 2003; Olson, Dollahite, & White, 2002; Marks & Dollahite, 2001; Dollahite, Marks, & Olson, 1998). The fathers' belief that family relationships can be perpetuated beyond the grave creates an expectation of an eternal relationship with their children that helps them commit to and care for their children, even in challenging times.

Additional research conducted with Christian, Jewish, and Muslim families demonstrates the important presiding role of fathers in the religious lives of their families (Marks & Dollahite, 2007; Dollahite & Thatcher, 2008; Dollahite & Marks, 2009). Whether it is a Jewish father blessing his children at the Sabbath table, a Catholic father taking his family to mass, a Muslim father leading his family in daily prayers, or a Latter-day Saint father gathering his family for scripture study, presiding in love and righteousness requires a deep and abiding commitment to the well-being of one's family.

Presiding in love requires faithful fathers to follow the example of their Heavenly Father. Each recorded time Heavenly Father's voice has been heard, he referred to his Son as "my beloved Son" and said that he was "well pleased" with him (Matthew 3:16–17; Matthew 17:5; 3 Nephi 11:7; Joseph Smith—History 1:17). This is a divine pattern that all faithful fathers can follow. Unfortunately, some children, teens, and young adults rarely hear the words "I love you," "I am pleased with you," or "I am proud of you" from their fathers. Faithful fathers will frequently communicate sincere and uplifting messages, verbally, in writing, and by their actions to show that they love their children and are pleased with them. It is helpful if children hear specific, accurate, and positive messages about their actions from their fathers. This can be difficult, especially for those who did not hear these messages from their own fathers. It is difficult, but it can be done.

As one who presides, a faithful father helps his children capture a vision of what the Lord expects for them. One of the best ways to do this is to give fathers' blessings on a regular basis. Some fathers have the tradition of blessing their children before each school year or before other special occasions. One father shared this example:

> On the Saturday before the first fast Sunday after the birthday, I take the birthday child out on a one-on-one date. We eat wherever she chooses and we talk about the highlights of the year just past. Then we converse about the upcoming year and consider special hopes, needs, and wants. After returning home from the meal, we start our fast, kneeling with the rest of the family in prayer and asking for the Lord's Spirit to be with us. The next day (fast Sunday), before breaking our fast, I give that child a blessing for the coming year. (Hill & Dollahite, 2005, p. 168)

Providing fathers' blessings is one way a faithful father can help his children capture the vision of what the Lord expects of them. Craig Dimond, © Intellectual Reserve, Inc.

As part of their stewardship to preside, fathers are responsible to organize the everyday activities of the home so that family members are brought together frequently to be nourished physically and spiritually. Elder Perry (2004) taught, "You preside at the meal table, at family prayer. You preside at family home evening; and as guided by the Spirit of the Lord, you see that your children are taught correct principles" (p. 71). A father's presence and participation in these activities unifies and strengthens his family. Faithful fathers recognize they cannot be replaced in this stewardship and recognize that in such moments the most meaningful aspects of family life can be experienced. Author Robert Bellah (1991) wrote, "The family meal . . .

is the chief family celebration, even a family sacrament" (p. 260). Research on highly religious Christian, Muslim, and Jewish parents and their adolescent children shows that one of the most important things a father can do is to engage his teenaged children in "youth-centered" religious conversations in which the father is particularly attentive to the needs, interests, and concerns of his child (Dollahite & Thatcher, 2008). Research on religiously diverse adolescents also demonstrates the importance of establishing and maintaining a strong relationship with one's teenage child in helping the youth to develop a strong commitment to his or her religious identity (Layton, Dollahite, & Hardy, 2011). For example, one Protestant young man recognized that his relationship with God the Father could be understood by relating it to his relationship with his parents (p. 403). A Muslim young woman valued fulfilling her duty to her religion as a way to help her parents fulfill theirs (p. 403–404).

Faithful fathers who serve as righteous priesthood holders are often called to preside in places besides the home. These fathers may find it difficult to find adequate time to fulfill both their ecclesiastical priesthood duties and their family responsibilities. While Church callings are important and should be a high priority, the work of a father is the greatest calling any man can ever have. The scriptures teach us an important lesson. The only time the Lord used the word *rebuke* to chasten the Prophet Joseph Smith was when Joseph failed to teach his children—even though it was at a time of compelling Church responsibilities (see D&C 93:47–48). If the head of the dispensation of the fullness of times was expected to make time for his fathering, fathers now ought to do the same.

Author George Durrant (1976) provides a perspective that serving one's family, even wholesome recreation, is Church work:

> While I was mission president, I would quite often resolve that it was again time for some more high-priority Church work. Then [our family] would all go to an amusement park. . . . I just walked around the park with a smile on my face, holding hands with my

children, eating all the cotton candy I could stand. Once in a while, a thought would enter my mind: "Hey, you're the mission president. You'd better get back to the office." But then I'd smile again and say to myself, "Well, I'm doing my Church work here. I'm with my children and my wife. We're having a fun day and tonight I'll be able to write in my journal that I did six hours of glorious Church work today. (p. 29)

As a faithful father learns to harmonize Church and paternal responsibilities, he can also reach out and assume a fathering role for others of God's children. The Lord has said, "Wherefore, be faithful; . . . succor the weak, lift up the hands which hang down, and strengthen the feeble knees" (D&C 81:5). Home teaching is a formal way to be a father figure, and there are many other informal settings as well. These fathers enrich the lives of others while being an example of service to their own children. When a father has a chance to home teach with his sons, he should take full advantage of the great blessing of being able to fulfill priesthood and fatherhood duties at the same time. During these few years of service while his son is a teacher and priest, he has the chance to build spiritual and emotional bonds with his son through doing the Lord's work together. Great care should be given to preparation for the visits, during which the father can lovingly and positively teach his son the doctrines of the priesthood and the joy of priesthood service. He can build the son's skills and confidence in home teaching and gospel-based service. The father should regularly express his love for and pride in his son for taking his priesthood duties seriously and his joy in being able to do this great service together.

With an appropriate vision of presiding in terms of stewardship, love, and service, faithful fathers are blessed to play a critical role within the family unit. A father's presiding role entails taking the lead in family worship within the home, expressing love through words and actions, using the power of the priesthood in the home, encouraging togetherness in daily family activities, and balancing and prioritizing the many demands he faces. When fathers act with accountability for these uniting rituals, they strengthen the bonds with their children. Their leadership, love, and attentiveness are special blessings to both immediate family members and others for whom they serve as a father figure and friend.

Providing

By divine design, fathers are . . . responsible to provide the necessities of life. (First Presidency, 1995, p. 102)

Faithful fathers are responsible to provide the necessities of life for their families. Providing the necessities of life involves providing income and living providently through the wise use of resources. President Hinckley (1998a) emphasized the importance of providing adequately: "It is your primary obligation to provide for your family" (p. 50). Recognizing that unique challenges or circumstances may conflict with this aspect of a father's role, President Howard W. Hunter (1994) taught, "You [fathers] have the responsibility, unless disabled, to provide temporal support for your wife and children" (p. 51).

Faithful fathers are responsible not only for providing an income but also for establishing sound financial management at home. President Hinckley (1998b) taught, "I urge you to be modest in your expenditures; discipline yourselves in your purchases to avoid debt to the extent possible. Pay off debt as quickly as you can, and free yourselves from bondage" (p. 54). Fathers should also be faithful tithe payers and should wisely use excess funds on establishing savings and providing for the poor and needy. When fathers employ this counsel to live providently, they provide security for their family. They also help their children learn self-discipline and the difference between wants and needs. Fathers should work as partners with their wives in tending to financial matters. In this joint responsibility, husband and wife should be respectful to each other, even when disagreements may arise.

Fathers must also teach their children principles of providing. President Benson (1987) said, "Teach your children to work . . . Establishing mission

Faithful fathers are responsible to provide the necessities of life for their families. Craig Dimond, © 2001 Intellectual Reserve, Inc.

funds and education funds for your children shows them what Dad considers to be important" (p. 51). Fathers can teach these principles by being an example of hard work and provident living as well as by involving their children appropriately in financial decision-making. They will thus teach their children to budget, save, and share.

One of the authors of this chapter gives the following example:

A few years ago, one source of income for the family budget unexpectedly dried up and we found ourselves with a $750 per month budget shortfall. I felt impressed to bring this problem to our family council to resolve. We held a family council and listed on a white board all of the ways we could think of to reduce our spending. Some of these included: increase the thermostat by five degrees in the summer and reduce it by five degrees in the winter, eliminate cable television, reduce or eliminate cell phones, eliminate summer camps, stop taking the newspaper, go on a camping vacation instead of staying in hotels, reduce the number of times we go out to eat, plan better where we drive so we reduce mileage on the cars, etc. Everyone then created a priority list of the cuts they would select. After this each person got to talk about their list and everyone could make modifications. We then tallied up the responses and decided on a new budget for the family with the agreed-upon cuts. I believe this taught our children many good lessons. The only thing I didn't like about it was that everyone wanted to stop the newspaper except for me. However, I graciously agreed to the cut on the condition that I could still buy the newspaper on occasion from the newsstand. (Hill, 2012)

Providing the necessities of life, however, should not be used as justification for spending excessive time and energy at work simply to provide a high standard of living. Sometimes hopes of achieving greater success, a higher salary, or a more powerful title lure men to spend more time in the workplace than in the home. One of the most important aspects of providing for one's children is to bestow upon them enough paternal time and enthusiastic involvement.

To find time for their children, fathers must make spending time with them a high priority. This usually involves a continual effort for fathers not to allow their careers or jobs to deplete their time and energy and turn attention away from their children. © Tyler Olson.

It is said that children spell *love* "t-i-m-e." To find time for their children, fathers must make spending time with them a high priority. This usually involves a continual effort for fathers not to allow their careers or jobs to deplete their time and energy and turn attention away from their children. One father learned the importance of putting family first when he chose to stay at work a little later than he had planned to finish up a relatively unimportant project. Traffic was heavier than expected, so he was late for his son's first swim meet. He arrived just as his son was getting out of the water. He had missed it! He reflected, "If this had been an important business meeting I would have given myself more lead time." He vowed he would never again let his job keep him from missing important events in his child's life (Hill, 1991). President Monson (2005) highlighted this point as he spoke to fathers, "I would encourage you to be available to your children. I have heard it said that no man, as death approaches, has ever declared that he wished he had spent more time at the office" (p. 20).

President Monson goes on to quote a powerful article entitled "A Day at the Beach" by Arthur Gordon.

> When I was around thirteen and my brother ten, Father had promised to take us to the circus. But at lunchtime there was a phone call; some urgent business required his attention downtown. We braced ourselves for disappointment. Then we heard him say, "No, I won't be down. It'll have to wait." When he came back to the table, Mother smiled [and said,] "The circus keeps coming back, you know."
>
> "I know," said Father. "But childhood doesn't." (p. 21)

Author George Durrant (1976) captured the relative importance of work and family:

> At your place of work, you are needed. But, sad as it may seem, there has never been a man who, when he leaves his daily job or when he retires, is not adequately replaced. As one man said, "I felt that if I left the company, it would take a month or so and then I'd be replaced and they wouldn't even miss me. But," he said, "I was wrong. It only took a week." . . . But there is a place where a man has no substitute. Not after a month or a year or a generation. That is the place where they call him "Father." When he leaves home [for work], he's missed. And until he returns, there will be an empty, unfilled space in the hearts of his family. (p. 15)

Providing the necessities of life is a great responsibility, and the Lord expects fathers to ensure the temporal security of their families. This role can be a great burden, especially during challenging economic times and conflicting responsibilities. However, fathers should not be discouraged. Through faithful living and with the help of their wives and the Lord, fathers can do it. The Lord recognizes the sacrifice such service requires and blesses fathers as they diligently do their best.

Protecting

By divine design fathers . . . are responsible to provide . . . protection for their families. (First Presidency, 1995, p. 102)

Protecting is closely related to presiding and providing. Both spiritual and temporal safety are elements of protection. President Hunter (1994) taught, "A righteous father protects his children with his time and presence in their social, educational, and spiritual activities and responsibilities" (p. 51). Elder Perry (2003) added, "We need to make our homes a place of refuge from the storm, which is increasing in intensity all about us. Even if the smallest openings are left unattended, negative influences can penetrate the very walls of our homes" (p. 40). Protection involves guarding the home from spiritually detrimental influences, providing emotional support, ensuring a physically safe environment, appropriately expressing physical affection, and teaching family preparedness.

We live in a world in which moral dangers confront children very early in life. Faithful fathers should actively protect their children by helping them make wise choices about the literature they read, the media they watch, and the friendships they establish. President Hinckley (2002) wrote, "Guard your homes. How foolish it seems to install bars and bolts and electronic devices against thieves and molesters while more insidious intruders stealthily enter and despoil" (p. 2–6).

Children also need emotional protection, especially during times of crisis. Research shows that children feel deep security and comfort from regular family routines in such times (Loser, Hill, Klein, & Dollahite, 2009). Consistent family meals, bedtime rituals, family recreation, and

Fathers are responsible to provide spiritual protection for their children by helping them understand and make wise choices about the media they watch, the literature they read, and the friends they associate with. Craig W. Dimond, © Intellectual Reserve, Inc.

other comforting consistencies can have a reassuring and stabilizing effect on children. Religious traditions and rituals such as regular prayer, church attendance, and other religious activities and devotions can be especially comforting in these increasingly dangerous and anxiety-provoking times.

Faithful fathers protect their children by setting clear boundaries about what is and is not allowed in the home. It is especially important that fathers are good examples in this respect. When the father of the home shuns evil and keeps his thoughts, words, and actions pure, his children will learn to do the same. It is helpful for parents to watch media with their children and turn it off with an explanation when it violates the standards of the home. Faithful fathers can also provide both spiritual and physical protection by surveying the environment and preparing their children ahead of time to meet known dangers.

Physical protection is also important. A faithful father, along with his wife, protects his family by wisely selecting a safe neighborhood in which to locate their home. The father can also take a protective lead by insisting upon seat belt use, installing smoke alarms, locking up dangerous chemicals, and seeing that bike helmets are worn. Appropriate physical affection between fathers and children helps with feelings of security. Hugging, holding hands, and sitting close give children a tangible sense of security that words alone cannot provide. Research confirms that children receive emotional and psychological benefits from meaningful physical affection from parents in particular (Blackwell, 2000).

While appropriate touch is important for healthy emotional and psychological development, the effects of inappropriate touching can be devastating. All forms of abuse are harmful to the development of the heart, mind, and relationship. Research among a sample of college students and their dating partners revealed that memories of childhood emotional abuse was negatively associated with relationship quality (Riggs, Cusimano, & Benson, 2011). It has also been found among a random sample of 2,225 women in a New Zealand community that a background with any type of abuse as a child was related to increased sexual difficulties, psychopathology, lower self-esteem, and interpersonal problems (Mullen et al., 1996). The Lord condemns any man who would abuse his children. President Hinckley (1998c) taught, "No man who abuses his wife or children is worthy to be a member in good standing in this Church" (p. 72). Spiritual abuse is another form of abuse that is often overlooked. It occurs when a man misuses his priesthood authority to unrighteously exert power and control over his wife or children. The Lord's warning in D&C 121:37 applies well to fathers: "[When] they . . . exercise control or dominion or compulsion upon the souls of the children of men, in any degree of unrighteousness, behold, the heavens withdraw themselves; the Spirit of the Lord is grieved, and when it is withdrawn, Amen to the priesthood or the authority of that man." A faithful father knows how to control his temper and never threatens his wife or children with actions, words, or thoughts. Where destructive abuse has occurred, the healing power of the Atonement can be applied through the difficult but achievable road of repentance, forgiveness, and healing.

Family preparedness is an additional way to protect family during times of need. Fathers should take the lead in ensuring that principles of preparedness are taught and lived in their families. President Monson (2008b) counseled, "We urge all Latter-day Saints to be prudent in their planning, to be conservative in their living, and to avoid excessive or unnecessary debt" (p. 61). President Hinckley (1998b) also warned Latter-day Saints that financial prosperity can be fleeting and has encouraged them to be cautious and prepared (pp. 52–53). For many decades, Church leaders have regularly counseled members to get out of debt, live modestly, and have a savings they can subsist on during a financial crisis. By heeding these prophetic warnings, fathers can protect their children from unnecessary fear, pain, and lack of opportunity.

Finally, a way for a faithful father to offer protection is to formally dedicate his home as a place of safety. The *Church Handbook of Instructions* (2010) helps us understand this process:

> Church members may dedicate their homes as sacred edifices where
> the Holy Spirit can reside and where family members can worship,

find safety from the world, grow spiritually, and prepare for eternal family relationships. Homes need not be free of debt to be dedicated. Unlike Church buildings, homes are not consecrated to the Lord. . . . [To dedicate a home], a family might gather and offer a prayer that includes the elements mentioned [above] and other words as the Spirit directs. (pp. 176–77)

Some fathers have transcribed their dedicatory prayer and displayed it in a prominent place as a reminder that their home is the Lord's. Remembering that the home has been dedicated can be a comfort to those living within its walls, and a reminder of what should and should not happen there. When the standards of the home are kept consistent with the aims and desires expressed in a dedicatory prayer, the adversary's attacks on the home can be thwarted and it can become a haven of growth, learning, and joy.

As the adversary increasingly seeks to destroy the good work accomplished in the home, the duty to protect is ever more important and challenging. Fathers can provide protection by being available to their children physically, emotionally, and spiritually. Through their actions they ensure physical safety, regulate entertainment, and practice family preparedness. Finally, a father may offer a dedicatory prayer on the home that can serve as a blanket of protection for the family, providing a vision for unity, purity, and peace among its members.

Partnering

In these sacred responsibilities, fathers and mothers are obligated to help one another as equal partners. (First Presidency, 1995, p.102)

In studying family proclamation–based principles of faithful fathering, we may be tempted to limit our focus to the three P's, preside, provide, and protect. However, the stewardship to partner with one's eternal companion is equally—if not more—important. Partnership in marriage means to be united in decision-making, to fully contribute and invite full contribution in both spiritual and temporal work in the home, and to bear and nurture children together as co-creators with God. President Boyd K. Packer (1998) stated, "However much priesthood power and authority the men may possess—however much wisdom and experience they may accumulate—the safety of the family, the integrity of the doctrine, the ordinances, the covenants, indeed the future of the Church, rests equally on the women. . . . No man achieves the supernal exalting status of worthy fatherhood except as a gift from his wife" (p. 73). With a vision of being united eternally as a family, fathers and mothers can and should help one another as companions in fulfilling their divinely appointed responsibilities.

For a man acting alone, the responsibility to be a faithful father may seem difficult, burdensome, and even overwhelming. "Fortunately, you are not required to preside and judge, and act without counsel, without assistance. You have a wife—a companion, a counselor, a partner, a helpmeet, a friend" (Quorum of the Twelve Apostles, 2002, p. 15). With a helpmeet to help bear this burden, the stewardship of being a faithful father may become light (see Mosiah 18:8).

The partnership of Joseph Smith with his wife Emma is an extraordinary illustration of the grand vision of equal partnership. Jesse Crosby (as cited in Andrus & Andrus, 1999), an early Latter-day Saint, observed this about Joseph Smith: "Some of the home habits of the Prophet—such as building kitchen fires, carrying out ashes, carrying in wood and water, assisting in the care of children, etc.—were not in accord with my idea of a great man's self-respect." So Brother Crosby gave Joseph what he called "corrective advice," telling him that such work was "too terrible a humiliation, for you who are the head, and you should not do it." Joseph responded, "If there be humiliation in a man's house, who but the head of that house should or could bear that humiliation?" (pp. 163–64). As a father, Joseph partnered with Emma in raising the children and in the everyday work of the home.

In keeping with the Prophet's example, President Packer (1989) taught, "There is no task, however menial, connected with the care of babies, the nurturing of children, or with the maintenance of the home that is not [a

Faithful fathers partner with their wives in all aspects of their marriage. Craig Dimond,
© Intellectual Reserve, Inc.

Perhaps partnering in parenting is the greatest responsibility and aspiration of all.
© *Kzenon.*

husband's] equal obligation" (p. 75). And President Hinckley (1992) said, "Marriage, in its truest sense, is a partnership of equals, with neither exercising dominion over the other, but, rather, with each encouraging and assisting the other in whatever responsibilities and aspirations he or she might have" (p. 6). Perhaps partnering in parenting is the greatest responsibility and aspiration of all. In this regard, fathers have a tremendously positive impact on children simply through expressing love and honor for their mother. President Hunter (1994) taught, "one of the greatest things a father can do for his children is to love their mother" (p. 50). A father can show his love for his wife by expressing appreciation to her, supporting her in her individual endeavors, and assisting her in every way possible. Fathers should both offer loving service and accept it as a gift from their wives in a spirit of humility and sacrifice. Faithful fathers seek help from their wives in their own stewardships to preside over their families in love and righteousness. President Hunter (1994) wrote, "Presiding in righteousness necessitates a shared responsibility between husband and wife; together you act with knowledge and participation in all family matters. For a man to operate independent of or without regard to the feelings and counsel of his wife in governing the family is to exercise unrighteous dominion" (p. 51). Shared family leadership means deciding all important matters together in humility. Decisions are made in a humble spirit of honoring agency, facilitating growth, bridging conflicts, forgiving, and healing. No decision of substance should be made except by consensus.

Faithful fathers assist their wives in nurturing and caring for their children as well as in the daily maintenance of the home. President Benson (1987) wrote, "Remember, brethren . . . to help with the dishes, change diapers, get up with a crying child in the night, and leave the television or the newspaper to help with the dinner. Those are the quiet ways we say, 'I love you' with our actions. They bring rich dividends" (p. 50). Scholarly research reveals that when the father is more involved in housework and childcare, both husbands and wives rate their intimate relationship as more satisfying (Coltrane, 2003).

Faithful fathers are also sacred partners in procreation. President Benson (1987b) wrote, "Husbands and wives, as co-creators, should eagerly and prayerfully invite children into their homes. Then, as each child joins their family circle, they can gratefully exclaim, as did Hannah, 'For this child I prayed, and the Lord hath given me my petition which I asked of him' (1 Samuel 1:27)."

Fathers must join with their partners in teaching their children the proper principles of procreation. President Hinckley (1996) wrote, "Let parents teach their children the sanctity of sex, that the gift of creating life is sacred, that the impulses that burn within us can be and must be disciplined and restrained if there is to be happiness, peace, and goodness" (p. 7).

While the assistance of a helpmeet is invaluable, there are circumstances in which a father is required to take on both the roles of nurturing and providing. Whether through death, disability, divorce, or other circumstances, a growing number of men are single parents. While they may feel overwhelmed, single fathers are fully capable of raising a righteous family with the Lord's help.

When fathers seek the assistance of their wives in presiding, providing, and protecting, and provide assistance to their wives in nurturing, the partnership thus created is a powerful strength in the home. Fathers should be full partners in day-to-day labors in the home as well as in the nurturing of their children. As they are fully invested in the home, they will reap great blessings of eternal relationships that can never be severed.

Summary

Year in and year out, faithful fathers do the everyday tasks, founded upon the gospel of Jesus Christ, that are necessary to establish, maintain, and strengthen their families. They endure to the end of their paternal stewardship in mortality and are then crowned with the glory of an eternal posterity. A faithful father does his best to fulfill his stewardships of presiding, providing, protecting, and partnering. Becoming a faithful father

Helping around the house is one way to say, "I love you" with your actions. Mark A. Philbrick. © 2013 BYU Photo.

is of transcendent importance. President Hinckley (2004) taught, "When life is over and you look back, you will not take any money with you. The only thing that will give you satisfaction is what you see in the lives of your children, [and] you will have an understanding that comes of the gospel that these children are also our Father in Heaven's children" ("Rear Children," para. 1).

The process of becoming a faithful father is, in essence, the process of becoming like God. It is an apprenticeship. As a man seeks God's help to preside, provide, protect, and partner in righteousness, he receives divine direction. Just as an apprentice learns line upon line from his master, so faithful fathers can look to God for guidance, and they too will learn. We believe that becoming a faithful father is within the grasp of every faithful man. Remember, "the most important of the Lord's work you and I will ever do will be within the walls of our own homes" (Lee, 1974, p. 255).

References

Andrus, H. L., & Andrus, H. M. (1999). *They knew the Prophet: Personal accounts from over 100 people who knew Joseph Smith.* Salt Lake City: Deseret Book.

Bellah, R. N., Madsen, R., Swidler, W. M., Swidler, A., & Tipton, S. M. (1991). *The good society.* New York: Vintage.

Benson, E. T. (1987a, November). To the fathers in Israel, *Ensign, 17*(11), 48–51.

Benson, E. T. (1987b). To the mothers in Zion. Retrieved from <http://www.byu.edu/fc/ee/w_etb87.htm>

Blackwell, P. L. (2000, July). The influence of touch on child development: Implications for intervention. *Infants and Young Children, 13*(1), 25–39.

Brotherson, S. E., Dollahite, D. C., & Hawkins, A. J. (2005, Winter). Generative fathering and the dynamics of connection between fathers and their children. *Fathering, 3*(1), 1–28.

Coltrane, S. (2003). Fathering: paradoxes, contradictions, and dilemmas. Paper presented at the second annual Work and Family Conference held at Boston, Massachusetts. Retrieved from http://www.powershow.com/view/c0d7-ZTE3Y/Fathering_Paradoxes_Contradictions_and_Dilemmas_powerpoint_ppt_presentation

Dollahite, D. C. (2003, March). Fathering for eternity: Generative spirituality in Latter-day Saint fathers of children with special needs. *Review of Religious Research, 44*(3), 237–251.

Dollahite, D. C., & Marks, L. D. (2009, June). A conceptual model of family and religious processes in highly religious families. *Review of Religious Research, 50*(4), 373–391.

Dollahite, D. C., Marks, L. D., & Olson, M. M. (1998, Fall). Faithful fathering in trying times: Religious beliefs and practices of Latter-day Saint fathers of children with special needs. *Journal of Men's Studies, 7*(1), 71–93.

Dollahite, D. C. & Thatcher, J. Y. (2008, September). Talking about religion: How religious youth and parents discuss their faith. *Journal of Adolescent Research, 23*(5), 611–641.

Durrant, G. D. (1976). *Love at home starring Father.* Salt Lake City: Bookcraft.

First Presidency and Council of the Twelve Apostles (1995). The family: A proclamation to the world. *Ensign, 25*(11), 102.

Handbook 2: Administering the Church (2010). Salt Lake City: The Church of Jesus Christ of Latter-day Saints, 176–177.

Hill, E. J. (2012). Lecture in SFL 100, Strengthening marriages and families, Brigham Young University, Provo, Utah.

Hill, E. J., & Dollahite, D. C. (2005). Faithful fathering. In C. Hart, L. D. Newell, E. Walton, & D. C. Dollahite (Eds.). *Helping and healing our families: Principles and practices inspired by "The family: A proclamation to the world"* (pp. 167–171). Salt Lake City: Deseret Book.

Hill, E. J., Whyte, R. O., Jacob, J. I., Blanchard, V. I., Duncan, S., Dollahite, D. C., & Wadsworth, L. (2008). Fathers' religious and family involvement at home: Work and family outcomes. *The Open Family Studies Journal, 1*, 56–65.

Hill, T. (1991). Please, put first things first. *DADS Newsletter, 9*, 5.

Hinckley, G. B. (1992, August). I believe. *Ensign, 22*(8), 6.

Hinckley, G. B. (1996, September). Four simple things to help our families and our nations. *Ensign, 26*(9). 2–8.

Hinckley, G. B. (1998a, May). Living worthy of the girl you will someday marry. *Ensign, 28*(5).

Hinckley, G. B. (1998b, November). To the boys and to the men. *Ensign, 28*(11), 51–54.

Hinckley, G. B. (1998c, November). What are people asking about us. *Ensign, 28*(11), 70–72.

Hinckley, G. B. (2002, January). Overpowering the Goliaths in our lives. *Ensign, 32*(1), 2–6.

Hinckley, G. B. (2004, January 3). Church news: Messages of inspiration from President Hinckley. Available at http://www.ldschurchnews.com/articles/print/44907/Messages-of-inspiration-from-President-Hinckley.html

Hunter, H. W. (1994, November). Being a righteous husband and father. *Ensign, 24*(11), 49–51.

Lamb, M. E. (1997). Fathers and child development: An introductory overview and guide. In M. E. Lamb (Ed.). *The role of the father in child development* (3rd ed., pp. 1–18). New York: Wiley.

Layton, E., Dollahite, D. C., & Hardy, S. A. (2011). Anchors of religious commitment in adolescents. *Journal of Adolescent Research, 26*(3), 381–413.

Lee, H. B. (1974). *Stand ye in holy places.* Salt Lake City: Deseret Book.

Loser, R. W., Hill, E. J., Klein, S. R., & Dollahite, D. C. (2009). Perceived benefits of religious rituals in the Latter-day Saint home. *Review of Religious Research, 50*(3), 345–362.

Loser, R. W., Klein, S. R., Hill, E. J., & Dollahite, D. C. (2008, September). Religion and the daily lives of LDS families: An ecological perspective. *Family and Consumer Sciences Research Journal, 37*(1), 52–70.

Marks, L. D., & Dollahite, D. C. (2001). Religion, relationships, and responsible fathering in Latter-day Saint families of children with special needs. *Journal of Social and Personal Relationships, 18*(5), 625–650.

Marks, L. D., & Dollahite, D. C. (2007). Fathering and religious contexts: Why religion makes a difference to fathers and their children. In S. E. Brotherson, & J. M. White (Eds.). *Why Fathers Count* (pp. 335–351). Harriman, TN: Men's Studies Press.

Monson, T. S. (2005, May). Constant truths for changing times. *Ensign, 35*(5), 20–21.

Monson, T. S. (2008a, May). Examples of righteousness. *Ensign, 38*(5), 66.

Monson, T. S. (2008b, November). To learn, to do, to be. *Ensign, 38*(11).

Monson, T. S. (2010, October). Blessings of the temple. *Ensign, 40*(10), 15.

Mullen, P. E., Martin, J. L., Anderson, J. C., Romans, S. E., & Herbison, G. P. (1996). The long-term impact of the physical, emotional, and sexual abuse of children: A community study. *Child Abuse and Neglect, 20*(1), 7–21.

Olson, M. M., Dollahite, D. C., & White, M. B. (2002). Involved fathering of children with special needs: relationships and religion as resources. *Journal of Religion, Disability, & Health, 6*(1), 47–73.

Packer, B. K. (1989, July). A tribute to women. *Ensign, 19*(7), 75.

Packer, B. K. (1998). The Relief Society. *Ensign, 28*(5), 72–74.

Perry, L. T. (2003). The importance of the family. *Ensign, 33*(5), 40.

Perry, L. T. (2004, May). Fatherhood, an eternal calling. *Ensign, 34*(5), 69–72.

Quorum of the Twelve Apostles. (2002, June). Father, consider your ways. *Ensign, 32*(6), 12–16.

Riggs, S. A., Cusimano, A. M., & Benson, K. M. (2011). Childhood emotional abuse and attachment processes in the dyadic adjustment of dating couples. *Journal of Counseling Psychology, 58*(1), 126–138.

8

A House of Faith:
How Family Religiosity
Strengthens Our Children

THE Apostle Paul warned that "in the last days perilous times shall come" (2 Timothy 3:1–4). His prophecies of the wicked conditions that will prevail in the last days are being realized before our very eyes. All manner of sin—including violence, crime, fraud, drug and alcohol abuse, pornography, and sexual immorality—can be seen in society. The Savior also prophesied concerning the conditions of the world that will precede his Second Coming when he stated "iniquity [does] abound" (Joseph Smith —Matthew 1:30). The "fiery darts of the wicked" are particularly aimed at families (Ephesians 6:16). Parents find themselves in the midst of the battle against sin and often worry that their children, who are surrounded by it, may be yielding to temptations. They wonder what they can do to protect their families from this onslaught of wickedness.

It is not just the parents who worry and wonder. Youth on the front lines in this battle against the growing wickedness of the world also are troubled by the temptations and challenges they face every day. "My parents really have no idea how hard it is to be a teenager today," one LDS high school student despaired. Another lamented the pressure he feels from his friends. He reported, "Almost all of my friends use alcohol and drugs and go to parties almost every weekend. Many are immoral and tell me how fun it is. When I tell them these things are against my religion, they make fun of me and call me names." LDS youth realize they are in the thick of perilous things.

Although parents cannot *isolate* their children from every evil influence, opposition, or peer pressure, they can *insulate* them. What can we, as parents, do to provide such *insulation*? What must occur within the walls of our own homes to help our children gain the spiritual and emotional strength to be righteous and responsible in these challenging times? Prophets of God continually raise their warning voices and lovingly give us counsel on how to strengthen our families. In addition, social science research confirms such counsel and gives further insight into how we can be better parents. This chapter reports many of the results of a large study (perhaps the largest ever done among LDS youth and families) on the influence of religion in the lives of LDS youth, and offers practical suggestions on how parents can strengthen the religiosity of their children.

The Power of Religion in the Lives of LDS Youth

In the landmark book *Soul Searching*, authors Christian Smith and Melinda Lundquist Denton (2005) reported the finds of the National Study of Youth and Religion (NSYR), the largest and most detailed study of religion in the lives of teenagers in the United States ever conducted. In contrast to earlier scholars who argued that religion has little or no influence on the behavior of adolescents (Stark, 1984; Hirschi & Stark, 1969), Smith and Denton (2005) found that "the empirical evidence suggests that religious faith and practice themselves exert significant, positive, direct and indirect influence on the lives of teenagers, helping to foster healthier, more engaged adolescents who live more constructive and promising lives" (p. 263). The NSYR study also reports that religiosity is positively correlated with academic achievement, moral development, and community volunteerism and is negatively linked to delinquency, alcohol, tobacco, and drug use, as well as illicit sexual activity among youth. Princeton professor

Kenda Creasy Dean (2010) in her book, *Almost Christian*, analyzed the NSYR study and concluded:

> Teenagers who say religion is important to them are doing "much better in life" than less religious teenagers, by a number of measures. Those who participate in religious communities are more likely to do well in school, have positive relationships with their families, have a positive outlook on life, and wear their seatbelts—the list goes on, enumerating an array of outcomes that parents pray for. . . .
>
> Highly devoted young people are much more compassionate, significantly more likely to care about things like racial equality and justice, far less likely to be moral relativists, to lie, cheat, or do things "they hoped their parents would never find out about." They are not just doing "okay" in life; they are doing significantly better than their peers, at least in terms of happiness and forms of success approved by the cultural mainstream. . . . So it comes as no surprise that young people who reported positive relationships with parents and peers, success in school, hope for the future, and healthy lifestyle choices were also more likely to be highly committed to faith as well. (pp. 20, 47)

The findings reported in the National Study of Youth and Religion are particularly interesting to Latter-day Saint parents. Although the number of LDS teens who were included in the NYSR sample was quite small, the researchers were clearly impressed with their devotion and behavior. In a chapter entitled "Mormon Envy," Professor Dean wrote:

> Mormon teenagers attach the most importance to faith and are most likely to fall in the category of highly devoted youth. . . . In nearly every area, using a variety of measures, Mormon teenagers showed the highest levels of religious understanding, vitality, and

congruence between religious belief and practiced faith; they were the least likely to engage in high-risk behavior and consistently were the most positive, healthy, hopeful, and self-aware teenagers in the interviews. (p. 20)

The results of this national study and the observations of these researchers confirm what we have found from studying Latter-day Saint youth and families for the past quarter of a century (Chadwick, Top, & McClendon, 2010; Top, Chadwick, & Garrett, 1999; Chadwick & Top, 1993). Our studies have clearly established that religion is a significant factor directly affecting the attitudes and actions of LDS adolescents. Importantly, we discovered that the religiosity of their parents and the spiritual environment of the home were significant influences in the religious development of the youth. Just as religion matters in shaping the character and behavior of youth, parents matter in shaping the faith and devotion of their children. "The best way to get most youth more involved in and serious about their faith communities," Smith and Denton (2005) wrote, "is to get their parents more involved in and serious about their faith communities" (p. 267).

A Study of Faith and Family among LDS Youth

With the cooperation of the Church Educational System, over a 20 year period we surveyed over 5,000 LDS high school students, ages 14 to 18, living in different regions of the United States, Great Britain, and Mexico to test the relationship of religion and family with delinquency, academic achievement, and feelings of self-esteem. The study focused on these three behaviors because of their importance in the lives of teenagers. To ascertain the influence of religion and family on these behaviors, we included other important factors in a model of delinquency, including academic achievement and self-esteem. The theoretical model tested is shown in Figure 1. As can be seen, the model required religiosity and family to compete with

Figure 1. Conceptual Model with Religiosity, Peer Influence, Personality Traits, and Family Characteristics Predicting Adolescent Delinquency

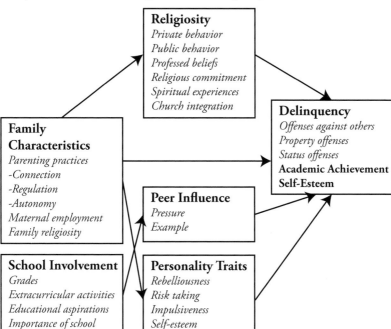

peer influences, personality traits, and school involvement to explain delinquency. Structural equation analysis was used to test the model since it identifies the relative strengths of each of the factors in explaining delinquency, academic achievement, or feelings of self-esteem.

Obviously, we cannot report all of the results of these extensive studies in the limited pages of this chapter. Rather, we will share only a few of the major findings and discuss their implications for us as parents. Detailed theoretical, methodological, statistical information, and conclusions from these studies have been published in a variety of other venues over the past several years (see Chadwick, Top, & McClendon, 2010; Top & Chadwick, 2006; Top & Chadwick, 2004; Top, Chadwick, & McClendon, 2003; Top & Chadwick, 1999; Top & Chadwick, 1998; Top & Chadwick, 1993).

Figure 2. Model of Significant Estimates for Delinquency (Utah County Young Men)

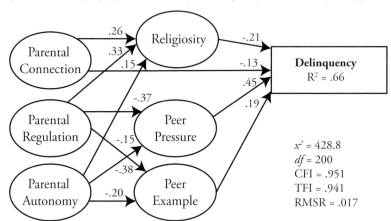

Faith, Family and Delinquency

The influence of faith and family on delinquency among LDS youth was ascertained utilizing the theoretical model shown in Figure 1. The model allowed peers, religion, personality traits, school activities and family characteristics to compete in explaining delinquency. Delinquent behavior included offenses against others, such as beating up other kids; property offenses, such as shoplifting and vandalism; and status offenses, including underage drinking, drug use, and premarital sex.

The results of the test of the model for young men living in Utah County are presented in Figure 2. Similar results were obtained for young men and young women residing in different regions of the United States, Great Britain, and Mexico. In the figure we see that peer influences are the strongest predictor of whether an LDS teenager will engage in delinquent behaviors. We were certainly not surprised by this result. There is a large literature that has identified peer pressure as the single most significant factor predicting delinquency. What is important to note, however, is that religiosity is also statistically significant. The beta coefficient is -.21, which means that the greater the religiosity of the teenagers, the less they were involved in activities that are immoral, illegal, or improper. The model accounted for two-thirds of the variation in the delinquency among LDS young men.

At first we were disappointed to discover that only one family characteristic, parental connection—a combination of both a mom and a dad's connection—was a significant predictor of delinquency in the multivariate model. Some social scientists have repeatedly contended that parents are largely irrelevant in accounting for the delinquent activities of their children (Harris, 2009). The problem with these previous studies is that they examined only the *direct effects* of family on delinquency and neglected the *indirect effects*. As noted in Figure 2, parental connection (love and support), parental regulation (rules, obedience and discipline) and parental autonomy (parents' acceptance of child's feelings, opinions, and ideas) have strong impacts on their teens' religiosity, resistance to peer pressures, and peer example. What these findings make clear is that parents who love and are concerned about their children; who set family rules, ascertain compliance, and discipline inappropriate behavior; and who allow their teens to develop their own sense of self have children with rather low delinquency.

Faith, Family, and Academic Aspirations and Achievement

Loving parents want to help their children be happy, confident, responsible, and successful in life. Sometimes they go to great lengths to achieve that—buying the latest product that claims to help children get an "edge" in school or involving them in activities that "build" young people. These things are good, but as shown in Figure 3, which focuses on academic aspirations, we found one thing that is better—religiosity. Social science research has long noted that the educational level of a teen's father is the strongest predictor of educational aspirations and accomplishments of adolescents.

The structural equation model presented in Figure 3 accounts for nearly 50% of the educational aspirations of the young men living in Utah County. As mentioned earlier, space constraints preclude presenting the various models predicting academic achievement and aspirations for LDS

Figure 3. Model of Siginificant Estimates for Educational Aspirations (Utah County Young Men)

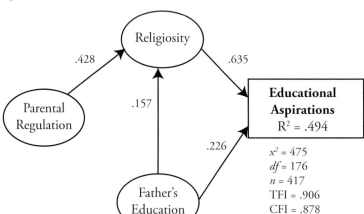

youth living in the different geographical areas. For our purposes in this chapter, we selected the model for Utah County young men because it is highly representative of the findings from the different populations.

Surprisingly, the strongest predictor of educational plans was the youths' religiosity. Among LDS youth, religious beliefs, practices, and spiritual experiences combined into a measure of religiosity that was the strongest factor to emerge in the multivariate model. The father's education was the only other factor to enter the equation. It should be noted that parental regulation made a strong indirect impact on educational aspirations through religiosity. The results for young women in Utah County and both young men and women in the other regions were very similar. There is no doubt that fostering their religiosity enhances LDS youths' academic performance and desire for higher education.

Faith, Family, and Feelings of Self-Esteem

The last several years have witnessed great attention directed to studying the importance of self-esteem or feelings of self-worth among adolescents.

Popular enthusiasm for self-esteem swelled to the point that many parents, school administers, and government officials came to believe that it was a social vaccine that increases desirable behaviors and decreases negative ones (Rosenthal & Jacobson, 1992; Rosenthal, 1973; Hansford & Hattie, 1982). Mary Pipher (1994), a clinical psychologist who works with young women, detailed the negative impacts of the eroding self-confidence of young women in American society.

Although fostering self-esteem seems to increase appropriate behavior among teenagers, some researchers have raised a serious concern. After conducting a thorough review of the self-esteem research, Baumeister, Campbell, Krueger, and Vohs (2003) cautioned that parents, teachers, and others who have endeavored to raise self-esteem in young people may have unintentionally fostered narcissism in their children. Young people thought to have high self-esteem may actually be self-absorbed and conceited. Narcissistic youth feel that they are so special they deserve special treatment by others and that the rules of society do not apply to them.

We were somewhat surprised to discover that LDS high school seniors have slightly lower self-esteem than a large national sample of high school seniors. There are two plausible possible explanations for these lower feelings of self-worth. One explanation is that the gospel and the Church place very high expectations and demands on its youth, which are difficult to accomplish, and failure to do so contributes to feelings of inadequacy. This lack of perfection is then expressed in response to the questions measuring self-esteem. The alternative explanation is that LDS youth are taught to be humble and avoid pride, so they are more modest praising themselves. We do not have the data necessary to test these two alternative explanations, but we hope LDS youths' lower feelings of self-esteem are explained by the humility hypothesis rather than the perfectionism/guilt hypothesis.

The results of the structural equation model predicting the self-esteem of LDS young men in the United States is presented in Figure 4. Acceptance at church produced by far the strongest impact on self-esteem for young men. It is not surprising to find that feeling accepted is closely linked to

Figure 4. Model of Significant Estimates for Self-Esteem among LDS Young Men in the United States

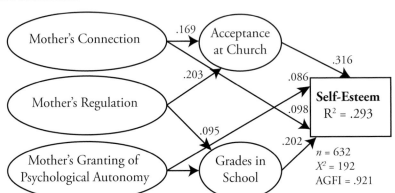

how adolescents value themselves. What is unique to these LDS teens is where and with whom they feel comfortable. It is not acceptance by friends at school, but rather, it is within their wards and branches with leaders, teachers, and fellow members that acceptance had such a powerful relationship to feelings of self-worth.

Not surprisingly, grades earned in school also made a significant contribution to self-esteem. Success in school gives youths' feelings of self-worth a boost.

Mothers' connection also produced a weak direct effect on feelings of self-worth. We included only the teens' mothers' behavior in the model because the behaviors of mothers and fathers were so highly correlated that including both created major statistical problems. Thus, even though the model identifies mothers' behavior, it represents the behavior of both parents. In addition, the *indirect* influence of mothers' connection, regulation, and granting of psychological autonomy on self-esteem through the two direct factors should be noted.

The results of this complex analysis make it clear that parents and Church leaders really do matter in how teens feel about themselves. What leaps out from this analysis is that parents and leaders need to make sure teens feel a spirit of love, acceptance, and warmth in the home and in the community of Saints. Parents and leaders must work together to make sure youth feel welcome in seminary, institute, priesthood quorum meetings, Scout groups, young women classes, Sunday School, sacrament meetings, and other Church-sponsored activities. Such acceptance is important in helping young people develop positive feelings about themselves.

Religious Ecology versus Personal Religiosity

When we published the good news that religiosity was a powerful influence for good in the lives of LDS teenagers, some critics responded that we had misinterpreted our findings. Stark (1984) argued that the LDS youth we had studied living in Utah, Idaho, and Southern California were surrounded by a powerful LDS religious ecology. Thus the theory was that youth had lower rates of delinquency and higher academic achievement because of the social pressures from their peers and from their entire community and not because of the religious principles they held.

In order to test the power of internalized religious principles against a religious ecology, we obtained data from samples of youth living in several regions of this country and Great Britain with differing religious ecologies. The communities ranged from a powerful religious ecology in Utah County to a low ecology in the Pacific Northwest and an extremely low ecology in Great Britain. We started with a sample of LDS high school students living along the East Coast because these teens were the only LDS students in their individual high schools. The results were almost identical with those obtained in the Utah-Idaho-California samples!

Critics responded that, while the LDS religious ecology was low, these East Coast students did live within a general Christian ecology that shaped their behavior. We asked our doubting colleagues where the lowest religious ecology in this country was. They readily identified the Pacific Northwest. Data were then collected from LDS youth in Seattle, Washington and Portland, Oregon. To provide an even stronger test of the religious ecology hypothesis, we collected data from LDS youth living in Great Britain. Space does not permit recounting the evidence of the low religious ecology in Great Britain, but these LDS youth lived in an extremely secular society and interacted with peers who were heavily involved in premarital sexual relations and alcohol and drug use.

The results for LDS youth living along the East Coast, in the Pacific Northwest and in Great Britain were very similar to those obtained in Utah. The religious ecology—where the adolescent lives and the religious culture of the community—did not matter nearly as much as did individual faith and religious conviction.

Internalized Religiosity

Most studies of the religion-delinquency connection have focused on affiliation and attendance, which are rather limited indicators of religious feelings and behaviors. In our study of LDS youth we examined five different dimensions of religiosity: professed religious beliefs, public religious behavior (attendance at meetings and involvement in church activities), private religious behavior (such as personal prayer and scripture study), spiritual experiences, and social acceptance at church. These different dimensions were included because we were convinced that internal feelings about the gospel are more important in the lives of teens than is mere attendance at church services.

Statistical tests were used to determine the relative strength of each of these factors. Because religious beliefs, private religious behavior, and spiritual experiences were so closely related, the confirmatory factor analysis combined them into one dimension of religiosity we called spirituality. Spirituality is the "stuff" of which a testimony of the gospel and commitment to the Church are made.

In model after model computed with different populations of young men and young women from different regions of the country and of the world, spirituality emerged as the strongest dimension of religiosity related to delinquency. To demonstrate the greater influence of spirituality as compared to public religious behavior and acceptance in church we computed a model in which only these three dimensions of religiosity competed to explain

Figure 5. Dimensions of Religiosity Predicting Delinquency among LDS Young Men in the United States

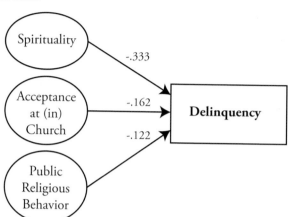

delinquency. As can be seen in Figure 5, each of these three dimensions of religiosity emerged as a significant predictor of delinquency. But the strongest factor by far was spirituality—the spirituality of the youth, the degree to which they had experienced and internalized the gospel into their lives—produced a beta coefficient of -.333. The negative number means an inverse relationship—the *higher* the spirituality, the *lower* the delinquency.

As mentioned earlier, what we anticipated would be important factors predicting delinquent behavior did not make a significant contribution in the multivariate model shown in Figure 2. Much to our surprise, family religiosity, which includes family home evening, family prayer, and family scripture reading, was not significant. What we learn from these results is that family religious practices and youth's attendance at church meetings apparently do not in and of themselves counteract peer pressures to engage in unworthy behavior. Rather, these practices are means to an end, not the end itself—the practices merely encourage and facilitate individual religious commitment and personal conversion. Youth that have their own spiritual experiences and engage in their own religious practices such as daily prayer and scripture study, above and beyond involvement in family religious practice, have greater strength to resist temptation and increased determination to live righteous lives.

Youth that have their own spiritual experiences and engage in their own religious practices such as daily prayer and scripture study, above and beyond involvement in family religious practice, have greater strength to resist temptation and increased determination to live righteous lives. Christina Smith, © Intellectual Reserve, Inc.

The results of our studies—not just the statistical findings, but also hundreds of comments by the youth themselves—validate the teachings of prophets of God given to the Church for generations: It is not enough to merely get our children into the Church; we must also make sure they gain a knowledge of the gospel and a personal testimony of its truthfulness. Our findings confirm what President James E. Faust (1990) declared:

> Generally, those children who make the decision and have the resolve to abstain from drugs, alcohol, and illicit sex are those who have adopted and internalized the strong values of their homes as lived by their parents. In times of difficult decisions they are most likely to follow the teachings of their parents rather than the examples of their peers or the sophistries of the media which

glamorize alcohol consumption, illicit sex, infidelity, dishonesty, and other vices. . . .

What seems to help cement parental [and Church] teachings and values in place in children's lives is a firm belief in Deity. When this belief becomes part of their very souls, they have inner strength. (pp. 42–43)

What Parents Can Do to Help Youth Internalize Gospel Principles

Youth should not be left on their own to make the gospel an integral part of their personal lives. While everyone must plant their own seed of faith, a fertile seedbed and nurturing environment is gained through a spiritually supportive family. Parents can do much to help their children internalize gospel principles. Elder M. Russell Ballard (1996) declared, "The home and family have vital roles in cultivating and developing personal faith and testimony. . . . The family is the basic unit of society; the best place for individuals to build faith and strong testimonies is in righteous homes filled with love. . . . Strong, faithful families have the best opportunity to produce strong, faithful members of the Church" (p. 81). The responsibility of parents to create a home environment that fosters spirituality and internalization of religious teachings is, to Latter-day Saints, God-given and divinely mandated. The First Presidency and Quorum of the Twelve Apostles (1995) have declared: "Parents have a sacred duty to rear their children in love and righteousness, to provide for their physical and spiritual needs, to teach them to love and serve one another, to observe the commandments of God, and to be law-abiding citizens wherever they live. Husbands and wives—mothers and fathers—will be held accountable before God for the discharge of these obligations" (p. 102).

From the results of our extensive study and from the anecdotal comments of hundreds of LDS teens and young adults, several important suggestions emerged as to how parents can specifically help their children make the gospel an important part of their lives. It is impossible to discuss at length all of these suggestions in this chapter. For our purposes here, we offer three general suggestions.

Practice What You Preach

The old adage "actions speak louder than words" is certainly true within the walls of a home. Nothing will undermine our efforts to create a spiritual home environment more than neglecting to practice what we profess. All that we teach as parents will seem hollow or trivial to our children if we don't evidence our beliefs and values in a comprehensive way of life. To use the language of our kids, "We must walk the walk, not just talk the talk." This doesn't mean parents have to be perfect. We aren't, and our children know it. They're smart enough to realize that we have weaknesses and at times we may not be as good as we desire. Parents do serious damage, however, when they deliberately go against the very teachings and standards they expect of their children. It seems that our children have a special radar system that can detect not only parental hypocrisy but also insincerity. Although teens may not notice a lot of things we wish they would—like the clutter and chaos in their bedrooms or the lateness of the hour when they are having fun with friends—they are quick to observe parental hypocrisy or attempts to live a double standard. When it comes to having a "house of faith," there can be no double standards.

If we want our children to have testimonies of the gospel, to internalize its principles and to live by high standards of purity and integrity, we must do the same. If we want them to be worthy to marry in the temple, we must strive to be temple worthy and demonstrate our love for the temple by frequent attendance. If we want them to study the scriptures and sincerely pray to our Heavenly Father each day, we need to do the same. If we want them to be committed to the gospel and actively involved in the Church, we must show them the way by our lives—by our activity in the Church and our faithfulness to callings and covenants. To do otherwise sends the signal to our children that the gospel we teach really isn't all that important to us after all. As a result, they likely won't take it seriously either. We can't give what we don't have! "We need to start with ourselves as parents," President Henry B. Eyring (1996) declared, "No program we follow or family tradition we create can transmit a legacy of testimony we do not have" (p. 63).

Teach the Gospel

In this dispensation the Lord has commanded parents to teach their children "the doctrine and repentance, faith in Christ the Son of the living God, and of baptism and the gift of the Holy Ghost by the laying on of hands. . . . And they shall also teach their children to pray, and to walk uprightly before the Lord" (D&C 68:25, 28). Failing to do so results in, as the Lord declared, "the sin be[ing] upon the heads of the parents" (D&C 68:25). This divine mandate has been reaffirmed by prophets in our own day. In a letter addressed to "Members of the Church throughout the World," dated February 11, 1999, the First Presidency declared, "We call upon parents to devote their best efforts to the teaching and rearing of their children in gospel principles which will keep them close to the Church." They further declared that "the home is the basis of a righteous life" and that no other agency, program, or organization can adequately replace parents in fulfilling their "God-given responsibility" of teaching the gospel (p. 80).

It would be easy, in light of these strong statements, for us as parents to feel overwhelmed by this sacred obligation. Some of us may feel that we lack sufficient gospel knowledge to properly teach our children. Some of us may feel we lack adequate teaching skills. Some of us may have other concerns. All parents have inadequacies, but the Lord has given us the responsibility to teach the gospel to our children nonetheless. Fortunately, the Lord never gives responsibilities without also providing "a way for them that they may accomplish the thing which he commandeth them" (1 Nephi 3:7). The Church has provided us with inspired programs and

No other agency, program, or organization can adequately replace parents in fulfilling their "God-given responsibility" of teaching the gospel. Matt Reier, © Intellectual Reserve, Inc.

counsel that can assist us in our responsibilities and make them far less intimidating. From our research, including hundreds of comments from LDS youth and young adults, we have found three simple things that parents can do to better teach the gospel to their children.

Hold Regular Family Prayer, Family Home Evening, and Family Scripture Study

"We counsel parents and children," the First Presidency (1999) stated, "to give highest priority to family prayer, family home evening, gospel study and instruction, and wholesome family activities" (p. 80). Even though the statistical results of our study showed no significant *direct* relationship between these family religious practices and delinquency, academic achievement, and feelings of self-worth, that doesn't tell the whole story. As previously discussed, we found that personal spirituality and religious conviction of LDS youth are directly linked to lower levels of delinquency. Family religious practices such as family home evening, family prayer, and family scripture study promote religious internalization and thus impact adolescent behavior. There is a spiritual power in family religiosity.

Despite the prophetic counsel to hold family religious activities, a surprising number of families do not avail themselves of the great blessings that family home evening, family prayer, and family scripture reading can yield. As can be seen in Table 1, only about half of the LDS families involved in our studies reported that they held regular family prayer and family home evening, and less than a third had regular family scripture study.

Table 1. Frequency of Family Home Evening, Family Prayer, and Family Scripture Reading among LDS Families in the United States

Frequency	FHE (N=3079)	Family Prayer (N=3079)	Family Scripture (N=3079)
Very Often	43%	59%	29%
Sometimes	19%	13%	19%
Rarely/Never	38%	28%	52%
	100%	100%	100%

Perhaps every parent feels frustrated at times in trying to faithfully hold these family religious practices when the children are restless and nothing seems to be "sinking in." The young people in our study made many comments that should be encouraging to parents. They readily admit that there is a more powerful influence in these practices than what may appear on the surface. These hindsight comments from the young adults we interviewed show the lasting influence of family religious practices:

I know that I was a pain in the neck of my parents when it came to family prayer and family home evening. But I am thankful now

Religious practices such as family home evening, family prayer, and family scripture study promote religious internalization and thus impact adolescent behavior. Matt Reier, © Intellectual Reserve, Inc.

that they didn't give up. It had more influence upon me than I was willing to admit at the time.

I pretended not to be listening when we had scripture study or lessons during family night, but more sank in than my parents thought. Even though my dad was inactive, he was always the one saying, "Time for family scripture reading" or "Prayer time." That showed me that he still wanted what was best for his family. It really helped our family.

The study results, coupled with hundreds of anecdotal comments from youth and young adults, confirm what prophets of God have long taught: Testimonies are strengthened, gospel knowledge is increased, and greater love and harmony within the family result when parents faithfully attend to these family religious practices. When the family home evening program was first introduced to the Church, the First Presidency (1915) promised the Saints "great blessings" if they would diligently seek to "gather their boys and girls about them in the home and teach them the word of the Lord." Undoubtedly, these promises apply today just as much, if not more so, than in 1915, and not just with regard to family home evening. It applies to all aspects of teaching and rearing of children in gospel principles.

> If the Saints obey this counsel, we promise that great blessings will result. Love at home and obedience to parents will increase. Faith will be developed in the hearts of the youth of Israel, and they will gain power to combat the evil influences and temptations which best them. (733–34)

Teach Practical Applications of Gospel Principles

The Lord has commanded parents to teach their children to "walk uprightly before the Lord" (D&C 68:28). There are two dimensions to this sacred parental duty—first, to teach the doctrines of the kingdom, and second, to teach their children *how to apply* those doctrines to their daily lives. As one of the young adults in our study observed, "I don't think parents teach the fundamental doctrines of the gospel enough—things like faith, repentance, and the Atonement and how these things work in daily life. Parents often teach doctrines and principles, but don't specifically talk about the why and the how."

Nephi spoke of "liken[ing the] scriptures" to ourselves (1 Nephi 19:23). This certainly applies to gospel teaching in our homes. Parents can do this by talking with their children about how the gospel can actually help us in our daily lives and apply it to dealing with specific temptations and challenges we face. An important way whereby we can teach practical application of gospel principles to our children is to ask them how they would apply or "liken" the gospel to their own unique circumstances. Practical application of the gospel can be a two-way street—we can share with our families how the gospel applies in our lives and learn from them on how they do the same.

One young woman in our study reported that her father would often talk to the children about challenges or problems he was having at work. "How would you handle this?" he would ask his family. Pretty soon a good discussion would ensue, focusing on how gospel principles solve life's real problems. The young lady observed, "Now I realize he was helping us to see how the teachings of the gospel actually work in life, rather than asking us to solve his problems." Youth are much more likely to live the standard of the Church when they know not only the doctrines but also why they should do as they are commanded, and what will be the practical benefits, right here and now, of living the gospel.

Discuss and Share Feelings about the Gospel at Times Other Than Sunday

A major challenge youth have to overcome in order to have strength to resist temptation is the tendency to view religion as merely a "church thing" or something that is done only on Sundays. This compartmentalization prevents them from seeing how the teachings of the gospel affect everyday lives and everyday situations. Seeing how the gospel is fully integrated into their parents' lives will help children understand how it can permeate every part of their own lives. In fact, the word "religion" has its root in a Latin word *ligare*, which means "to bind," "to connect," or "to hold together." It is the same root found in the word "ligament." Religion exerts power in our families when it is fully attached to or connected with all aspect of our lives.

Not all opportunities to teach the gospel to our children occur on Sundays, Monday evenings, or during early morning scripture study. In fact, some of the most important gospel teaching moments may come at unscheduled or unexpected times. They may come when a daughter faces a difficult challenge at school or when a son is debating the merits of serving a mission—anytime a child is worrying, wondering, or questioning.

Seizing these teaching moments whenever they occur and talking about religious principles when needed shows our children that the gospel has everyday application. Often these informal discussions help our children to better connect the dots, so to speak, and see how the doctrines and principles of the gospel really fit together and apply to daily life. One young woman in our study made the following astute observation as to how informal gospel discussion can yield unexpected and unintentional, yet powerful, gospel learning experiences:

> There are two places that I hold dear to my heart and see as great gospel learning places. This may sound strange, but they are my parents' king-size bed and the kitchen table. We almost always ate dinner together, and there we would talk about our daily activities, but there was much more than that. We often would get into in-depth gospel discussions or talk about how we felt about something. Just these little things taught me so much. As for the bed— it had to be a king-size so all six of us kids could fit on it. This was a place where we could talk with Mom and Dad. I received so much comfort, guidance, and spiritual teaching there.

Help Your Children Come to Know for Themselves

The cement that holds gospel teachings in place in the lives of our children (as well as ourselves) is personal spiritual experience. As was cited previously, the most powerful component of religiosity on behavior is personal spirituality—feeling the Spirit in one's own life and experiencing the fruits of gospel living. Two scriptural accounts, though not specifically teaching parenting practices, illustrate this principle well.

The first comes from the ministry of John the Baptist. His foreordained mission was to be an Elias—one who prepares the way for someone even greater. He did not merely draw disciples to himself with his teachings and testimony. Rather, because those who listened to him were inspired by his words and touched by his love, they accepted his direction to their most important relationship—a relationship with the Savior of the world. "He must increase," John testified of Christ, "but I must decrease" (John 3:30).

As parents, we must be like John—preparers of the way for our children to come to know the Master for themselves. We can teach, love, nurture, strengthen, serve, and exemplify, but ultimately only the Savior can save. The religious environment of our home—teaching both by precept and example—ultimately must lead our children to him.

This leads to the second scriptural account that testifies of this—the account of Lehi's dream of the tree of life (see 1 Nephi 8). We are familiar with the story and symbols of his dream: the iron rod, the strait and narrow path, the mists of darkness, the great and spacious building, and the fruit of the tree, which "was desirable to make one happy" (1 Nephi 8:10). From Nephi's later commentary, we learn the spiritual meaning of the symbolic elements of the dream (see 1 Nephi 11–12). One particular element of the story, however, has particular application to parents. It is what Father Lehi says and does *after* he arrived at the tree of life and partook of its fruit.

> And it came to pass that I did go forth and partake of the fruit thereof; and I beheld that it was most sweet, above all that I ever before tasted. Yea, and I beheld that the fruit thereof was white, to exceed all the whiteness that I had ever seen.
>
> And as I partook of the fruit thereof it filled my soul with exceedingly great joy; wherefore, *I began to be desirous that my family should partake of it also;* for I knew that it was desirable above all other fruit.
>
> And as I cast my eyes round about, that perhaps I might discover my family also. . . .
>
> [And] I beheld your mother Sariah, and Sam, and Nephi; and they stood as if they knew not whither they should go.

Lehi realized that he could not force his children to partake of the fruit of the tree of life or even desire to come unto it. He recognized that all people, including our own children, must come to the tree on their own. © Kazuto Uota, courtesy of Church History Museum.

And it came to pass that I beckoned unto them; and I also I did say unto them with a loud voice that they should come unto me, and partake of the fruit, which was desirable above all other fruit. (1 Nephi 8:11–15; emphasis added)

Any loving parent can relate to Lehi's desire that his family also partake of the love of Christ. Virtually every parent would do anything in their power to ensure that their children would partake of the fruit. Lehi did all he could. However, he understood that there are some things that parents cannot do.

Lehi exhorted his children "with all the feeling of a tender parent" (1 Nephi 8:37), but he could not compel his children to hold to the iron rod, come to the tree, and partake of its fruit. He could not eat the fruit *for* them or "force-feed" them or provide some special "short-cut" through the mists of darkness. He knew—and we must know also—that all people, including our own children, must come to the tree on their own. There is no other way to partake of the saving love of the Savior. What can we, as parents, do besides just desiring that our children come to know for themselves the love of God, the truthfulness of the gospel, and the sweetness of the Atonement of Jesus Christ? From our study and through years of observation and experience, we have found three specific things that parents do that are most effective in helping their children come to experience for themselves the blessings of personal testimony and living gospel principles.

Provide Opportunities for Spiritual Experiences

While real spiritual experiences cannot be manufactured or contrived, parents can provide opportunities and settings in which their children may more easily feel close to the Lord and the companionship of the Holy Spirit. In this way, youth are not limited to simply learning about the gospel and seeing it in action; they can actually *experience* it. Many young people in our study identified special moments—many of which were spontaneous and unexpected—when they felt an outpouring of the Spirit. One young woman told of an experience in which her family went to the temple and did baptisms for the dead for some of their ancestors. Afterward, she said her parents talked to the children about the importance of the temple: "They told us how much they loved the temple and how thankful they were to have us sealed to them," she remembered. "We had heard these things before, but because of what we had just been doing as a family, their testimonies had a powerful impact on us."

Others reported similar, strong spiritual feelings as they had father's blessings, witnessed the blessing of a sick family member, performed meaningful service for those in need, or held impromptu testimony meetings. Sometimes simple things yielded the most profound spiritual feelings.

Encourage Personal Prayer and Scripture Study

If we were to identify one thing as the single most important factor in helping our children internalize gospel principles, it would undoubtedly be personal prayer. It is the catalyst for the development of all other spiritual traits and strengths. Those youth in our study who consistently prayed privately had significantly lower levels of delinquency, including immorality and drug and alcohol use. In contrast, those youth who didn't live the standards of the Church and who engaged most frequently in delinquent behaviors, rarely if ever prayed privately. Ironically, however, even among this latter group, the majority reported that they participated regularly in family prayer. As important as family prayer, family scripture study, and family home evening are, they are, nonetheless, *external* religious activities. Personal prayer and individual scripture study are *internal* religious behaviors that can have even greater power in the lives of our children.

There are prophetic promises attached to those internal private religious practices. President Ezra Taft Benson (1977) promised the youth of the Church, "If you will earnestly seek guidance from your Heavenly Father, morning and evening, you will be given the strength to shun any temptation" (p. 32). Likewise, he promised that regular study of the scriptures, particularly the Book of Mormon, will yield "greater power to resist temptation" and "power to avoid deception" (1988, p. 54). Many of the young people in our study gratefully acknowledged the encouragement they received from their parents in this regard.

My dad always reminds me, "Say your prayers." This reminds me that it is not enough to have family prayer. I must pray on my own.

I am so blessed now because parents encouraged me when I was young to pray and read my scriptures on my own. Reading the scriptures and having personal prayer are things not to be done without.

Encourage our Children to Gain Their Own Personal Testimony of the Gospel

Perhaps the most important component of the shield of faith is personal testimony and conversion. The results of our research confirm that those youth who have their own personal conviction of the gospel have fewer behavioral problems, have a stronger sense of self-worth, and do better in school. They possess an inner strength that enables them to resist temptation and stand firm against negative peer pressures. "I am satisfied . . . that whenever a man [or woman or youth] has a true witness in his heart of the living reality of the Lord Jesus Christ all else will come together as it should," President Gordon B. Hinckley (1997) said. "That is the root from which all virtue springs among those who call themselves Latter-day Saints" (p. 648). The comments of many of the young people we have surveyed through the years provide powerful witness to that fact:

> I wish I had developed a strong testimony earlier in life. I found that [by] the time I had strengthened my testimony or experienced my personal conversion, I had already given in to many temptations which I regret to this day. I wish I had not acted "too cool" for the gospel and instead softened my heart so a testimony could have entered in.
>
> A testimony of the Savior and the gospel's truth is so necessary to resist temptation. In my eyes a testimony is the best prevention

The single most important factor in helping our children internalize gospel principles is personal prayer. Matt Reier, © Intellectual Reserve, Inc.

against Satan's temptations and is the most important thing parents can teach.

My parents' top priority was that we develop our own personal testimonies.

Because Satan targets our children at younger and younger ages, they must internalize the teachings of the gospel they receive at home and at Church by developing a meaningful relationship with God and testimony of the truthfulness of the Restoration sooner rather than later. It's never too early, but it can become too late. We may be seeing the fulfillment of the prophecy uttered by President Heber C. Kimball (Whitney, 1967) in the mid-nineteenth century. His warning should echo in our ears and burn in our hearts as we daily strive to lead our children to God:

> To meet the difficulties that are coming, it will be necessary for you to have a knowledge of the truth of this work for yourselves. The difficulties will be of such a character that the man or woman [or youth] who does not possess this personal knowledge or witness will fall. . . . The time will come when no man or woman will be able to endure on borrowed light. Each will have to be guided by the light within himself. If you do not have it, how will you stand? (p. 450)

Conclusion

The religious environment of our homes plays a significant role in helping our children "put on the whole armour of God that [they] may be able to stand against the wiles of the devil" (Ephesians 6:11). President Boyd K. Packer (1995) taught:

> The plan designed by the Father contemplates that man and woman, husband and wife, working together, fit each child individually with

a shield of faith made to buckle on so firmly that it can neither be pulled off nor penetrated by [Satan's] fiery darts.

It takes the steady strength of a father to hammer out the metal of it and the tender hands of a mother to polish it and fit it on. Sometimes one parent is left to do it alone. It is difficult, but it can be done.

In the Church we can teach about the materials from which a shield of faith is made: reverence, courage, chastity, repentance, forgiveness, compassion. In church we can learn how to assemble and fit them together. But the actual making of and fitting on of the shield of faith belongs in the family circle. (p. 8)

As Latter-day Saints, we should not need scientific studies to validate the teachings of the scriptures or the counsel of living prophets. However, the results of our large study of LDS youth provide a powerful second witness. Religiosity—personal and family—connects like a ligament the various aspects of the lives of Latter-day Saint youth. The results clearly show that LDS adolescents who internalize gospel teachings are less involved in delinquent behaviors, do better in school, and feel a stronger sense of self-worth. Religion matters in the lives of LDS young people. Likewise, parents matter, and so does the "house of faith" they provide for their children.

References

Ballard, M. R. (1996, May). Feasting at the Lord's table. *Ensign, 26*(5), 81.

Baumeister, R. F., Campbell, J. D., Kreuger, J. I., & Vohs, K. D. (2003). Does high self-esteem cause better performance, interpersonal success, happiness, or healthier lifestyles? *Psychological Science in the Public Interest, 4*(1), 1–44.

Benson, E. T. (1977, November). A message to the rising generation. *Ensign, 7*(11), 30–32.

Benson, E. T. (1988). *The teachings of Ezra Taft Benson.* Salt Lake City: Bookcraft.

Chadwick, B. A., & Top, B. L. (1993). Religiosity and delinquency among LDS adolescents. *Journal for the Scientific Study of Religion, 32*(1), 51–67.

Chadwick, B. A., Top, B. L., & McClendon, R. J. (2010). *Shield of faith: The power of religion in the lives of LDS youth and young adults.* Provo, UT: Religious Studies Center, Brigham Young University.

Dean, K. C. (2010). *Almost Christian: What the faith of our teenagers is telling the American church.* New York: Oxford University Press.

Eyring, H. B. (1996, May). A legacy of testimony. *Ensign 26*(5), 63.

Faust, J. E. (1990). The greatest challenge in the world—good parenting. *Official Report of the 160th Semiannual General Conference of The Church of Jesus Christ of Latter-day Saints.* Salt Lake City: The Church of Jesus Christ of Latter-day Saints.

First Presidency of The Church of Jesus Christ of Latter-day Saints. (1915, June). Home evening. *Improvement Era, 18*(8), 733–734.

First Presidency and Council of the Twelve Apostles of The Church of Jesus Christ of Latter-day Saints. (1995, November). The family: A proclamation to the world. *Ensign, 25*(11), 102.

First Presidency of The Church of Jesus Christ of Latter-day Saints. (1999, June). *Keeping children close to the Church. Ensign, 29(6), 80.*

Hansford, B. C., & Hattie, J. A. (1982). The relationship between self and achievement/performance measures. *Review of Educational Research, 52*(1), 123–142.

Harris, J. R. (2009). *The nurture assumption: Why children turn out the way they do.* New York: Simon & Schuster.

Hinckley, G. B. (1997). *Teachings of Gordon B. Hinckley.* Salt Lake City: Deseret Book.

Hirschi, T., & Stark, R. (1969). Hellfire and delinquency. *Social Problems, 17* (2), 202–213.

Packer, B. K. (1995, May). The shield of faith. *Ensign, 25*(5), 8.

Pipher, M. (1994). *Reviving Ophelia: Saving the selves of adolescent girls.* New York: Ballantine Books.

Rosenthal, R. (1973). The Pygmalion effect lives. *Psychology Today, 7*(4), 56–63.

Rosenthal, R., & Jacobson, L. (1992). *Pygmalion in the classroom: Teacher expectations and pupils' intellectual development.* Norwalk, CT: Irvington Publishers; Sheffield, South Yorkshire: Ardent Media.

Smith, C., & Denton, M. L. (2005). *Soul searching: The religious and spiritual lives of American teenagers*. New York: Oxford University Press.

Stark, R. (1984). Religion and conformity: Reaffirming a sociology of religion. *Sociological Analysis, 45*(4), 273–282.

Top, B. L., & Chadwick, B. A. (1993). The power of the word: Religion, family, friends, and delinquent behavior of LDS youth. *BYU Studies, 33*(2), 41–67.

Top, B. L., & Chadwick, B. A. (1998). *Rearing righteous youth of Zion: Great news, good news, not-so-good news*. Salt Lake City: Bookcraft.

Top, B. L., & Chadwick, B. A. (1999, March). Helping teens stay strong. *Ensign, 29*(3), 27–34.

Top, B. L., & Chadwick, B. A. (2004). *10 secrets wise parents know*. Salt Lake City: Deseret Book.

Top, B. L., & Chadwick, B. A. (2006, February). Helping children develop feelings of self-worth. *Ensign, 36*(2), 32–37.

Top, B. L., Chadwick, B. A., & Garrett, J. (1999). Family, religion, and delinquency among LDS youth. *Religion, Mental Health and the Latter-day Saints*. D. K. Judd (Ed.). Provo, UT: Religious Studies Center, Brigham Young University, 129–168.

Top, B. L., Chadwick, B. A., & McClendon, R. J. (2003). Spirituality and self-worth: The role of religion in shaping teens' self-image. *Religious Educator, 4*(2), 77–93.

Whitney, O. F. (1967). *Life of Heber C. Kimball* (3rd ed.). Salt Lake City: Bookcraft.

9

Helping Children Put On the Whole Armor of God: A Proactive Approach to Parenting Teenagers

MANY of us have adverse reactions to just hearing the word "teenager" and dread the day that our children cross that threshold and become what is often perceived as an uncontrollable force. This stereotype of teenage storm and stress dates back to the early 1900s when the term "adolescence" was first used by G. Stanley Hall, and it continued to dominate into the late 1950s (Arnett, 2012). Despite historical and current public opinion, research in the field of adolescence (which includes children and teens ages 10–18) does not consider this time to be a universal period of storm and stress. Indeed, fully 80% of adolescents mention thinking highly of their parents, and 60% report wanting to be like their parents when they grow up (Larson & Richards, 1994). Although many of us fall prey to stereotypes of adolescent angst, perhaps when we think of this age period we should also think of the many youth that the Lord called at a young age to do miraculous things. David, Nephi, Mormon, and Joseph Smith were all young, yet all were capable of amazing feats, and all were instruments in the hands of the Lord.

So how do we help our children transition from the awkward, sometimes rebellious teens into the strong men and women of faith that we desire them

It is essential that we help our children put on the whole armor of God so they will be able to face the temptations of the adversary with the proper protection. © Don Christensen, courtesy of Church History Museum.

to be? In 1 Nephi 2:16, Nephi refers to himself as "exceedingly young" and "large in stature." In 1 Nephi 4:31, he refers to himself as "a man large in stature." What happened between those two chapters to transform him from exceedingly young to a man? In 1 Nephi 3:7, Nephi responds to the call of the Lord to "go and do" what he is asked. He is obedient to the Lord's command, and this action secures his transformation to manhood. In order to help our children make this same transition from being exceedingly young to being men and women in the gospel, it is essential that we help them to put on the whole armor of God so they will be able to face the temptations of the adversary with the proper protection. Putting on the armor of God includes girding one's loins with truth, donning the breastplate of righteousness, shoeing one's feet with the gospel of peace, and arming oneself with the shield of faith, the helmet of salvation, and the sword of the Spirit (see Ephesians 6:14–17). If we desire our children to be prepared for battle and poised for triumph, we need to help them understand what they will encounter in the world today. We need to help them develop truth, righteousness, peace, faith, and the influence of the Spirit in their own lives and arm them with these weapons to fight the battles that will keep them on the strait and narrow path. One key way we can do this is through proactive parenting.

Proactive Parenting

Perhaps some of you reading this do not have teenagers yet, so you might think it best to put this counsel aside for a few years and come back to it once you are in the thick of things. However, those with young children are often the best audience to address, since raising healthy teenagers requires a proactive approach of starting when children are young and building relationships of openness and communication over time. In this chapter I will focus on what I call *proactive parenting*, which is a parent's active attempt to socialize a child's values and behaviors *before misbehavior or transgression has occurred* (Padilla-Walker & Thompson, 2005). The vast majority of research on parenting focuses on *reactive parenting*, or parental discipline. This is what parents do *after* a child has done something wrong or transgressed and is typified by giving time-outs, spanking, and familiarizing children with consequences. When comparing reactive and proactive parenting, it is suggested that proactive parenting is often a more effective way to communicate parental messages than is reactive parenting. Indeed, proactive parenting, in one form or another, has been linked to less media use (Nathanson, 1999), higher levels of academic achievement (Seyfried & Chung, 2002), later age of sexual debut (Dittus, Miller, Kotchick, & Forehand, 2004), and lower levels of drug use and delinquency (Fletcher, Steinberg, & Williams-Wheeler, 2004). The effectiveness of proactive parenting is due in part to the lack of strong emotions, on the part of both the parent and the child, that are often present with reactive parenting. Few of us internalize messages when we are being yelled at or scolded, and proactive parenting allows for discussion and teaching in a safe environment without anger or sadness. Think of the last time you yelled at your child or were yelled at by someone. All you likely remember is that you did not like how you felt, which supports research suggesting that the socialization message is often lost in reactive parenting situations (Grusec & Goodnow, 1994). Indeed, proactive parenting may help to decrease the need for extensive reactive parenting by anticipating challenges the child might face and communicating values and parental expectations to the child before misbehavior occurs.

With young children, proactive parenting is a pretty straightforward process. For example, my day out shopping with my children goes very differently when I am proactive and tell them ahead of time that today we will *not* be purchasing any toys or candy at the store. If I somehow fail to give this important warning, the day usually ends in me dragging screaming children out of the store and leaving an abandoned shopping cart at the checkout counter while I desperately try not to yell at my children in public. With adolescents, however, proactive parenting takes time, and starting sooner rather than later is always better. As children reach adolescence they will be increasingly faced with values that may be contrary to those held by your family. In fact, as the mother of a 12-year-old, 9-year-old, and 1-year-old, I have been surprised that exposure to conflicting values starts much earlier than the adolescent years. Being proactive in the face of these ever-increasing conflicting messages of values (whether they be from peers, teachers, or media) requires that parents clearly communicate their values to their children and, as necessary, provide them with tools to combat these potentially conflicting messages.

At face value, this argument is intuitive. Why wait until your child is sexually active, getting into physical fights with others, or involved in drugs to talk to him or her about these behaviors? While the need for a proactive approach is logical, research shows that many parents wait until their children are sexually active before talking to them about sexuality or until their teens are in serious trouble before trying to address their problematic behavior (see Eisenberg, Sieving, Bearinger, Swain, & Resnick, 2006). Although some teens may still manage to avoid trouble on their own, for others this is simply too late, and this delay can have serious consequences. Indeed, teens note that when they have questions about topics such as sexuality, the most common sources they turn to in an attempt to learn more are friends and the media (Steinberg, 2010). As a parent, I know that those sources are not where I want my children to learn about issues that I feel strongly about. Thus it is important that we talk to our children early and frequently so we do not miss the opportunity to teach our children what is important to us and what we hope will also be important to them. While this approach certainly applies to issues that are of great importance to us, such as the law of chastity and the Word of Wisdom, proactive parenting also applies to everyday expectations that we have for our children, including chores, homework, and behavior in public (for example at the grocery store or church). When I think of scriptural examples of good proactive parenting, I think of Lehi and Alma, who both spoke at length to their children not only about their current behaviors but also about what they needed to do for their futures. They gave their children suggestions and counsel regarding how each of them might avoid pitfalls in their futures, and they addressed their children individually and according to their own needs (see 2 Nephi 1; Alma 36–42).

Specific Proactive Parenting Practices

I will now discuss three common proactive parenting practices I have identified in my research (Padilla-Walker & Thompson, 2005; Padilla-Walker, Christensen, & Day, 2011). These practices can also be identified in the teachings of the Savior, who is certainly the best manifestation of exemplary proactive parenting. The first proactive parenting practice is called *cocooning*. This is the most restrictive form of proactive parenting and is typified by parents who try to protect or shelter their children from any source outside the family that poses a potential threat. Examples of cocooning include forbidding certain television shows or not allowing children to hang out with particular friends. By appropriately cocooning young children, parents teach children *what* is right and wrong. When examining the Savior's teaching of his disciples, we see his cocooning behavior early on in their development as men of God when he encouraged them to avoid or leave behind the things of the world and follow him—"Follow me, and I will make you fishers of men" (Matthew 4:19). It was first necessary that they remove themselves from worldly pursuits before they could embrace the Savior's mission. Thus, the disciples left their nets and their ships, or shielded themselves from worldly pursuits, for the pursuit of heavenly things.

A second approach to proactive parenting is called *prearming*, and involves a parent's active attempts to teach values by providing some strategy, or "advance arming," to help teens when they are faced with conflicting messages of values. This strategy is common among parents who feel their values are threatened by society and may include talking and discussing specific situations adolescents might encounter. However, prearming is varied and can also be characterized by seemingly benign value-laden comments we make as parents, such as commenting on how someone wears his hair or how immodestly someone is dressed. For example, the other day my daughter saw a picture of one of her favorite cartoon characters who happened to be very skinny and a bit immodestly dressed, and she commented, "Wow, Mom! That girl needs some clothes and a sandwich!" And last year when my family was visiting Las Vegas, my son was saying goodbye to all of the sights of Vegas as we passed them. He said, "Good-bye, M&M World! Good-bye, Belagio Buffet!" And as we drove by a billboard, he ended with, "Good-bye, inappropriately dressed ladies!" My children's comments sounded familiar—clearly my husband and I had been using prearming to communicate values about modesty and body image without even knowing it! By using prearming, we teach our children *why* something is wrong. This is an absolutely essential step, as pointed out by President Dieter F. Uchtdorf: "The 'why' of obedience sanctifies our actions, transforming the mundane into the majestic. It magnifies our small acts of obedience into holy acts of consecration" (Uchtdorf, 2011). As we examine the Savior's interactions with his disciples, his use of prearming is extensive, in that he uses discussion and teaches by example time and time again. In both the Bible and the Book of Mormon he directs parables and teachings directly to his disciples in an attempt to prepare them for what they will face once he is no longer with them, and they must make decisions and choose their actions without his physical presence (see 3 Nephi 15).

The final proactive strategy is called *deference*, which is characterized by parents who allow their children to make their own decisions. This is often an attempt to show trust in their children, and it is usually used when adolescents are older, after many years of using strategies like prearming and cocooning. For example, this might be represented by parents allowing their child to choose his or her own media or allowing their child to hang out with a friend they may not yet know. By using this strategy, parents allow children to use their agency to practice *choosing* between right and wrong. This approach is indicative of Joseph Smith's oft-cited quote, "We teach them correct principles and allow them to govern themselves" (Clark, 1965–1975). At first glance this approach might not seem proactive, but it by no means suggests that parents are no longer involved or aware of what their children are doing. Indeed, most parents who effectively use deference are ready at a moment's notice to step in and redirect their children should parents see them consistently choosing incorrectly, but allowing this agency is key to development and harmony in the parent-child relationship during the teen years. If parents always make decisions about media and friends for their children, it will eventually feel controlling to teenagers (Nathanson, 1999, 2002), and more importantly, they will not have a chance to practice making correct decisions without parental supervision, which may lead to struggles once teens leave home (Steinberg, 2010). The Savior used deference in a more absolute sense when he finally left the presence of his disciples and allowed them to use what they had learned to preach the gospel and lead the Church. He was still with them and was ready to help when they needed it, but he largely allowed them to apply what they had learned and to use their agency, thus showing his trust in them.

As you might expect, parents use these three strategies (cocooning, pre-arming, and deference) to varying degrees as their children age and become more mature and responsible. Indeed, in a recent study we found that over a period of three years (when children were ages 12 to 14), parents' rates of prearming and cocooning both decreased over time, and rates of deference increased (Padilla-Walker, Coyne, Fraser, Dyer, & Yorgason, 2012). Prearming is the most commonly used proactive parenting strategy at every age, but by age 14 deference is nearly as common as prearming. In addition, parents usually do not use only one proactive approach to parenting, but more often combine several and are quite flexible in their use. My colleagues and I have found several patterns of proactive parenting, the most common of which include what we call *reasoned cocooning* and *reasoned deference*. Reasoned cocooning is when parents combine cocooning and prearming by sheltering or protecting their adolescents from outside influences, while also taking time to talk with their children about these decisions. Reasoned deference is when parents combine deference and prearming and allow their adolescents to make their own decisions while parents talk to them extensively about those decisions. Thus research suggests there are three main approaches to proactive parenting, which can be used alone or in combination. An effective parent is a flexible parent, so it is common for parents to use a combination of proactive approaches depending on the individual child and the situation being faced.

Finding the Most Effective Proactive Approach for Your Child

The next logical question to pose, and perhaps the most important, is which of these strategies is most effective at promoting positive teen outcomes? The answer to this difficult question depends on many factors, but those most relevant include (a) the source of the influence (for example, media versus peers) and (b) a host of characteristics of the child (such as temperament, gender, and age).

Source of the Influence

When considering the source of influence, research suggests that parents feel more threatened by the influence of media on their children than they do by the influence of peers (Padilla-Walker & Thompson, 2005). I think many of us remember being forbidden to hang out with certain friends or groups who were involved in particular behaviors, and this is still a relatively easy thing for parents to cocoon. However, research suggests that parents take a number of approaches to proactively parenting their teens and that cocooning or prohibiting involvement with peers is not nearly as effective a strategy as is prearming or guiding one's children regarding the types of friends they should choose *before* the child has gotten into trouble with peers (Mounts, 2002). Parents who are proactive have children with higher quality relationships with peers, as well as higher levels of cooperation, self-control, and social skills (Mounts, 2011). The Church also takes a proactive approach to teaching about peers and friends as exemplified in the *For the Strength of Youth* pamphlet, which uses extensive prearming by suggesting that youth should choose their friends carefully: "Choose friends who share your values so you can strengthen and encourage each other in living high standards. A true friend will encourage you to be your best self" (p. 12). Indeed, many negative behaviors can be avoided by proactively keeping our children away from individuals who would encourage negative behavior but also by discussing with our children the importance of surrounding oneself with righteous friends.

Although there is a body of research focusing on proactive parenting in response to peers, I would like to focus primarily on the influence of media, as it is much more difficult for parents to regulate. Although some forms of media are not appropriate at any age, research suggests that strict cocooning of media is not very effective, especially as adolescents get older and can view media at a friend's house or on their portable media device (Nathanson, 2002). It seems to be more effective to use prearming strategies, which include talking to adolescents about media that they may encounter and offering them strategies to deal with inappropriate media. Part of the reason prearming is so important is because despite parents' best efforts, it is nearly inevitable that children will be exposed to inappropriate media content. Indeed, recent reports suggest that nearly 100% of boys and 65% of girls are exposed to online pornography during adolescence, and nearly two-thirds of that exposure is unwanted (Brown & L'Engle, 2009; Rideout, Foehr, & Roberts, 2010; Sabina, Wolak, & Finkelhor, 2008).

That being said, over 50% of teens report learning about sexuality on the Internet (Kaiser Family Foundation, 2010), which raises two important points. First, it is essential that we provide our children with the critical thinking skills or tools to deal with inappropriate media when they come across it. If we merely avoid talking about these issues and just hope our children miraculously avoid exposure, our children will be left defenseless when they come into contact with inappropriate information. Second, and on a related note, it is very important that our children learn about sexuality from parent-child discussions before they are sexually mature and long before they are sexually active. In this venue, hopefully questions can be adequately answered and principals of chastity and sexuality can be taught gradually and in the safety of the family home. Elder M. Russell Ballard 1999 said: "As our children grow, they need information taught by parents more directly and plainly about what is and is not appropriate. Parents need to teach children to avoid any pornographic photographs or stories . . . [and] talk to them plainly about sex and the teaching of the gospel regarding chastity. Let this information come from parents in the home in an appropriate way" (p. 86).

In addition to prearming children against inappropriate media influences, another helpful approach that facilitates proactive parenting is to participate in appropriate media with your children. For example, we have found in our research that playing video games or watching movies with teens, or even texting teens, can help to strengthen family ties (Coyne, Padilla-Walker, Stockdale, & Day, 2011). In addition, engaging in media as a family creates opportunities for prearming to occur by providing a platform for parent-child conversation about media content (Padilla-Walker, Coyne, & Fraser, 2012).

One approach to proactive parenting is to participate in appropriate media with children. © *Scott Griessel.*

Indeed, I remember numerous conversations I had with my parents as a teenager that began as a result of something we watched together on television. In turn, our family has numerous phrases or "mantras" we use to help encourage one another that we took from songs or movies that we watched as a family.

Although watching inappropriate or violent media with teenagers can unintentionally act as an endorsement of negative behavior, watching television shows appropriate for teens or playing appropriate video games rated T and below have been shown to lead to greater levels of parent-child connection. This connection is key to opening channels of communication and allowing for discussion about important issues (Coyne et al., 2011). So although parental cocooning of media during early childhood may be appropriate, reasoned cocooning or prearming seem to be more effective approaches to dealing with conflicting messages of values from media during the adolescent years.

Characteristics of the Child

Our Heavenly Father knows each of us individually, and our experiences are "tailored to the individual's capacities and needs, as known by a loving Father in Heaven" (Hunter, 1990). As loving earthly parents, we too must carefully consider our child's individual characteristics when determining what proactive approach might be most appropriate for that individual child. More specifically, it is important to consider the temperament and age of the child.

Individual temperament. Temperamental differences are influenced by biological factors and are reflected in behavioral tendencies such as fearfulness, aggression, or extroversion. Some children are temperamentally more susceptible to peer influences or to media influences than others are, so reasoned cocooning in childhood may be appropriate for this type of child, as any exposure might negatively influence behavior. For example, when my son was younger, he was prone to aggressive behavior. We found that any exposure to violent television resulted in his behavior becoming much more aggressive, so we tended to cocoon him from such programs as much as possible, while still providing an explanation for why we thought he should avoid certain media. In contrast, a child who is very good at regulating emotions and behaviors may not need as much cocooning, especially as he displays an ability to make good choices in regard to media and friends.

In addition, some children might be more or less receptive to different forms of proactive parenting as a function of their temperaments. For example, some children are particularly resistant to parental authority and might not be very responsive to cocooning of any kind. This type of child would require a parent to use increased levels of prearming to ensure that the child is prepared with the appropriate protection against conflicting values. Other children might be quite amenable to parental control, and while at younger ages reasoned cocooning might be appropriate, it may be tempting to continue to shelter children because they will allow it. However, this approach may not serve children well, as eventually they will be on their own and will need the tools necessary to face a variety of influences. Although it is our task as parents to get to know our children individually, ultimately our Heavenly Father knows our children far better than we do, so it is important to seek for his help often when trying to determine what approach will work best for each individual child.

Age of the child. The Lord teaches us "line upon line, precept upon precept" (2 Nephi 28:30). In Doctrine and Covenants 50:40, he states, "Behold, ye are little children and ye cannot bear all things now; ye must grow in grace and in the knowledge of the truth." We need to take the same gradual and individually tailored approach with our children. In addition to temperament, how effective each proactive strategy is depends largely upon the age of the child. Although I will be discussing age in terms of numbers, it is worth mentioning that developmental age (or level of maturity) is probably more accurate for parents to use as a gauge than is chronological age. Because each individual child, regardless of age, will develop on his or her own personal timetable, it is possible that the age ranges used in research do not apply to each practical situation, so please keep that in mind.

Early adolescence (preteens). Research on early adolescents (children ages 10–14) suggests that any strategy that contains prearming, or discussing issues with teens, seems to be positively associated with healthy outcomes (Mounts, 2011; Nathanson, 1999; Padilla-Walker & Coyne, 2011). This includes cocooning combined with prearming (reasoned cocooning), deference combined with prearming (reasoned deference), and prearming alone. Proactive parenting that includes prearming has been associated with adolescents who have a greater ability to understand the needs of others and to control their own impulses. Prearming has also been linked to lower levels of both depression and problem behaviors. In other words, whether parents allowed their early teens more autonomy (deference) or whether they sheltered their children a bit more (cocooning) did not seem to matter as much as whether or not parents combined these strategies with discussion about potential influences. This is likely because as parents have open conversations with their teens about value-laden topics, parents are not only communicating values but are also allowing their children to engage in dialogue that will impact both moral reasoning abilities and feelings of self-generation. Self-generation means that adolescents feel *they* are choosing their own values and behaviors. Despite the importance of autonomy in promoting adolescents' feelings of self-generation, it is also clear from this research that deference (or allowing nearly complete autonomy) during early adolescence is not associated with positive outcomes if used without the accompanied parent-child conversation. This may be because deference is developmentally inappropriate if used as the sole proactive approach before adolescents' values are adequately internalized. Indeed, the need to consider a child's age when using deference is highlighted by research suggesting that deference and autonomy granting are more appropriate as children get older (Nelson et al., 2011).

Mid to late adolescence. Research with children in middle adolescence (about ages 14–16) focuses on adolescents' development of personal values or the internalization of values (Grusec & Goodnow, 1994; Padilla-Walker, Fraser, & Harper, 2012). General Authorities have counseled that our teens cannot live on borrowed light, or that it is important that they internalize testimonies and values of their own (Bednar, 2012). If proactive parenting is an attempt to avoid misbehavior in the face of potentially conflicting values, then being proactive is one way that we as parents, leaders, or teachers attempt to promote family or societal values in our children. *Values* are defined as broad, stable goals or motivational constructs that communicate what is important to an individual (Bardi & Schwartz, 2003). For example, one might value being kind and honest to those around him or her, a value that researchers term a benevolent or prosocial value. Others might value achievement, defined as striving to excel in an area such as school or athletics. If adolescents value benevolence, they should be more likely to volunteer and be kind to their neighbors. If other adolescents value academic achievement, they should be more likely to do well in school. This is called value-congruent behavior, or behavior that is congruent with one's internalized values.

Internalization of values is the process whereby children acknowledge values and integrate them into their identities (Grusec & Goodnow, 1994). More specifically, if values are externally regulated (that is, we value something only insomuch as we would get punished for *not* doing it), then those values are less likely to be reflected in our behaviors. However, if our values are internally regulated (we value something because we enjoy it or because it is part of who we are and how we define ourselves) then those values are much more likely to be reflected in our behaviors. This pattern applies to our children's development of spiritual values as well. Are our children engaging in church activities and communication with the Lord because they are sanctioned to do so (external regulation), or are they doing such because they enjoy it and it is becoming part of who they are (internal regulation)? In Matthew 15:8 the Lord speaks of this condition when he says, "This people draweth nigh unto me with their mouth, and honoureth me with their lips, but their heart is far from me." Internalization suggests not only external behavioral obedience but obedience with all our might, mind, and strength as well.

Although internalization of values is clearly a gradual process in teens and even in adults, proactive parenting has been found to be associated with internalization of values during mid- to late adolescence (Padilla-Walker, Fraser, & Harper, 2012). More specifically, parental use of deference and reasoned deference were associated with the most consistent value-congruent behaviors across a variety of values and behaviors. In other words, parents who talked to their adolescents, but also allowed autonomy in the face of potentially conflicting values in an attempt to show trust in their children, had teens whose values were more strongly tied to their behaviors. This might be reflected in a parent who allowed their child to read a book without the parent reading it first or to attend a party without the parent attending. Now, for many of us, this finding may be difficult to digest. Is doing nothing really the best way to help our teens make correct

When our children internalize eternal values, they engage in church activities and communication with the Lord because they enjoy it and it helps them become who they are.
© *Intellectual Reserve, Inc.*

choices? Absolutely not. Remember that parents who use deference before misbehavior has occurred have often spent years using reasoned cocooning and prearming to teach their children values, and they are now giving those children the autonomy necessary to make their own decisions (and to practice what their parents have taught them). If parents want to be capable of allowing the freedom that many adolescents and young adults desire, they are better served to begin the work of teaching values much earlier than adolescence. Early preparation will keep lines of communication open throughout the teenage years.

This allowing for agency with continued oversight is again consistent with the teachings of the Savior. After his feeding of the 5,000, the Savior went to a mountain to pray, and his disciples headed out to sea. Soon, the ship was caught in a storm, so the Savior walked across the water to the disciples, who were unsure of who was approaching them. He told them, "Be of good cheer; it is I; be not afraid" (Matthew 14:27). Now, at this point, a controlling parent might say, "It is I; end of discussion." But the Savior is never controlling. He taught his disciples a great deal before this point, and he allowed Peter to experience a great lesson. Peter said to the Lord, "If it be thou, bid me come unto thee on the water," and he left the ship to walk on the water. As Peter used his agency and began to be afraid and to doubt, he began to sink. Again, the Savior did not allow him to sink, but immediately reached out his hand and rescued Peter, with a mild rebuke (see Matthew 14:28–31). Peter learned much more from this experience than he would have if the Lord had said, "It is I; end of discussion." As parents, this is a pattern that we too should follow. This means extensive teaching initially and then the allowance of autonomy with our continued willingness to immediately reach out and save our children should they begin to sink. As children get older and gain more autonomy (especially as they leave the parental home; see chapter 12, this volume; Nelson, Padilla-Walker, Christensen, Evans, & Carroll, 2011), this earlier support will help provide a secure foundation from which parents can then step back even further and defer to their child.

Adolescence is a time of transition where many teens want to make their own decisions. Welden Andersen, © Intellectual Reserve, Inc.

Helping Children Become Agents unto Themselves

Adolescence is a time of transition, and most teens balk at the idea of being controlled or may even interpret well-meant parental suggestions as annoying lecturing that is infringing upon their abilities to make their own decisions. If parents start when their children are young and talk to them about values, behaviors, and different situations they may be faced with and how to respond to them, it is likely that once teens hit mid-adolescence (about age 14 or 15), their values will be beginning to solidify and will be at least moderately reflected in their behaviors. As such, parents will be able to stand back and increasingly defer to their child. Elder David A. Bednar (2010) highlights the need for parents to be watchful and discerning in regard to their children; one of the ways he suggests that parents do this is by inviting their children to become agents until themselves; to act, and not merely be acted upon. He said:

> Parents have the sacred responsibility to help children to act and seek learning by faith. And a child is never too young to take part in this pattern of learning.
>
> Giving a man a fish feeds him for one meal. Teaching a man to fish feeds him for a lifetime. As parents and gospel instructors, you and I are not in the business of distributing fish; rather, our work is to help our children learn "to fish" and to become spiritually steadfast. This vital objective is best accomplished as we encourage our children to act in accordance with correct principles—as we help them to learn by doing. (pp. 42–43)

This clearly is one of the strongest weapons parents can give to their children against negative influences from media or other sources: not just enforcing rules that do not apply to every situation, but by encouraging the use of moral agency to think critically about what is being learned and to then choose to act in accordance with the will of the Lord.

Proactive parenting, especially prearming, during childhood and early adolescence will also increase the chances that adolescents will come to parents when they are faced with conflicting values or situations that they are not sure how to deal with. For example, I knew a couple that was very open about discussing sexuality with their children. As their children got older, they always went to their parents to discuss these types of issues rather than talking to peers or looking on the Internet for answers. Alternatively, those parents who do not lay this foundation in childhood and early adolescence may find themselves struggling to help teens who have been thrust into a world with numerous conflicting values from countless sources, have very little advanced armor with which to protect themselves, and do not feel they can discuss difficult issues with their parents. If parents find themselves in this position, it is not too late to start opening lines of communication and increasing parent-child connection. Although long-standing patterns of communication and family interaction are difficult to change, acknowledgement of the need to change is an important first step.

It is important to note, however, that when given autonomy, not all children will make good choices. Many of us are all too aware that despite our best efforts, our children continue to make poor choices. Even proactive parenting is not a fail-safe approach, and although I can share with you what research suggests is the most effective for teens "on average," clearly there are individual situations that require special measures. Elder Howard W. Hunter (1983) said:

> A successful parent is one who has loved, one who has sacrificed, and one who has cared for, taught, and ministered to the needs of a child. If you have done all of these and your child is still wayward or troublesome or worldly, it could well be that you are, nevertheless, a successful parent. Perhaps there are children who have come into the world that would challenge any set of parents under any set of circumstances. Likewise, perhaps there are others who would bless the lives of, and be a joy to, almost any father or mother. (p. 65)

Thus, taken together, we can conclude that the most effective approach to proactive parenting is a flexible approach that may change depending on the source of influence, on the individual child, and on the type of outcome being measured. This flexibility highlights the need for parents to prayerfully follow the Spirit as they contemplate which approach might be best for each of their children. No one loves our children and knows their needs better than our Father in Heaven, and if parents earnestly seek his guidance in rearing their children he will lovingly provide the advice and direction needed.

Raising Children in Enemy Territory

Regardless of what stage of life each of us is in, being proactive can benefit us in many ways, as being proactive is essential to our successful temporal and spiritual progression. Many sinful patterns can be avoided by being proactive against the influences of the adversary. Avoiding our own personal pitfalls requires that we are aware of them and willing to face them, just as helping our children to avoid their pitfalls requires that we take the time to get to know our children and their vulnerabilities. Anticipating vulnerability and taking the necessary precautions *before* serious sin occurs is always easier than repenting afterward.

Counsel to be prepared both temporally and spiritually is not something that we are unfamiliar with in the Church, and being self-reliant in these ways requires us to be proactive. As mentioned previously, being proactive should be likened to putting on the whole armor of God. "Put on the whole armour of God, that ye may be able to stand against the wiles of the devil. For we wrestle not against flesh and blood, but against principalities, against powers, against the rulers of the darkness of this world, against spiritual wickedness in high places. Wherefore take unto you the whole armour of God, that ye may be able to withstand in the evil day, and having done all, to stand" (Ephesians 6:11–13). Whether we apply this principle to ourselves, or help to provide our children with these tools, this proactive approach helps us and our children to stand strong in both temporal and spiritual situations. We have been counseled to be in the world, but not of the world. Elder Quentin L. Cook said, "We cannot avoid the world. A cloistered existence is not the answer. In a positive sense, our contribution to the world is part of our challenge and is essential if we are to develop our talents" (Cook, 2006, 54). He mentioned that one way for us to do this is to be confident about our beliefs and to live them. We must proactively prepare ourselves and our children to do so.

Church leaders have increasingly warned us that the youth of the Church are being raised "in enemy territory" (Packer, 2011, 16), in a world where moral standards are blurred or even nonexistent (Monson, 2011, 60). Elder Jeffrey R. Holland (2003) said:

> Some days it seems that a sea of temptation and transgression inundates [our children], simply washes over them before they can successfully withstand it, before they should have to face it. And often at least some of the forces at work seem beyond our personal control.
>
> Well, some of them may be beyond our control, but I testify with faith in the living God that they are not beyond His." (p. 85)

With the help of Almighty God, we can seize the opportunity to be proactive today in the lives of our children and help them to be agents in their own lives. A proactive approach to parenting provides our children with the armor needed to enter enemy territory with protection and to ultimately return with honor.

References

Arnett, J. J. (2012). *Adolescence and emerging adulthood: A cultural approach* (5th ed.). Upper Saddle River, NJ: Pearson Prentice Hall.

Bardi, A., & Schwartz, S. H. (2003). Values and behavior: Strength and structure of relations. *Personality and Social Psychology Bulletin, 29*, 1207–1220.

Ballard, M. R. (1999, May). Like a flame unquenchable. *Ensign, 29*(5), 85–87.

Bednar, D. A. (2010, May). Watching with all perseverance. *Ensign, 40*(5), 40–43.

Bednar, D. A. (2012, November). Converted unto the Lord. *Ensign, 42*(11), 106–109.

Brown, J. D., & L'Engle, K. L. (2009, February). X-rated: Sexual attitudes and behaviors associated with U.S. early adolescents' exposure to sexually explicit media. *Communication Research, 36*(1), 129–151.

Cook, Q. L. (2006, February). Lessons from the Old Testament: In the world but not of the world. *Ensign, 36*(2), 53–55.

Clark, J. R. (1965–1975). *Messages of the First Presidency*. Salt Lake City: Bookcraft.

Coyne, S. M., Padilla-Walker, L. M., Stockdale, L., & Day, R. D. (2011). Game on . . . girls: Associations between co-playing video games and adolescent behavioral and family outcomes. *Journal of Adolescent Health, 49*, 160–165.

Dittus, P., Miller, K. S., Kotchick, B. A., & Forehand, R. (2004). Why parents matter!: The conceptual basis for a community-based HIV prevention program for the parents of African American youth. *Journal Of Child And Family Studies, 13*(1), 5–20.

Eisenberg, M. E., Sieving, R. E., Bearinger, L. H., Swain, C., & Resnick, M. D. (2006). Parents' communication with adolescents about sexual behavior: A missed opportunity for prevention? *Journal of Youth and Adolescence, 35*(6), 893–902.

Fletcher, A. C., Steinberg, L., & Williams-Wheeler, M. (2004). Parental influences on adolescent problem behavior: Revisiting Stattin and Kerr. *Child Development, 75*(3), 781–796.

For the strength of youth: Fulfilling our duty to God. (2001). Salt Lake City: The Church of Jesus Christ of Latter-day Saints.

Grusec, J. E., & Goodnow, J. J. (1994). Impact of parental discipline methods on the child's internalization of values: A reconceptualization of current points of view. *Developmental Psychology, 30*, 4–19.

Holland, J. R. (2003, May). A prayer for the children. *Ensign, 33*(5), 85–87.

Hunter, H. W. (1983, November). Parents' concern for children. *Ensign, 13*(11), 63–65.

Hunter, H. W. (1990, November). Come unto me. *Ensign, 20*(11), 17–18.

Larson, R., & Richards, M. (1994). *Divergent realities: The emotional lives of mothers, fathers, and adolescents.* New York: Basic Books.

Monson, T. M. (2011, November). Dare to stand alone. *Ensign, 41*(11), 60–67.

Mounts, N. S. (2002). Parental management of adolescent peer relationships in context: The role of parenting style. *Journal of Family Psychology, 16*, 58–69.

Mounts, N. S. (2011). Parental management of peer relationships and early adolescents' social skills. *Journal of Youth and Adolescence, 40*, 416–427.

Nathanson, A. I. (1999). Identifying and explaining the relationship between parental mediation and children's aggression. *Communication Research, 26*(2), 124–143.

Nathanson, A. I. (2002). The unintended effects of parental mediation of television on adolescents. *Media Psychology, 4*, 207–230.

Nelson, L. J., Padilla-Walker, L. M., Christensen, K. J., Evans, C. A., & Carroll, J. A. (2011). Parenting in emerging adulthood: An examination of parenting clusters and correlates. *Journal of Youth and Adolescence, 40*(6), 730–743.

Packer, B. K. (2011, November). Counsel to youth. *Ensign, 41*(11), 16–19.

Padilla-Walker, L. M. (2006). "Peers I can monitor, it's media that really worries me!" Parental cognitions as predictors of proactive parental strategy choice. *Journal of Adolescent Research, 21*, 56–82.

Padilla-Walker, L. M., Christensen, K. J., & Day, R. D. (2011). Proactive parenting practices during early adolescence: A cluster approach. *Journal of Adolescence, 34*(4), 203–214.

Padilla-Walker, L. M., & Coyne, S. M. (2011). "Turn that thing off!" Parent and adolescent predictors of proactive media monitoring. *Journal of Adolescence, 34*, 705–715.

Padilla-Walker, L. M., Coyne, S. M., & Fraser, A. (2012). Getting a high speed family connection: Associations between family media use and family connection. *Family Relations, 61*, 426–440.

Padilla-Walker, L. M., Coyne, S. M., Fraser, A. M., Dyer, W. J., & Yorgason, J. B. (2012). Parents and adolescents growing up in the digital age: Latent growth curve analysis of proactive media monitoring. *Journal of Adolescence, 35*(5), 1153–1165.

Padilla-Walker, L. M., Fraser, A. M., & Harper, J. M. (2012). Walking the walk: The moderating role of proactive parenting on adolescents' value-congruent behaviors. *Journal of Adolescence, 35*(5), 1141–1152.

Padilla-Walker, L. M., & Thompson, R. A. (2005). Combating conflicting messages of values: A closer look at parental strategies. *Social Development, 14*, 305–323.

Rideout, V. J., Foehr, U. G., & Roberts, D. F. (2010). *Generation M2: Media in the lives of 8- to 18-year olds.* Menlo Park, CA.

Sabina, C., Wolak, J., & Finkelhor, D. (2008). The nature and dynamics of Internet pornography exposure for youth. *Cyber Psychology and Behavior, 11*(6), 691–693.

Seyfried, S. F., & Chung, I. (2002). Parent involvement as parental monitoring of student motivation and parent expectations predicting later achievement among African American and European American middle school age students.

In D. de Anda (Ed.), *Social work with multicultural youth* (pp. 109–131). Binghamton, NY: Haworth Social Work Practice Press.

Steinberg, L. (2010). *Adolescence* (9th ed.). New York: McGraw-Hill Companies.

Uchtdorf, D. F. (2011, November). Forget me not. *Ensign, 41*(11), 120–123.

JEFFREY S. REBER & STEVEN P. MOODY

IO

Perils and Prospects of Parenting LDS Youth in an Increasingly *Narcissistic Culture*

AMERICAN culture is marked by a growing desire for special status, recognition, and achievement (Reber & Moody, 2013). As one manifestation of this trend, consider the increasing number of people seeking the spotlight of fame through the medium of reality television programs. In 2000 there were only four reality television programs on air. One decade later, there were 320, each one with a cast of supposedly everyday people like you and me trying to become famous and often doing so in the most outrageous ways (Ocasio, 2012). An even greater number of people are seeking the recognition of their so-called friends and followers through social media outlets like Facebook and Twitter. In 2011 there were over 800 million active Facebook users, and every day two billion posts received "likes" and comments and 250 million photos were posted. At the time, the average US Facebook user spent 7 hours and 46 minutes on Facebook each month (Parr, 2011).

Researchers at UCLA's Children Digital Media Center (CDMC) have found that the media is participating in these social trends, especially in television programming directed toward preteens. Uhls & Greenfield (2011), for example, said that for the last 26 years that values in preteen television have been measured: the top values were community feeling and benevolence, with fame ranked among the least important. In 2007, for the first time ever, the trend flipped, with fame at the top and community feeling and benevolence dropping nearly to the bottom. One of the study coauthors found this trend disconcerting, stating that "the rise of fame in preteen television may be one influence on the documented rise in narcissism in our culture" (CDMC@UCLA, 2011).

Some psychologists disagree with the suggestion that these trends toward fame lead to narcissism. They assert that the rising concern with fame is harmless or nothing new and argue that the youth of every generation have behaved similarly before growing up and growing out of this life phase (for example, Trzesniewski & Donnellan, 2010). However, these psychologists are in the minority. A growing number of mental health professionals are concerned that our culture is becoming more self-absorbed, self-indulgent, and narcissistic than any previous generation (Cushman, 1995; Richardson, 2005; Pinsky & Young, 2009). Psychologists Twenge & Campbell (2009) believe we live in an unprecedented age of entitlement that is contributing to a narcissism epidemic, afflicting many more people than ever before. Support for their argument can be found in a number of studies. Among these studies are those identifying a strong relationship between participation on reality television programs and narcissism (Young & Pinsky, 2006), and studies that have found evidence of a strong positive correlation between Facebook use and subclinical levels of narcissism (Buffardi & Campbell, 2008).

A number of researchers agree that adolescents are at a particularly high risk for developing the characteristics of narcissism that mark this rising social tide (Barry, Kerig, Stellwagen, & Barry, 2010). They note that measures of adolescent and young adult narcissism have steadily risen since the 1970s, and more young people are receiving diagnoses of Narcissistic Personality Disorder than in the past. These trends led psychologist W. Keith Campbell (2011) to conclude, "You can look at individual scores of narcissism, you can look at data on lifetime prevalence of Narcissistic Personality

Disorder, you can look at related cultural trends, and they all point to one thing. Narcissism is on the rise" (p. 64).

This rise in narcissism is disconcerting because narcissism has a number of negative effects on psychological well-being and the quality of interpersonal relationships. It also contributes to a number of problems in society (Twenge & Campbell, 2009). With regard to psychological well-being, researchers have found that narcissism correlates with increased aggression (Bushman & Baumeister, 1998) and hostility (Rhodewalt & Morf, 1995) and is linked to extreme emotional instability and strong outbursts, which include anger and rage (Emmons, 1987). These psychological effects not only negatively impact the individual, but can be distressing to others. Psychologists Brown and Zeigler-Hill (2004) noted that "narcissists often go to great lengths to glorify themselves even when doing so undermines their relationships with others" (p. 585). Narcissists often demand that their concerns be the focal point of relationships, and they show little concern for the needs of others. As one psychologist put it, "Narcissists have a lack of insight about understanding and processing feelings [and] . . . are slow to learn the all-important skills of commitment such as sympathy, understanding the intentions and motives of their partner, compassion and empathy" (Namka, 2005, "Intimacy Skill Defects," para. 1). This insensitivity to the feelings of others often damages relational well-being and may hasten the termination of relationships (Miller, Campbell, & Pilkonis, 2007).

Narcissism also negatively impacts society. Namka (2005) notes that "people with narcissistic behavior have a sense of entitlement that allows them to break the rules of society" ("Narcissistic Person in Relationship," para. 4). In this sense, it is not surprising that researchers have found a strong positive correlation between narcissism and white-collar business crime (Blickel, Schlegel, Fassbender, & Klein, 2006). Narcissistic people are less likely to feel guilt than non-narcissistic people, which can loosen the restraints on immoral behavior (Brunell, Staats, Barden, & Hupp, 2011) and contribute to the deterioration of societal morals and values. Given the troubling individual, interpersonal, and societal consequences that can accompany narcissism, a number of social scientists have begun to look more closely at the factors that may contribute to the development of narcissistic tendencies in adolescents, including the media, technology, and the topic of this chapter: parenting.

Narcissism and Parental Indulgence

A relationship between parenting and narcissism has been presupposed since at least the time of Freud (1914). However, the systematic empirical study of the specific aspects of parenting that might contribute to adolescent narcissism has a fairly short history. While more study is needed, the contours of the relationship between parenting and adolescent narcissism are beginning to come into relief. Researchers have found that parenting styles, specifically the authoritarian and permissive forms, may play an important role in the development of adolescent narcissism (Watson, Little, & Biderman, 1992), as can such things as excessive parental control and monitoring. Mixed messages of public praise and private belittling from parents may also contribute to this disconcerting social trend (Horton, Bleau, & Drwecki, 2006).

One factor that has shown a particularly sustained and strong correlation across multiple studies and among both adolescent males and females is parental indulgence. According to Horton (2011), "parents who indulge their children by caving into their every whim and lavishing them with affection regardless of their behavior are facilitating their children's sense of superiority and entitlement, critical ingredients in narcissism." The key concern with indulgent parenting is that children learn via their parents' modeling that there is "a disconnect between self-evaluation and performance such that the positive view of the self exists independent of behavior (that is, 'I am great no matter what I do')" (p. 129).

Parental indulgence is a particularly paradoxical phenomenon. Parents want to show their children their support and encouragement. They want to strengthen their children's self-concepts and raise their self-esteem, and they certainly do not want to curtail their potential. However, these

Parents who indulge their children by caving into their every whim and lavishing them with affection regardless of their behavior are facilitating their children's sense of superiority and entitlement, which are critical ingredients in narcissism. © Andres Rodriguez.

healthy parental intentions can easily turn into something more troubling. As Twenge and Campbell (2009) described it, "It is increasingly common to see parents relinquishing authority to young children, showering them with unearned praise, protecting them from their teachers' criticisms, giving them expensive automobiles, and allowing them to have freedom but not the responsibility that goes with it" (p. 73). In cases such as this, when parents give their children praise that is not connected to performance and block or dismiss negative or critical feedback of their children that comes from others (for example, a coach or a teacher), they may overinflate the confidence of their children and contribute to their sense of self-importance and superiority (Reber & Moody, 2013).

These tendencies to indulge children only increase when parents' own sense of worth and self-esteem are tied up in their children. It was Freud (1917) who first described an unconscious defense mechanism—that is, a method of protecting oneself from feelings of shame, guilt, and embarrassment—known as identification, which can manifest itself in the tendency for some parents to live vicariously through the successes and accomplishments of their children. If their child excels academically, athletically, musically, or in some other way that speaks to the repressed unmet wishes of the parents, the parents may unconsciously take much of the credit for their child's excellence and feel better about themselves as a result. This can fuel parents' overinvestment in their child's activities and accomplishments. Narcissistic identification can also drive parents to push their children into activities that the parents, not the children, care about and can facilitate the behavior of giving praise without critical feedback that marks problematic parental indulgence. After all, if the parent identifies with their child, any negative or critical feedback the child receives will also be taken personally by the parent whose own self-worth may be too fragile to tolerate any criticism or failure.

Are Parents to Blame?

It can be easy to point the finger at parents and blame them for the behaviors and personalities of their children. After all, they are typically the people who spend every day with the children, and they are responsible for teaching them and helping them mature into fully functioning persons. Of all the factors that play a role in a child's life, it is the parents who are most easily seen and are most likely to receive the credit or blame for the child's actions. But there are many other influences at play here, the majority of which are implicit and go unnoticed, both by parents and by those who might blame them. Indeed, we would argue that parents are in a uniquely difficult position. Parents, along with their children, are caught in the middle of a virtual perfect storm of implicit sociocultural and psychological forces that press parents toward indulgence and encourage a sense of entitlement and superiority in their children; and many parents are completely unaware of these forces and pressures acting on them and their children.

We are not suggesting that parents or children are determined by these factors. However, to the extent they are unaware of them it is easier for certain sociocultural and psychological ideas and practices about parenting to be taken for granted as the way things are or the way things are supposed to be. Without recognition that these commonly accepted sociocultural influences and ideas are assumptions, not facts, and without consideration of viable alternative ways to conceptualize parenting, parents may be unlikely to engage in the important critical thinking process that would help them see the role these assumptions play in their children developing a heightened sense of specialness or even narcissistic tendencies.

Implicit Sociocultural Influences on Parental Indulgence

To facilitate greater critical thinking about parental indulgence and the sociocultural influences acting upon it, we make explicit here several of the implicit assumptions that influence parents and press their children toward a heightened sense of self-importance and entitlement. Over time these assumptions have likely become taken for granted by many parents, as they seem to have been by many mental health professionals and our society generally. We critically examine these ideas to show their status as assumptions, not facts, and then we briefly consider an alternative set of assumptions that are based on the gospel of Jesus Christ and provide a contrast to the taken-for-granted assumptions of the conventional view. This critical evaluation of assumptions and alternatives is designed to provide parents with a model for conducting their own critical examination of their assumptions about parenting and may help parents make a more informed decision about their parenting practices.

Humanistic psychology and self-centeredness. In the 1950s and '60s Abraham Maslow, Carl Rogers, and other psychologists in the humanistic tradition grew dissatisfied with the deterministic and negative psychologies of psychoanalysis and behaviorism. They sought to emphasize the positive potential in persons to become fully functioning, flourishing human beings and developed a number of important theories to that effect. The result was a psychological movement with sufficient impact to become known as the third force in psychology (Goble, 1970). This third force emphasized the unique, inherent potential of every individual which can be actualized only if the individual is allowed to discover his or her potential and develop it without the forced societal expectations of parents and other institutions.

Carl Rogers (1961), for example, believed that if children are given unconditional positive regard by their parents and other significant people in their life, then the inner voice of their authentic self—their genuine potential—will not be drowned out by outer voices of parental expectation or societal demands. Parents who show conditional positive regard, on the other hand, will press children to live for the sake of others instead of for the sake of their own potential. As children conform to parental and societal expectations, they will develop incongruence between the authentic self and this socially developed self, the result of which is inauthenticity, which will ultimately bring about some kind of disorder in the person. For Rogers, in order to raise fully functioning persons, parents must let children be their genuine selves, showing positive regard for the child without limitation or condition. Otherwise, as the humanist sees it, children will develop neurotic or psychotic conditions that may stay with them their entire life and will hinder their self-actualization.

Humanistic psychology's conceptualization of self-actualization has been criticized for its potential for self-centeredness (Myers, 2009; Seligman & Csikszentmihalyi, 2000). The heart of the criticism is that if the self-actualization needs of the individual are primary, then the needs of others must inevitably be secondary (Slife & Williams, 1995). This strongly suggests that parents must set aside their expectations for their children and cater to the needs of their children as their children define those needs and endeavor to pursue them. In this way, parents and other people are instrumentalized and serve as the means to their children's ends, which can promote a sense of entitlement in children and may encourage indulgence by parents (Cushman, 1990; Vitz 1994).

Postmodernism and moral and epistemological relativism. A number of historians and philosophers describe contemporary western culture as postmodern (for example, Best & Kellner, 1997). Postmodernism has many themes and meanings, but one prominent focus of this perspective is the critique of absolute truth and morality (Franks & Keller, 1996). For many postmodernists there are no capital "T" truths that transcend all cultures and times. Grand, all-encompassing, authoritative narratives like religion, science, and democracy are not taken to be universal and certain. Instead all truth and morality claims are viewed as particular and tentative. For the relativistic postmodern, all truth is culturally constructed within each culture's unique context (Burr, 1995). This means the things we think of as capital "T" truths are only culture-bound little "t" truths that have application and value only within the culture in which they are constructed.

If every culture constructs its truths according to its particular context, history, and goals one culture cannot say another culture is wrong or immoral because it would be judging that culture according to its standards of truth and morality, which are only true for that unique culture. To impose one culture's truths on the truths of another culture is intolerant. Tolerance is probably the closest thing to a universal truth or moral value in a relativistic postmodern society (Wong, 1984). From the postmodern perspective, when cultures tolerate one another they honor and preserve the different truths of other cultures (Carson, 2012).

There is no principle reason why relativism would not seep very easily down to the individual level. Indeed, a number of postmodern thinkers assert that truth is ultimately in the eye of the beholder (Christman, 2009). After all, just as cultures emerge in unique sociocultural historical contexts, so too do individuals. No one has the same genetic makeup, environment, experiences, contexts, and so forth, as any other person, so how can anyone really know what it is like to be another person? How can anyone know another person's truths? From this perspective, even parents don't fully know the unique contexts of their children. Therefore parents should tolerate their children's burgeoning truths rather than impose their own truths upon them. Anything short of that would be intolerant and overbearing. Children may have always complained that their parents don't know what it is like to be them and to live in their time and place, but now, with the support of the postmodern worldview, kids can back up their complaints with a culturally reinforced ideology. If parents are to steer clear of imposing their truths on their children, which would be a sure sign of intolerance for the postmodern, they must let their children ultimately decide what is true and good for themselves.

Moral and epistemological relativism is seen by many scholars as a significant threat to the health of society, and for this reason postmodernism has been widely criticized for its potentially destructive influence (see Fisher, 2005; Baumann, 1992). Relativism denies any claim to authority over others by any culture or person, including parents. This means that every person, including a child, is ultimately an authority unto himself or herself, and that individual authority must be tolerated. Within this framework, parents may offer suggestions or advice to their children, but they cannot impose their will on them and certainly cannot with any justification tell their children no.

American psychology and self-esteem. The term "self-esteem" is an invention of American psychology first described by William James (1890) just over a century ago. Since that time it has grown in popularity and has become reified as one of the attributes or characteristics of children that is of great concern to parents and educators (Twenge & Campbell, 2009). There are now literally thousands of manuals and handbooks that teach parents and teachers how to enhance and monitor children's self-esteem and how to identify signs of trouble when it is low. Research on self-esteem development suggests that childhood and adolescence are key stages of self-esteem formation and parents play a very important role in that formation (Shaffer, 2005). Many parents feel responsible for helping children cultivate high positive evaluations of themselves and for watching out for warning signs of low self-esteem, including depression and loneliness.

If parents are successful in fostering high, secure self-esteem in their children, as opposed to high defensive self-esteem or low self-esteem, their

Many parents feel responsible for helping children cultivate high, positive evaluations of themselves and for watching out for warning signs of low self-esteem, including depression and loneliness. Matt Reier, © Intellectual Reserve, Inc.

children will be in a position to enjoy many lifelong benefits, including greater confidence, greater capacity for happiness, more friends, stronger values, greater enjoyment of activities, increased resilience, resistance to manipulation and peer pressure, and many more (Baumeister & Bushman, 2008; Baumeister, Campbell, Krueger, Vohs, 2003). And how are parents taught to cultivate high self-esteem in their children? The self-esteem literature encourages parents to practice unconditional positive regard, indulgence, and tolerance. Twenge and Campbell (2009) warn about the negative consequences that often follow from these messages, stating:

If parents are successful in fostering high, secure self-esteem in their children, as opposed to high defensive self-esteem or low self-esteem, their children will be in a position to enjoy many lifelong benefits, including greater confidence, greater capacity for happiness, more friends, stronger values, greater enjoyment of activities, increased resilience, resistance to manipulation and peer pressure, and many more. © Iuliia Gusakova.

Many of today's parents . . . seek to raise children high in self-admiration and self-esteem, partially because books and articles have touted its importance. Unfortunately, much of what parents think raises self-esteem—such as telling a kid he's special and giving him what he wants—actually leads to narcissism. (p. 74)

It is important to note that high self-esteem need not be connected to the reality of a person's circumstances or performance in any way. In fact, researchers have found that people with high self-esteem often tend to be unrealistically optimistic (Armor & Taylor, 2002). For example, when asked about the likelihood of divorce or suffering from a terminal illness or a catastrophic event at some point in their lives, people with high self-esteem significantly underestimate the probability that such things would ever happen to them. Researchers have also found that people with high self-esteem will sometimes handicap their performance on a task in order to preserve their positive self-evaluations (Tice & Baumeister, 1990).

Because high self-esteem does not have to correlate positively with ability, performance, or skill, then criticism, punishment, negative feedback, or even realistic feedback from parents is not required. If the goal is high self-esteem, then only praise and positive reinforcement is needed, no matter what the child does. Critical or realistic feedback, particularly when given to a child in a low self-esteem state might sow the seeds of an enduring habit of negative self-evaluation. Negative self-evaluation often correlates with a number of other negative aspects of life, including pessimism and depression, self-doubt and heavy self-criticism, perfectionism, hostility and defensiveness, fear of failure and rejection, and envy of others (Donnellan, et al., 2005; Mruk, 2006). If critical or realistic feedback could lead to such unwanted consequences, parents may decide it is better to avoid criticism altogether and show only self-esteem boosting unconditional praise.

The concept of self-esteem has been criticized for its ethnocentrism, the lack of evidence showing a causal relationship between self-esteem and academic achievement, and its individualism and overemphasis on self-actualization (for a review, see Kohn, 1994). Indeed, laboratory research shows that people who have high self-esteem are more likely to get angry and aggressive when their high opinion of themselves is threatened than are people with low self-esteem (Papps & O'Carroll, 1998). This concept of ego-threat defense is one subtle implication of an emphasis on self-esteem that parents are unlikely to anticipate when they indulge their children. In their indulgent efforts to strengthen their children's positive evaluation of themselves parents may also strengthen the children's resistance to any feedback or criticism, however constructive, which might threaten their optimistic, if not always realistic beliefs about themselves.

Positive psychology and happiness. Like their humanistic forebears, positive psychologists are interested in those aspects of human psychology that relate to flourishing and human potential. No topic is more important to positive psychologists than happiness (Seligman, 2002). Happiness has been defined in a variety of ways but it is generally undergirded with the assumption of hedonism (Veenhoven, 2003). Hedonism is the idea that pleasure in its varied manifestations is desirable and ought to be pursued, whereas pain in its many forms is undesirable and ought to be avoided. Accordingly, a happy person has maximal pleasure (that is, satisfaction, enjoyment, and wellbeing) and minimal pain (suffering, anxiety, and regret). Parents are in a unique position to influence this form of happiness in their young children. They can create positive experiences that feel good to their children and create a smile on their face. They can also try and protect children from negative experiences that would annoy them or cause them sadness. The important thing is that parents maximize the number of their children's pleasurable experiences and minimize the number of their painful experiences.

Positive psychology's shift of focus from the negative, disordered aspects of life to those positive aspects that accentuate happiness corresponds with a cultural trend in which parents are more focused on the hedonistic happiness of their children than ever before (Hooper, 2012; Wang, 2011). In this hedonistic culture, it is easy for parents to believe that if they put a great deal of time and effort into an elaborate birthday party for a child, for example, the

Parents are in a unique position to create positive experiences and influence the happiness of their young children. © Szefei.

party is only successful if the child gives the "good feeling" stamp of approval to it. If parents ask if the child had a good time on his or her special day and the child says he or she did not, then from a hedonistic perspective the parents have failed to deliver the pleasurable experience the child deserves. On this view, everything hinges on the hedonistic emotional satisfaction of the child (Slife & Richardson, 2008).

When considering this form of hedonistic happiness, one cannot help but think of Veruca Salt from *Charlie and the Chocolate Factory*, who wielded her mood like a whip to manipulate her father into giving her whatever she claimed she needed in order to be happy. If, as hedonism implies, a child should have a happy childhood, and if happiness is defined by the child's hedonistic emotional satisfaction, then parents really have no choice but to provide experiences that are pleasurable and enjoyable for the child and to protect the child from experiences that cause suffering and pain. But is hedonism as fundamental to happiness and psychological flourishing as many positive psychologists, economists, evolutionary theorists, and other scholarly disciplines assume? A number of critics of positive psychology argue that neither hedonism nor emotional satisfaction is a necessary criterion of wellbeing and happiness (for a review, see Held, 2004). On the contrary, the pursuit of pleasure and minimization of pain might lead to a number of problematic psychological consequences, including selfishness, narcissism, and psychological disorders (Slife & Richardson, 2008). In this way, the negative aspects of psychology that positive psychologists deemphasize may rear their head precisely because of the efforts to accentuate the positive. Parents who strive to indulge their children's hedonistic emotional desires may unknowingly feed a number of unwanted psychological tendencies in their children, like narcissism.

Consumer culture and affluenza. Today's adolescents live in one of the wealthiest eras ever known in the history of the world. Never before have there been so many goods and services available to meet our every need and desire, and never before has there been consumption on so grand a scale. Even the most frugal parents today have more stuff than the parents of any previous generation. Whether they intend to or not, parents often model the indulgence of their desires for more material goods and are doing so at an ever earlier age. Indeed, there are more young adult millionaires than ever before in history. More young parents live in the large homes, drive the expensive cars, and travel on the costly vacations that would have previously been reserved for those mature individuals who spent a lifetime accruing the wealth necessary for such indulgences in their later life. Is it possible that the children of younger, wealthier parents are learning by social observation to have similar desires and even expectations for themselves despite their young age (Seiter, 1995)?

Today it is not unusual at all to see children as young as seven or eight years old with fully functional smart phones and access to every kind of technology imaginable, including video games and fully motorized scooters, bikes, and go-karts. Toddlers can be found sporting Air Jordan booties and Ralph Lauren onesies. Every kind of food is available for consumption,

There is a growing sense of entitlement to these many goods and services among youth in our culture, and if parents do not meet the demands of their children, they may be viewed as authoritarian and unfairly withholding. © Goodluz.

especially junk food, and adolescent obesity has reached epidemic levels (Jelalian & Steele, 2008). There is a growing sense of entitlement to these many goods and services among youth in our culture and if parents do not meet the demands of their children they may be viewed as authoritarian and unfairly withholding (Twenge & Campbell, 2009). Even if, as many researchers have argued (for example, DeGraaf, Wann, & Naylor, 2005), this materialistic entitlement is a kind of sickness that like influenza can reach epidemic levels, indulgent parents may unknowingly act as if their children have as much right to be sick in this way as anybody else.

Affluenza, as DeGraaf et al. (2005) have labeled it, is a significant cultural trend that results in a number of problematic psychological and social outcomes, including debt, waste, excess, and anxiety that result from the constant pursuit of more and better things. It may also facilitate feelings of entitlement and greed in children. As Philip Cushman (1990) describes it, this constant pursuit of things which cannot ultimately satisfy what people really need (that is, meaningful relationships with others) results in a growing emptiness in the self, which people may continue to mistakenly believe can best be filled by increased consumption of material things. The result is ever more emptiness. Might parents who model affluenza for their children set their children up for this kind of narcissistic emptiness that Cushman describes?

Noble and Great Ones

Parents in the LDS Church may face an additional temptation toward indulgence that is worth mentioning here. LDS parents and their children have been told many times that the youth who are coming forth in this the last hour of the dispensation of the fullness of times are among the most noble and great spirits of our Heavenly Father. These children have many great gifts and talents and have been prepared to come into the world in a time of great challenges and opportunities. To what extent might LDS parents be prone to adopt a view of their children as being foreordained to a great calling or purpose? To what extent might they feel unqualified to parent children with such advanced abilities and talents? Could this uniquely LDS understanding of children make it easy for some LDS parents to overemphasize their children's strengths and to underemphasize their weaknesses? Might it make constructive criticism and honest feedback hard to come by and unbounded praise the norm? To what extent does this knowledge lead to more permissive parenting where children are allowed to govern themselves too early and without properly enforced limits?

Narcissism and Parents of LDS Youth

Though we are not aware of any published studies that examine parental indulgence and narcissistic tendencies among LDS youth specifically, we see no reason to expect that parents of LDS youth are immune to the influences just reviewed. On the contrary, each of these sources may present a particular vulnerability for LDS parents. For example, similar to humanistic psychologists, LDS parents believe their children are unique. They believe they existed as unique intelligences and then spirits prior to earth life where they now exist as unique souls—united spirits and bodies (see Abraham 3:22). LDS parents, like humanistic psychologists, also believe their children have a potential which is of primary importance to their healthy growth and development. As children of a divine king, they have the potential to become like God (see D&C 88:107). These overlapping ideas are quite positive. However, if LDS parents are influenced by the perspective of humanistic psychology in their parenting they may forget that our children's ultimate purpose, as children of God, is to glorify him and serve others, not to focus primarily on meeting their unique potential and needs, no matter how divine their origin may be.

LDS parents may also have a particular vulnerability with regard to relativism. Although LDS parents don't embrace moral and epistemological relativism per se, they can face a relativism-like challenge when dealing with the personal revelations their children claim to receive, particularly when they are older. For example, when a young adult reports that he or she has received an answer to prayer about attending a certain college, taking a job, going on a mission, or getting married parents may not feel comfortable countering the decision if they disagree. They may find it appropriate to counsel, consult, and cajole, but in a postmodern culture they would stop short of telling the child his or her decision is wrong. To tell the child his or her revelation is wrong would not only be intolerant of the child's truth but might also undermine the lesson on personal revelation that many LDS parents try to teach their children. Thus once the child's trump card of personal revelation has been played, it can feel like all other hands must fold.

Parents in the Church are also especially likely to desire high self-esteem for their children. They have been taught and also teach their children that every person is a child of God of inherent worth (see D&C 18:10; Lockhart,

1995). Children are princes and princesses of a divine King and are highly esteemed by their Heavenly Father. Given their inherent value LDS parents may believe their children ought to also have high self-esteem. They ought to value themselves as God values them and know that they are among his noble and great ones. From this perspective, low self-esteem would not accord with their divine nature and must at some level be seen as a denial of the love God has for the child. To the extent that these beliefs lead parents to focus primarily on developing the esteem of the child toward himself or herself, parents risk deemphasizing the importance of esteeming God first and foremost in the child's life.

The scriptures teach that God's plan for his children is a plan of happiness (see Alma 42:8; 2 Nephi 9:13). Insofar as LDS parents' understanding of happiness consists of hedonistic emotional satisfaction, it will be difficult for them not to desire the current and/or ultimate hedonistic happiness of their children. They may strive to protect or rescue their children from suffering even when that suffering may be part of God's plan and could help the children grow and progress. In his book *Faith Precedes the Miracle*, President Spencer W. Kimball quoted Orson F. Whitney, who stated:

> No pain that we suffer, no trial that we experience is wasted. It ministers to our education, to the development of such qualities as patience, faith, fortitude and humility. All that we suffer and all that we endure, especially when we endure it patiently, builds up our characters, purifies our hearts, expands our souls, and makes us more tender and charitable, more worthy to be called the children of God . . . and it is through sorrow and suffering, toil and tribulation, that we gain the education that we come here to acquire and which will make us more like our Father and Mother in heaven (pp. 97–98).

Affluenza may also present unique challenges to LDS parents, particularly if they believe their prosperity is a sign of their being blessed by God for their righteousness and hard work. When parents believe God has blessed them with many material possessions they are more likely to model a focus on material consumption and may also nourish a sense of entitlement in children who may come to believe that if they live an obedient and righteous life God will bless and prosper them in a similar manner.

We remind the reader that none of these influences alone or in combination necessarily create indulgent parenting or lead to narcissism in children. However, they can facilitate and justify parental indulgence where inclinations toward it are already present. Parents who are uncomfortable giving honest feedback to their children or cannot tolerate their children feeling bad, for example, can find a supportive rationale for their indulgent actions in the self-esteem literature. Parents who like lavishing their children with praise will receive reinforcement for those actions in the concept of unconditional positive regard in humanistic psychology. And parents who tend to aggrandize the gifts and talents of their children will find able justification for that focus in one of the major goals of positive psychology, which is "to find and nurture genius and talent" (Compton, 2004, p. 5). For LDS parents, further reinforcement for these indulgences can come from their awareness of their children's divine potential and their knowledge of their children's gifts and talents, including those described in their children's patriarchal blessings. With all these influences and all the things LDS parents know about their children and what they can become, how can LDS parents help but lift their child up onto a pedestal?

Fight Back the Tide of Narcissism

We offer two suggestions that may aid LDS parents in their efforts to critically examine their own tendencies toward parental indulgence and to fight back the rising tide of narcissism that poses a particular threat to their children. The first suggestion is for parents to study, exemplify, and teach their children the attributes of Christ. The second suggestion is for parents to study Heavenly Father's parenting of his children and then compare and contrast that parenting style with their own.

Teach Children the Attributes of Christ

There is no better role model for children than Christ. This is true in all respects, but it is particularly significant with regard to narcissism. After all, Christ is the Firstborn of the Father in the spirit and the Only Begotten of the Father in the flesh. He is both fully God and fully human and has available to him all power and knowledge. His talents and gifts are innumerable, and his potential is unlimited. He has more reason than any other being to aggrandize himself above all others, yet he does not do it. On the contrary, when he lived on earth, he abased and condescended himself for our sakes, allowing himself to be a little child, wholly dependent on parents and others. As he grew into adulthood, he maintained his meekness and humility before the Father and others. Even when he was thoroughly exhausted from his long fast in the wilderness, he did not succumb to the temptations of the adversary to exercise his godly powers and lift himself above others. Though falsely accused, brought before Pilate for judgment, and sent to Golgotha to be crucified, he chose to be a lamb instead of a lion, gentle of spirit and lowly of heart.

When thinking of Christ's example, one is reminded of his words to Joseph in the Doctrine and Covenants where he warned Joseph about the tendency to lift oneself above others: "We have learned by sad experience," the Lord taught Joseph, "that it is the nature and disposition of almost all men, as soon as they get a little authority, as they suppose, they will immediately begin to exercise unrighteous dominion" (D&C 121:39). In contrast to that worldly self-aggrandizement over others, the Lord made it clear to Joseph that "no power or influence can or ought to be maintained by virtue of the priesthood" (v. 41) but only by the application of Christlike attributes, "by persuasion, by long-suffering, by gentleness and meekness, and by love unfeigned; by kindness and pure knowledge. . ." (vv. 41–42).

During his earthly sojourn, Christ refused to manifest the form of power Satan and many people expected of a Messiah, knowing that his influence upon the hearts of people across the world and over generations

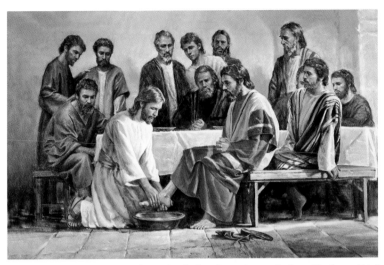

Christ maintained meekness and humility before the Father and others. He showed his love for his disciples in this instance by serving them. Del Parson, © Intellectual Reserve, Inc.

of time would be greater if it stemmed from his meekness and humility. Consider as an example the incredible influence Christ had on Peter (and on each of us who read the story) when he knelt down and washed Peter's feet. If Christ had commanded Peter to wash his feet, Peter would have happily obeyed his Lord and would have felt honored to do so, but it would not have left the same lasting impression on Peter's heart as did Christ's humble act of self-abasement. Because Christ acted in humility, Peter, knowing full well who Christ was, must have uncomfortably sat there in utter amazement that a God would deign to wash his dirty feet; and he and the other apostles surely never forgot the lesson they learned that day as they went on to serve others in like manner for the rest of their lives.

Similarly, parents can teach their children by word and by example that true and lasting power and influence comes not from worldly fame, prestige, or self-aggrandizement, but from the attributes of Christ that are developed and instilled in their hearts as they humble themselves before God and serve others in a spirit of meekness (see 1 Peter 3:4). On this point Elder Neal A. Maxwell (1983) has said, "The meek go on fewer ego trips, but they have far greater adventures. Ego trips, those 'travel now and pay later' indulgences, are always detours. The straight and narrow path is, after all, the only path which takes us to new and breathtaking places" (p. 72).

Albert Bandura's (1977) well-known theory of social learning provides a great deal of evidence supporting the idea that children learn from and often follow the model of their parents in their own conduct. Thus, if parents model the attributes of Christ, their children are more likely to practice those attributes as well. On the other hand, if parents indulge their children, then their children will be more likely to indulge themselves. Elder Lynn G. Robbins (2011) of the Seventy said, "To be good parents, one of the most important things we can teach our children is how to be more like the Savior" (p. 104). Teaching and modeling Christlike attributes can be a great spiritual inoculation against the development of narcissistic tendencies in our children

Follow Heavenly Father's Example

A second spiritual resource that can aid parents in their efforts to fight back the rising tide of narcissism is the example of Heavenly Father's parenting that is manifest in the scriptures and through our personal experiences with him. Two relevant questions can be asked. First, does Heavenly Father lavish praise on his children? Second, is Heavenly Father's praise unrelated to performance? Recall that parental indulgence includes an overabundance of praise with little critical feedback as well as praising children regardless of their successes or failures. Does Heavenly Father indulge us, his children, in similar ways?

The answer to the first question regarding God lavishing praise on his children is answered regularly in the relationship of Heavenly Father to his close associates, the prophets. Praise rarely exceeds a simple "blessed art thou" (Matthew 16:17; Luke 1:28, 42). Consider again the example of Joseph Smith. He was given some praise as seemed reasonably needed to lift his spirits and energize his work, but he was also regularly chastised and occasionally rebuked for his misdeeds, particularly when he was young and learning to submit his will to God. For example, after losing the 116 pages of the Book of Mormon manuscript, the Lord let Joseph know his disapproval in no uncertain terms, stating, "For although a man may have many revelations and have power to do many mighty works, yet if he boasts in his own strength, and sets at naught the counsels of God, and follows after the dictates of his own will and carnal desires, he must fall and incur the vengeance of a just God upon him" (D&C 3:4). Father in Heaven also did not remove obstacles from Joseph's path or make things easier for him. He allowed him to suffer because it would strengthen Joseph and because it was more important for Joseph to learn to esteem his Heavenly Father than to esteem himself. Even the Savior, a child of God without blemish or sin, was allowed to endure the great suffering of the atonement without a reprieve from his father, crying out "My God, My God, why hast thou forsaken me?" (Matthew 27:46). Surely, his father felt a great desire to indulge his innocent son in this time of great suffering, to ease his pain, and remove his burden, but he stayed his comforting hand, knowing that it was necessary for Christ to experience his absence for a time so he could in turn succor us when we feel abandoned and alone. Elder Maxwell (1997) said:

> Jesus' perfect empathy was ensured when, along with His Atonement for our sins, He took upon Himself our sicknesses, sorrows, griefs, and infirmities and came to know these "according to the flesh" (Alma 7:11–12). He did this in order that He might be filled with perfect, personal mercy and empathy and thereby know how to succor us in our infirmities. He thus fully comprehends human suffering. Truly Christ "descended below all things, in that He comprehended all things" (D&C 88:6). (p. 7)

Heavenly Father allowed his only begotten son to suffer body and spirit so he could lift us up, not so he could aggrandize himself.

As to God's parenting and the relationship of performance and praise there is little room for debate. God tells us that he is pleased when we do his will and keep his commandments and that he is not pleased when we are disobedient or ungrateful. He promises blessings for righteous action and punishment for sin. If he did not manifest his pleasure and displeasure in response to our performance of our duties, it would be difficult for us to learn his ways and to align our will with his. As Elder Maxwell (1995) has said, "Only by aligning our wills with God's is full happiness to be found" (p. 23). Without God's genuine feedback, it would be all but impossible for us to know how to return to him.

Unlike what might seem to be the case with some people, God's love for us is in no way diminished when he shows us his displeasure or punishes us by, for example, removing the presence of the Holy Spirit. On the contrary, he manifests his great love to us by his displeasure and punishments. Such actions give us an opportunity to be humbled and to repent and to more fully become his true disciples. They help us to have the companionship of the Spirit more regularly and more strongly in our lives. Our Heavenly Father does not praise or punish us willy-nilly but responds perfectly to our actions in a manner that gives us the best opportunity to grow closer to him. Surely, there is no better model of parenting for us to emulate than that.

Conclusion

Much more could be written about the differences between indulgent parenting in an increasingly narcissistic culture and a gospel-based approach to parenting that is exemplified by Christ and our Heavenly Father. Suffice it to say at this point, that the cultural influences toward indulgence and the teachings of the gospel have fundamentally different sets of core assumptions. The gospel is not principally concerned with the actualization of the self but with the glorification of God and the celestial actualization of others through selfless service. Elder William R. Bradford (1987) of the First Quorum of the Seventy said, "The only way under the heavens whereby a person can be sanctified is in selfless service" (p. 76). The gospel does not localize truth and morality in the individual, but in a God who speaks to us individually and

Even the Savior, a child of God without blemish or sin, was allowed to endure the great suffering of the atonement without a reprieve from his father. Harry Anderson, © Intellectual Reserve, Inc.

309

The gospel encourages us to use our talents and gifts to bless the lives of others with humility and meekness. Welden Andersen, © Intellectual Reserve, Inc.

communally through his prophets and, in the case of children, often through their parents (see Proverbs 22:6). Elder L. Tom Perry (2012) said, "According to the great plan of happiness, it is goodly parents who are entrusted with the care and development of Heavenly Father's children" (p. 27).

The gospel also does not focus esteem on ourselves but on our God who deserves all the glory and gratitude for who we are and what we can do. "True teachers of the word of God always seek to give God the glory and turn attention away from themselves" (*New Testament: Gospel Doctrine Manual*, 2002, p. 127). The plan of happiness is not the plan of the absence of suffering or the plan of feeling good, nor is the accrual of wealth and material goods the entitlement of those who keep the commandments. On the contrary, the gospel is the pure love of Christ, or charity, that leads us to submit ourselves to God and others in a spirit of humility and meekness and to use the talents and gifts with which God has blessed us to uplift and edify others, not to aggrandize ourselves or our children.

References

Armor, D. A., & Taylor, S. E. (2002). The dilemma of unrealistic optimism. In T. Gilovich, D. Griffin, & D. Kahneman (Eds.), *Heuristics and biases: The psychology of intuitive judgment*. New York: Cambridge University Press, 334–347.

Bandura, A. (1977). *Social learning theory*. Englewood Cliffs, NJ: Prentice Hall.

Barry, C. T., Kerig, P. K., Stellwagen, K. K., & Barry, T. D. (Eds.). (2011). *Narcissism and Machiavellianism in youth: Implications for the development of adaptive and maladaptive behavior*. Washington, DC: APA.

Baumann, Z. (1992). *Intimations of postmodernity*. London: Routledge.

Baumeister, R. & Bushman, B. (2008). *Social psychology and human nature*. Belmont, CA: Wadsworth Publishing.

Baumeister, R., Campbell, J., Krueger, J., & Vohs, K. (2003). Does high self-esteem cause better performance, interpersonal success, happiness, or healthier lifestyles? *Psychological Science in the Public Interest, 4*, 1–44.

Best, S., & Kellner, D. (1997). *The postmodern turn*. New York: Guilford Press.

Blickel, G., Schlegel, A., Fassbender, P., & Klein, U. (2006). Some personality correlates of business white-collar crime. *Applied Psychology, 55,* 220–233.

Bradford, W. (1987, November). Selfless Service. *Ensign, 13*(11), 76.

Brown, R. P., & Zeigler-Hill, V. (2004). Narcissism and the non-equivalence of self-esteem measure: A matter of dominance? *Journal of Research in Personality, 38*(6). 585–592.

Brunell, A. B., Staats, S., Barden, J., & Bupp, J. M. (2011). Narcissism and academic dishonesty: The exhibitionism dimension and the lack of guilt. *Personality and Individual Differences, 50*(3). 323–328.

Buffardi, L. E., & Campbell, W. K. (2008). Narcissism and social networking web sites. *Personality and Social Psychology Bulletin, 34,* 1303–1314.

Burr, V. (1995). *An introduction to social constructionism.* New York: Routledge.

Bushman B. & Baumeister, R. (1998). Threatened egotism, narcissism, self-esteem, and direct and displaced aggression: Does self-love or self-hate lead to violence? *Journal of Personality and Social Psychology, 75*(1), 219–229.

Campbell, W. K. (2011). Cited in *Reflecting on narcissism: Are young people more self-obsessed than ever before? Monitor on Psychology, 42,* 64.

Carson, D. A. (2012). *The intolerance of tolerance.* Grand Rapids, MI: Wm. B. Eerdmans.

CDMC@UCLA (2012). I want my fame TV: UCLA study finds that tweens receive a clear message from their favorite TV shows: Fame is the most important value. Retrieved December 19, 2012, from http://www.cdmc.ucla.edu/Welcome_files /CDMCpressreleaseUhls%26Greenfieldfinal4.pdf

Christman, J. (2009). *The politics of persons: Individual autonomy and socio-historical selves.* New York: Cambridge University Press.

The Church of Jesus Christ of Latter Day Saints. (2002). God is no respecter of persons. *New Testament: Gospel Doctrine Teacher's Manual,* lesson 30, 125–28.

Compton, W. C. (2004). *An introduction to positive psychology.* Belmont, CA: Wadsworth Publishing.

Cushman, P. (1990). Why the self is empty: Toward a historically situated psychology. *American Psychologist, 45,* 599–611.

De Graaf, J., Wann, D., & Naylor, T. H. (2005). *Affluenza: The all-consuming epidemic* (2nd Ed.). San Francisco: Berrett–Koehler.

Donnellan, M.B., Trzesniewski, K. H., Robins, R.W., Moffitt, T.E., & Caspi, A. (2005). Low self-esteem is related to aggression, antisocial behavior, and delinquency. *Psychological Science, 16*, 328–335.

Emmons, R. A. (1987). Narcissism: Theory and measurement. *Journal of Personality and Social Psychology, 52*, 11–17.

Fisher, L. (2005). The nature of law: Universal but not uniform. In A. Jackson, L. Fisher, & D. Dant (Eds.), *Turning Freud upside down: Gospel perspectives on psychotherapy's fundamental problems.* Provo, UT: Brigham Young University Press, 36–50.

Franks, D. D., & Keller, C. (1996). Thoughts on the postmodern rejection of truth. *Michigan Sociological Review, 10*, 32–50.

Freud, S. (1914). On narcissism. *The standard edition of the complete psychological works of Sigmund Freud, volume XIV (1914–1916): On the history of the psycho-analytic movement, papers on metapsychology and other works*, 67–102.

Freud, S. (1917). Mourning and melancholia. *The standard edition of the complete psychological works of Sigmund Freud, volume XIV (1914–1916): On the History of the Psycho-Analytic Movement, Papers on Metapsychology and Other Works*, 237–258.

Goble, F. (1970). *The third force: The psychology of Abraham Maslow.* Chapel Hill, NC: Maurice Bassett Publishing.

Hooper, J. (2012). *What children need to be happy, confident, and successful: Step by step positive psychology to help children flourish.* London: Jessica Kingsley Publishers.

Horton, R. S. (2011). On environmental sources of child narcissism: Are parents really to blame? In C. Barry, P. Kerig, K. Stellwagen, & T. Barry (Eds.), *Narcissism and Machiavellianism in youth: Implications for the development of adaptive and maladaptive behavior.* Washington, DC: APA, 125–143.

Horton, R. S., Bleau, G., & Drwecki, B. (2006). Parenting Narcissus: What are the links between parenting and narcissism? *Journal of Personality, 74*, 345–376.

James, W. (1890). *The principles of psychology.* New York, NY: Henry Holt and Company.

Jelalian, E., & Steele, R. (2008). *Handbook of Childhood and Adolescent Obesity.* New York, NY: Springer Science + Business Media.

Kimball, S. W. (1972). *Faith Precedes the Miracle.* Salt Lake City: Deseret Book.

Kohn, A. (1994). The truth about self-esteem. *Phi Delta Kappan, 76*, 272–283.

Lockhart, B. (1995, June). Our divinely based worth. *Ensign, 25*(6), 50–54.

Maxwell, N. A. (1983, March). Meekness—A dimension of true discipleship. *Ensign, 13*(3), 70–74.

Maxwell, N. A. (1995, November). Swallowed up in the will of the Father. *Ensign, 25*(11), 22–24.

Maxwell, N. A. (1997, April). Enduring well. *Ensign, 27*(4), 6–10.

Miller, J. D., Campbell, W. K., & Pilkonis, P. A. (2007). Narcissistic personality disorder: Relations with distress and functional impairment. *Comprehensive Psychiatry, 48*, 170–177.

Mruk, C. (2006). *Self-esteem research, theory, and practice*. New York, NY: Springer Publishing.

Namka, L. (2005). Selfishness and narcissism in family relationships. Retrieved April 17, 2013, from http://www.angriesout.com/grown17.htm

Ocasio A. (2012). Reality TV by the numbers. Retrieved December 19, 2012, from http://screenrant.com/reality-tv-statistics-infographic-aco-149257/

Papps, B. P., & O'Carroll, R. E. (1998). Extremes of self-esteem and narcissism and the experience and expression of anger and aggression. *Aggressive Behavior, 24*, 421–438.

Parr, B. (2011). Facebook by the numbers. Retrieved December 19, 2012, from http://mashable.com/2011/10/21/facebook-infographic/

Perry, L. T. (2012, November). Becoming goodly parents. *Ensign, 42*(11), 26–28.

Pinsky, D., & Young, S. M. (2009). *The mirror effect: How celebrity narcissism is seducing America*. New York: Harper Collins.

Reber, J. S., & Moody, S. P. (2013). *Are we special? The truth and the lie about God's chosen people*. Salt Lake City: Deseret Book.

Richardson, F. C. (2005). Psychotherapy and modern dilemmas. In B. Slife, J. Reber, & F. Richardson (Eds), *Critical thinking about psychology: Hidden assumptions and plausible alternatives*. Washington, DC: APA Books, 17–38.

Rhodewalt, F., & Morf, C. C. (1995). Self and interpersonal correlates of the narcissistic personality inventory: A review and new findings. *Journal of Research in Personality, 29*, 1–23.

Robbins, L. G. (2011, May). What manner of men and women ought ye to be? *Ensign, 41*(5), 103–105.

Rogers, C. (1961). *On becoming a person: A therapist's view of psychotherapy.* New York: Houghton Mifflin.

Seiter, E. (1995). *Sold separately: Parents & children in consumer culture.* Princeton, NJ: Rutgers University Press.

Seligman, M. (2002). *Authentic happiness: Using the new positive psychology to realize your potential for lasting fulfillment.* New York, NY: The Free Press.

Shaffer, D. (2005). *Social and personality development. (6th Ed.).* Belmont, CA: Wadsworth Publishing.

Slife, B. D., & Richardson, F. C. (2008). Problematic ontological underpinnings of positive psychology: A strong relational alternative. *Theory & Psychology, 18*, 699–723.

Tice, D., & Baumeister, R. (1990). Self-esteem, self-handicapping, and self-presentation: The strategy of inadequate practice, *Journal of Personality, 58*, 443–464.

Trzesniewski, K. H., & Donnellan, M. B. (2010). Rethinking "generation me": A study of cohort effects from 1976–2006. *Perspectives in Psychological Science, 5*, 58–75.

Twenge, J. M., & Campbell, W. K. (2009). *The narcissism epidemic.* New York: Free Press.

Uhls, Y. T., & Greenfield, P. M. (2011). The rise of fame: An historical content analysis. *Cyberpsychology: Journal of Psychosocial Research on Cyberspace, 5*(1), article 1.

Veenhoven, R. (2003). Hedonism and Happiness. *Journal of Happiness Studies, 4*, 437–457.

Vitz, P. C. (1994). *Psychology as religion: The cult of self-worship (2nd Ed.).* Grand Rapids, MI: Wm B. Eerdmans.

Wang, S. (2011). Hedonic and Eudaimonic Happiness. Retrieved April 17, 2013, from http://harmonist.us/2011/03/hedonic-and-eudaimonic-happiness/

Watson, P. J., Little, T., & Biderman, M. D. (1992). Narcissism and parenting styles. *Psychoanalytic Psychology, 9*, 231–244.

Wong, D. B. (1984). *Moral relativity.* Berkeley, CA: University of California Press.

Young, S. M., & Pinsky, D. (2006). Narcissism and celebrity. *Journal of Research in Personality, 40*, 463–471.

11

Emerging Adulthood:
A Time to Prepare for One's "Ministries" in Life

A T the beginning of my doctoral studies at a large school in the eastern United States, I met some fellow students and introductions ensued. From our conversation they discovered that I was 26 years old and seeking a graduate degree while already married and the father of two children. With disbelief and a hint of disdain that I was already married and a father, one of my peers blurted out, "You are a fool!" I have told that story several times in professional settings, and people are usually in complete agreement that I was not a typical 26-year-old in the United States.

In the present Western culture, most young people between the ages of 18 and 27 do not get married, have children, or settle into a career. In fact, in the United States, the average age of marriage has reached an all-time high—28 for males and 26 for females (US Census Bureau, 2010). As a result of these demographic changes, the late teens to mid-to-late twenties is a time period focused on the individual and is characterized as the time to explore possible life directions in areas such as education, work, relationships, and worldviews (Arnett, 2000). Given society's view of what is "normal" today, it is understandable that many Latter-day Saint young people feel a great deal of opposition as they make their way into adulthood.

The late teens to mid-to-late twenties is a time period focused on the individual and is characterized as the time to explore possible life directions in areas such as education, work, relationships, and worldviews. © Rido.

It is also easy to see why parents feel an increase in pressure to assist their children in successfully navigating the pitfalls of this age period. So what can young people (and parents alike, see chapter 12) do during this time of intense change and challenge? The purpose of this chapter is to help young people have a proper perspective of what this period of their lives is about and how best to use this time to prepare for future adult roles, including, but not limited to, marriage.

Emerging Adulthood

As noted, the years between 18 and 27 look very different today compared to this period of development in past decades in Western cultures such as the United States. Indeed, one of the most unique aspects of this developmental period is the ambivalence that young people have about their status as adults. Numerous studies have shown that few young people this age consider themselves to be adults yet (Arnett, 1998; Nelson & Barry, 2005; Nelson et al., 2007). Parents tend to concur with this assessment of not-yet adulthood (Nelson et al., 2007). Given these perceptions, the term "emerging adulthood" has been coined (Arnett, 2000) to capture this in-between status of no longer being an adolescent but not yet feeling completely like an adult.

In studying the unique features of this period of life, researchers (Arnett, 2004) have characterized emerging adulthood as including five important features. First, it is an *age of feeling in-between*, as most emerging adults do not see themselves as either an adolescent or an adult. Second, emerging adulthood is an *age of possibilities*, as most young people are extremely optimistic and have high hopes for the future. Third, this period of development is an *age of instability* because it tends to be marked by instability in work, relationships, education, and residential status. Next, emerging adulthood is characterized as an *age of identity exploration* because many emerging adults are free to explore identities in the areas of education, work, love, and worldviews. Finally, emerging adulthood is a *self-focused age of life*. This is not meant to suggest that emerging adults are necessarily self-centered; rather, they are free from social obligations and other responsibilities that allow for a productive focus on the self.

As part of the exploration, instability, experimentation, and self-focus that are typical for this age period, a number of trends, many of them disturbing, are now prevalent during emerging adulthood. More and more young people are engaging in premarital intercourse (see Regnerus & Uecker, 2011), and cohabitation is preceding more than half of all marriages in the United States (Whitehead & Popenoe, 2001). It is taking longer for emerging adults to finish their education (Arnett, 2000). Emerging adulthood is the peak period for risk behaviors such as binge drinking, experimenting with drugs, and unprotected sex (Arnett, 2000). For example, in a report on drinking patterns, college-age males were overrepresented in the groups high in alcohol usages (Schulenberg & Maggs, 2001). Another trend seen in emerging adulthood is that dating in the more traditional sense has been replaced by "hanging out and hooking up" (for instance, hanging out with a group and then pairing off for uncommitted sexual relationships). One study reported that "only 50% of college women seniors reported having been asked on six or more dates by men since coming to college, and a third of women surveyed said they had been asked on two dates or fewer" (Glenn & Marquardt, 2001, p. 5). Finally, many emerging adults hold pessimistic views about marriage (Bachman, Johnston, & O'Malley, 2009). A negative view of marriage and a desire to postpone it until the late twenties or even thirties has been found to be linked with numerous harmful behaviors during emerging adulthood (for example, see Carroll, Willoughby, Badger, Nelson, Barry, & Madsen, 2007).

Taken together, the negative attitude towards marriage and family and the harmful behaviors that young people tend to engage in during this period of life might best be summarized as an approach of "eat, drink, and be merry, for tomorrow you will marry." These attitudes and behaviors make up the society in which Latter-day Saint emerging adults are living, working, attending school, and, in general, trying to make correct choices. It is not easy for them to stay on gospel paths as they transition into adult roles, but it is possible and important that they do so.

Implications for Latter-day Saint Emerging Adults

Understanding the period of emerging adulthood is important in order to better grasp the context in which young Latter-day Saints are making the transition to adulthood, and thereby assist them. They are receiving very conflicting messages from their religious community versus the larger society in which they live. From the media, peers, and other sources, they hear the message that marriage should be the furthest thing from their minds and that they should behave as though they are only young once and therefore should engage in as many "now-or-never" behaviors as possible (Ravert, 2009). Ravert examined the behaviors young people engaged in because they thought they would not be able to do them later in life after they had settled down as adults.

The most common theme that emerged was travel/adventure, followed by social events, alcohol/tobacco/drug use, relationships (for example, multiple sexual experiences), carefree lifestyle (such as being lazy, enjoying not having a real job), sports/action, academic/career (being able to change schools or change jobs), and independence/personal expression (2009).

Again, these findings highlight the message of the culture that surrounds young Latter-day Saints today. Unfortunately, some of these cultural values and behaviors are affecting too many Latter-day Saints, causing them to stray from gospel paths. As adolescents and emerging adults, a percentage of Latter-day Saint young people have participated in acts of delinquency (for example, offenses against people or property), cheating in school, risk behaviors (such as alcohol and drug use), and pornography use (Chadwick, Top, & McClendon, 2010; Nelson Padilla-Walker, & Carroll, 2010). In sum, although doing better as a group than their non–Latter-day Saint peers, Latter-day Saint emerging adults are not immune from the larger culture's views of what this time period should be about.

Unfortunately, not all of the challenges facing Latter-day Saint emerging adults come solely from outside influences. Many young people receive negative messages and pressure from within the Latter-day Saint community. Well-intentioned but misguided pressure from members of a ward or community may lead many emerging adults to feel uncomfortable or become casual in attending church. For example, my female students tell me story after story of returning home after a semester at Brigham Young University and attending church with their families only to be peppered with questions, jokes, and comments related to their empty ring finger or slothfulness in getting engaged. Again, much of this occurs in the context of good-natured kidding, but far too often it leads to discomfort, sadness, and self-doubt within the emerging adults. Another result is a broader level of misunderstanding among the Latter-day Saint culture of just what the focus of this time period should be. Therefore, a good starting point for the healthy transition into adult roles is for young people (as well as parents and leaders) to understand the purpose of this age period.

Preparing for Our Ministries

Many within our religious community are often given the false impression that the *only* purpose of emerging adulthood is to marry and start a family. If this is the case, then every day that young people wake up unmarried, they will feel a sense of failure. Furthermore, not everybody will marry in their twenties, if at all during this life. Parents and young people should see this time as a time to *prepare* for marriage (and other important "ministries" that I will discuss later). Then, whether individuals marry at age 20, 25, 30, or later, they can still feel assured that their actions are preparing them to choose a spouse. We all need to remember that there is no set age by which one *must* be married. Rather, President Gordon B. Hinckley (1999) counseled to "marry the right person in the right place at the right time" (p. 2).

In taking the approach that emerging adulthood is a time to prepare to marry rather than a time to marry, I do not wish to diminish the importance of marriage in any way. President Hinckley (1997) declared, "The most important decision of life is the decision concerning your companion" and Elder M. Russell Ballard (2012) recently admonished young people to "pay careful attention to finding your eternal companion," (p. 100). Young people should not unduly delay marrying, as it is indeed the most important undertaking of one's life (see Monson, 2011; Oaks, 2011; and Scott, 2011; these talks are from the April 2011 general conference that specifically admonishes young men to not delay marriage). My purpose in taking the approach that emerging adulthood is a time to prepare to marry is meant to help young people be better prepared for making and keeping the marriage covenant. Furthermore, it is meant to help young people be prepared for the demands of all aspects of adulthood, especially for those who through no fault of their own find themselves not married. In sum, this approach is not meant to devalue the importance of eternal marriage but to acknowledge its sacredness by the preparations we make for it in our lives leading up to it.

With the perspective that emerging adulthood is a time to prepare to marry as opposed to a time that they *must* marry, young people can view every day as an opportunity to prepare for future roles including, but not limited to, that of spouse. We know very little about the Savior's emerging adult years except that he "increased in wisdom and stature, and in favour with God and man" (Luke 2:52). During emerging adulthood, young people should emulate the Savior and focus on these four areas of their lives (wisdom, stature, favor with other people, and favor with God).

Wisdom

First, emerging adults should make strides to grow in wisdom. They should read from the "best books words of wisdom" and "seek learning, even by study and also by faith" (D&C 88:118). They should pursue as much education as possible. In a general Young Women meeting, Mary N. Cook (2012) quoted President Hinckley and his charge to the youth of the Church regarding the pursuit of knowledge:

> The pattern of study you establish during your formal schooling will in large measure affect your lifelong thirst for knowledge. . . . You must get all of the education that you possibly can. . . . Sacrifice anything that is needed to be sacrificed to qualify yourselves to do the work of [this] world. . . . Train your minds and hands to become an influence for good as you go forward with your lives. (p. 120)

Lest some think this counsel applies only to young men, President Hinckley (2001) has given the following counsel specifically to young women:

> Find purpose in your life. Choose the things you would like to do, and educate yourselves to be effective in their pursuit. For most it is very difficult to settle on a vocation. You are hopeful that you will marry and that all will be taken care of. In this day and time, a girl needs an education. She needs the means and skills by which to

Emerging adults should pursue as much education as possible. Mark A. Philbrick, © BYU Photo.

earn a living should she find herself in a situation where it becomes necessary to do so. (p. 95)

Both of these quotes speak to men and women about the necessity of getting the best education possible and developing the skills needed to earn a living. Emerging adulthood is the critical time to acquire the skills that are necessary to become financially self-reliant. Research shows the economic challenges facing young people today. For example, in 1969, 23.1% of 25-year-old men earned less than those in poverty. However, in 2004, it took until age 30 for there to be "only" 23.2% of the age group below the poverty line (Danziger & Rouse, 2007). In other words, this research shows that it is taking longer for young people, young men in particular, to earn enough money to support a family. In order to demonstrate the role that obtaining an education can have in preparing individuals to earn an income, the following table displays the average income for men and women, respectively, ages 25–34 with varying levels of education.

Table 1. Average Earnings in Dollars of Year-Round, Full-Time Workers Ages 25 to 34 Years by Educational Attainment, 2009.

	Males	Females
Less than 9th grade	$25,067	$18,278
9th to 12th grade (no diploma)	27,074	21,996
High school graduate	38,037	27,993
Some college, no degree	44,020	32,229
Associate's degree	48,313	36,202
Bachelor's degree or more	67,555	52,102

Source: US Census Bureau. (2010, September). Income, poverty and health insurance coverage in the United States: 2009, Current population reports *(Series P60-238, and Detailed Tables—Table PINC-04). Retrieved from http://www.census.gov/ compendia/statab/2012/tables/12s0703.pdf*

In sum, the evidence suggests that the requisite skills to earn a sufficient income comes from education received during emerging adulthood (for instance, college education, vocational training) rather than during adolescence (that is, high school). Hence, emerging adults may leave themselves unprepared for ministries (for example, providing for a family, having a career) if they choose to postpone, or avoid altogether, the pursuit of knowledge (strictly speaking, education) during emerging adulthood. Although I have focused on the importance of getting a college education, there are certainly other ways to acquire forms of knowledge that will enable one to become financially capable of caring for a family, including vocational schools, apprenticeships, and job-training programs. Regardless of the pathway one takes, the emphasis needs to be on acquiring knowledge and skills during emerging adulthood that will equip the person for long-term stability (not just short-term income) within his or her adult roles.

A final note is needed on the importance of following our Savior's example of growing in wisdom. Although acquiring an education plays a central role in the preparation to earn a living, the blessings that accompany the acquisition of knowledge extend well beyond the ability to make money. For example, attending college has been linked to a number of other positive outcomes including better critical thinking skills, greater participation in political and community activities, a more positive self-image, and greater interpersonal and intellectual competence (Pascarella & Terenzini, 2005; Rabow, Choi, & Purdy, 1998). In other words, an education can broaden ideas, insights, and abilities to relate to others and make important decisions. An education will help one think more clearly and make wise choices. Emerging adults who seek knowledge will have more tools at their disposal for problems that arise in their lives, including problems in their marriages and among their families.

Caring for Bodies

Second, just as the Savior "increased in . . . stature," emerging adults should give attention to their physical bodies. This does not simply mean to "grow up" physically. Rather, we are taught to care for our bodies in order to provide our spirits with a proper mortal dwelling. As noted previously, heavy drinking, alcohol-related problems, drug use, and risky sexual behaviors (such as number of sexual partners, low or improper use of condoms) often reach some of the highest levels during emerging adulthood (for examples, see Bachman, Johnston, O'Malley, & Schulenberg, 1996; Lefkowitz & Gillen, 2006; Schulenberg & Maggs, 2001). All of these behaviors are spiritually damaging, but they also pose serious threats to the health of the physical body. Therefore, the law of chastity and the Word of Wisdom are particularly important anchors for Latter-day Saint young people in maintaining both spiritual and physical well-being.

Drugs, alcohol, and premarital sex are not the only common issues during emerging adulthood that go against the charge to care for our bodies. Among those ages 18 to 25, approximately 36% of individuals have a tattoo and 30% have pierced their bodies in a place other than their ear lobe (Pew Research Center, 2007). Although an exact prevalence rate is difficult to pin down because of its private nature, estimates of adolescents and emerging adults who engage in self-harm (for instance, intentional harm to one's body without suicidal intent such as cutting, burning, or self-bruising) range from 4% to 38% (Briere & Gil, 1998; Favazza, 1996; Gratz, Conrad, & Roemer, 2002; Muehlenkamp & Guiterrez, 2004). It has been found that an alarming 25% of college-attending women engage in binging and purging (throwing up or using laxatives) as a weight-management strategy (The Renfrew Center Foundation for Eating Disorders, 2013). In sum, emerging adulthood is a time during which the health of and respect for the physical body is under attack.

Fortunately, the majority of Latter-day Saints are able to avoid the more obvious and serious threats to physical well-being. Our own data, drawn from a sample of active Latter-day Saint college students, shows that fewer than 5% engage in drug use, drinking, smoking, or self-harm, respectively (Nelson, 2012). Again, the sample from which these numbers are drawn does not capture the full range of Latter-day Saint young people. The numbers also are not meant to suggest it is always easy for young people to avoid these temptations or to downplay the challenges faced by those who may be struggling with addictions, eating disorders, or other challenges mentioned previously. However, the numbers do suggest that the challenges facing young people in regard to caring for their physical bodies may come in more subtle forms as they strive to prepare for future adult roles.

When I ask students in my classes about the challenges they face in regard to caring for their bodies, there are always some that squirm uncomfortably in their chairs and express a look of understanding on their faces as they begin to respond. One of their first answers is always about controlling their schedules and choices in order to get enough sleep. They talk about relying on substances such as energy drinks that are not expressly forbidden by the Word of Wisdom but are not particularly good for the body either. Indeed, our own data shows that approximately 20% of young men and nearly 10% of young women use energy drinks at least once a month. My students admit that often the use of these substances is to compensate for their poor choices regarding sleep. Students also

Students face many challenges in regards to taking care of their bodies. One of the most common challenges is controlling their schedules and choices in order to get enough sleep. © Nyul.

describe the challenges of eating a healthy diet, finding time to exercise, and managing stress. Thus emerging adulthood is certainly a time for young people to begin to form habits that will help them develop and maintain the health and vigor needed to fulfill the physically demanding requirements of adult roles (for example, running a household, caring for children, earning a living).

Finally, young people, especially women, should be cautious about the numerous terrible messages they get about their bodies. Many individuals believe that physical beauty is of utmost importance in life. This may be why over 51% of Latter-day Saint young women in our study admitted to avoiding food once a month to several times a month in order to lose weight (Nelson, 2012). As taught in the scriptures, we all need to come to know that the most important aspect about us is not our external qualities but rather our internal characteristics (see 1 Samuel 16:7). Emotional suffering can afflict individuals who place too much emphasis on physical appearance. Elder Jeffrey R. Holland (2005) cautioned:

> I plead with you young women to please be more accepting of yourselves, including your body shape and style, with a little less longing to look like someone else. We are all different. Some are tall, and some are short. Some are round, and some are thin. And almost everyone at some time or other wants to be something they are not! But as one adviser to teenage girls said: "You can't live your life worrying that the world is staring at you. When you let people's opinions make you self-conscious you give away your power. . . . The key to feeling [confident] is to always listen to your inner self— [the real you]." (p. 29)

It is a common practice in today's fashion industry to take pictures of models and improve them via computer technology. As a result, the finished product that we see on magazine covers is not a real person. The model who had his or her photograph taken does not in reality look like the image on the magazine. Satan has successfully made it so that many people strive for beauty that cannot be attained and, therefore, has caused individuals to feel poorly about themselves. Instead of reaching for such unattainable goals, young people should see that beauty comes from working on having a beautiful interior or heart, because that is attainable and can be seen in one's countenance. In summary, emerging adulthood is a time during which there is quite an extensive attack on the physical body. Learning to care for the physical body that we have each been given is an important stewardship. The body will be essential in fulfilling one's ministry as spouse, parent, provider, protector, and in other adult roles and responsibilities. Therefore, emerging adults should set goals to care for their bodies through healthy diet and exercise, sensible sleep schedules, modest dress, and avoidance of things that would harm or otherwise desecrate their bodies in any way.

Emerging adults should cultivate the invaluable abilities to communicate, listen, empathize, understand the perspectives of others, control their tempers, and think how their actions will affect themselves and others. © Intellectual Reserve, Inc.

Social Competence

Third, just as the Savior grew in "favour with . . . man" (Luke 2:52), emerging adults should work on their social skills and relationships with other people. They should cultivate the invaluable abilities to communicate, listen, empathize, understand the perspectives of others, control their tempers, and think how their actions will affect themselves and others. These abilities will help them interact with others and will better prepare them for marriage. If emerging adults use this time in their lives to work on these attributes, they will be well on their way to becoming prepared for future roles especially that of spouse.

The big question is how can individuals develop these interpersonal skills? They must be practiced. However, in an era in which face-to-face interactions have been replaced with social networking technology (for example, through phones and computers), and one-on-one dating has gone the way of simply hanging out (Glenn & Marquardt, 2001), there are fewer contexts where young people can practice and develop the skills needed for the formation and maintenance of successful relationships.

So again the question may be asked, how and where should young people learn these skills? Certainly an initial and important response is "on a mission." While there is no doubt that a mission helps in developing social competence, even a mission does not provide all of the skills necessary to succeed in marriage. Learning to communicate with a companion of the same sex, although important in the overall learning-to-communicate process, is not the same as communicating with a member of the opposite sex. Therefore, young people need to be proactive in placing themselves in one-on-one settings with members of the opposite sex as a way of developing and practicing the skills that will prepare them for marriage. Dating is the ideal setting for the acquisition and honing of these skills. Young people should actively date as a way to find out their strengths and weaknesses (to improve upon them) and the type of person with whom they want to make temple covenants.

It is important to reiterate how careful we need to be regarding the accuracy of the message we convey to young people. When adult members of the Church tell emerging adults they need to date in order to marry, many young people who do not yet feel ready to marry (for example, they do not yet feel they have the communication skills and other skills needed to be successful in marriage) may think they need to stop dating until they are ready to marry. In doing so, they stop doing the very thing that will help them prepare. This is why it is so important to understand that dating to marry is just *one* of many reasons to date. When we see emerging adulthood as a time to prepare for marriage, dating will be viewed by many Latter-day Saint emerging adults as much less ominous.

By dating, emerging adults can begin to prepare for marriage in a number of ways. First, dating provides young people the opportunity to observe in their dates the skills and abilities (or lack thereof) they may wish to either

Dating is the ideal setting for acquiring and practicing communication and other skills needed in marriage. Christina Smith, © Intellectual Reserve, Inc.

incorporate into their own social interactions (such as, listening, empathy, eye contact, verbal give-and-take, humor, the ability to generate new topics of conversation) or *eliminate* from their own behaviors (for example, talking only about oneself, excessive sarcasm). In other words, the process of dating will help make emerging adults aware of the areas in which they need to practice on subsequent dates.

Indeed, a second important purpose of dating is to provide individuals the opportunity to practice communication and other important relationship skills. Researchers have pointed at communication as being an important determinant in relationship satisfaction (see Meeks, Hendrick, S., & Hendrick, C., 1998; Troy, 2000). Specifically, they have pointed out the importance of aspects of communication such as engaging in eye contact, listening, allowing one's partner to talk, asking questions, expressing empathy, and, self-disclosing information as appropriate (for examples, see Davis & Oathout, 1987; Prager, 2000; Sprecher & Hendrick, S., 2004).

Therefore, dating provides a setting in which young people can develop and improve skills that they will need, most importantly, in their roles as spouses and parents, but also in the work place, callings within their wards and stakes, and roles within their communities.

Finally, dating helps young people learn to commit. By going on dates, young people practice committing to another individual by giving the individual their full attention. Some things that people can do to show their focused attention (i.e., commitment) would include being devoted to that person's interests, needs, and welfare over their own and would exclude personal distractions, such as their phones.

President Hinckley (1995) stated: "When you are married, be fiercely loyal one to another. Selfishness is the great destroyer of happy family life. If you will make your first concern the comfort, the well-being, and the happiness of your companion, sublimating any personal concern to that loftier goal, you will be happy, and your marriage will go on throughout eternity" (p. 67). Although this statement pertains specifically to marriage, dating provides the opportunity to practice placing the comfort, well-being, and happiness of another person above one's own for a couple of hours so that he or she is better prepared to do so within the covenant relationship of marriage.

In sum, a date with a particular person may not lead to marriage or even another date with that person, but that is not the only purpose of the date. It is important to understand that dating serves multiple important purposes for emerging adults, including helping them build important social skills and practice the ability to commit that will help them better prepare themselves to be able to "marry the right person at the right time in the right place." There are certainly other ways in which young people can and should develop communication and other relationship skills, including reading books on the topic, taking college and institute classes that focus on relationship skills, and observing others who possess good interpersonal skills. Even hanging out can serve an important function in this regard. However, none of these practices can replace dating. The process of dating provides the one-on-one setting

Dating serves multiple important purposes for emerging adults, including helping them build important social skills and practice the ability to commit that will help them better prepare themselves to be able to "marry the right person at the right time in the right place." Welden Andersen, © Intellectual Reserve, Inc.

with a member of the opposite sex that will best identify the skills and attributes (such as kindness, communication skills, selflessness) needed to succeed in a relationship, allow them to practice those skills, and help them learn to commit. In addition to these important functions served by dating, young people need to be dating because it provides the context in which they can, most importantly, find a spouse.

Spiritual Growth

Finally, emerging adults can follow the example of the Savior in preparing for their ministries by striving to grow spiritually (see Luke 2:52). They should use this time to strengthen their testimonies and their relationships with the Savior. They should make it a habit to study the scriptures, pray daily, attend their church meetings, pay full tithes, and, if possible, visit the temple. If developed early, these habits will carry over into their marriages and be a blessing to them throughout their lives.

Another essential part of spiritual development is service to others. This age should not be a time completely devoted to oneself. Individualism (that is, a focus solely on oneself) is a major theme in most Western societies today. This is especially so for many 18- to 27-year-olds who often feel it is a time to enjoy life before they have to settle down to the responsibilities that come with a family and career (Ravert, 2009). Hence, they tend to do whatever pleases them. Indeed, narcissism (or selfishness) is seen to be particularly high among today's emerging adults (Twenge, 2006).

Our young people cannot fall into that trap. I once learned a powerful lesson about passing up opportunities to serve. While climbing aboard a train in Romania in preparation for a three-hour train ride, I found myself without a seat and packed in the small entryway with numerous others in my unfortunate situation. While figuring out what to do for the long journey without a seat, I was approached by a small child begging for food and money. Romanian trains were at that time notorious for beggars going from compartment to compartment. I gave her a few pieces of candy, and she continued on her way. In an attempt to find a place to get out of the crowd and sit for the long ride, I crawled into a small luggage compartment.

Later, while I was trying to find a comfortable position in my cramped space and was complaining to myself about my predicament, the small child returned. I am sure she had canvassed the entire train and returned to me because she perceived that I had more to give. She seated herself in front of me and proceeded to plead with me for more. I was so full of self-pity and was so focused on my own predicament (which was not really that bad) that I was more concerned about my own comfort than this small girl's needs. I thought that if I gave her food or money, I would soon be surrounded by other beggars, and, with nowhere to hide, I would be "bothered" for the rest of my ride. Therefore, I decided to wait until my stop and *then* I would give her some food, money, clothing, and a blanket that I had for just such an occasion. However, a few stops before my own, the train came to a halt and there was a rush of people towards the exit. When the din settled, I saw that the girl was no longer there. She had given up waiting on me. She had left the train and returned to the extreme cold of that Romanian winter day without the food, clothing, and money that she so desperately needed and that I so selfishly had kept because I did not want to be bothered. I was so concerned about myself that I missed the opportunity to give to somebody in need. I pictured her small, coatless, hungry body out in the cold and will never forget how terrible I felt. The words of the Savior concerning those who are hungry, thirsty, and naked echoed in my head, "Inasmuch as ye have done it unto one of the least of these my brethren, ye have done it unto me" (Matthew 25:40).

Just as I was focused solely on myself in this situation, this time of emerging adulthood, when young people have so few responsibilities to and for others (for example, spouse, employer, children), can lead some young people to focus almost exclusively on themselves. Our young people should not be so focused on their own comfort during emerging adulthood that they pass up opportunities to serve. They need to accept callings and magnify them, be faithful visiting teachers and home teachers, and share their time and talents with others. Because of the growth that sacrifice brings, I

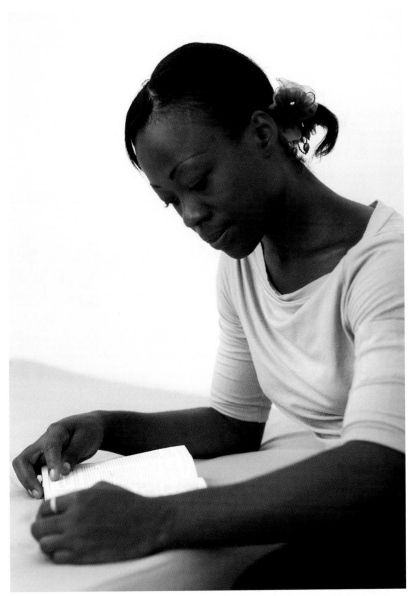

Emerging adults can follow the example of the Savior in preparing for their ministries by striving to grow spiritually (see Luke 2:52). They should use this time to strengthen their testimonies and their relationships with the Savior. Matt Reier, © Intellectual Reserve, Inc.

encourage young people to consider tithing their time in addition to their income. In other words, I challenge young people to give a "tithe" of their time (not literally 10% of one's day but whatever amount weekly or monthly that would reflect a true sacrifice in the service of others) in volunteering to work with children, the homeless, the elderly, or even their roommates, family, and friends. Regardless of how or where the service is given, young people will enjoy the spiritual growth that comes through caring for our Heavenly Father's children, and doing this will prepare them for a life of service to spouse and children.

Prepared For Your Ministry

In emulating the Savior in each of these areas, young people can follow the Lord's example and use this time to improve themselves physically, mentally, socially, and spiritually. These improvements will not only bless their own lives but it will prepare them for their "ministry" as a spouse and parent. Because of the significance of marriage, I have directed my words mainly towards preparing for one's ministry as spouse (i.e., preparation for marriage). However, there is certainly a much broader application to this principle. Indeed, in growing in wisdom, stature, and favor with God and men (see Luke 2:52), the Lord prepared himself for his mortal ministry. Young people, too, can prepare for their own ministries here in mortality, which may include being a spouse and parent, serving in callings in the Church, pursuing and maintaining careers, and providing community service. Again, while the most important ministries one will ever serve in will be as a wife and mother or as a husband and father, they are not the only ministries young people may find themselves in throughout their lives. Attempting to "become the right person" in the areas outlined previously will certainly prepare individuals for a family ministry, but improvement in these areas will likewise help them become prepared for other ministries along the way. The same skills of seeking an education, taking care of one's body, improving one's social skills, and growing spiritually

During emerging adulthood, young men have many opportunities to serve and grow in the form of missions, priesthood responsibilities and quorums, and temple ordinances. Matt Reier, © Intellectual Reserve, Inc.

will prepare one for success in the workplace, service in the Church, and being a contributing member of the community.

A Word to Young Men

Latter-day Saint young men have a great deal of structure provided for them during emerging adulthood. They have many opportunities to serve and grow in the form of missions, priesthood responsibilities and quorums, and temple ordinances. One challenge facing our young men today is the tendency to avoid utilizing this structure to their advantage. Instead, a focus on pleasurable leisure pursuits fills up too much time during the average day of many young men. In a recent study of non–Latter-day Saint emerging adults (Nelson & Padilla-Walker, 2012), my colleague and I attempted to examine the characteristics of emerging adults who are flourishing and who are floundering. We identified three types of young people—one group that was flourishing and two types who were floundering. The criteria that distinguished the first floundering group (we labeled this group the "externalizing group") were high levels of alcohol, drug, pornography, and video game use, as well as a high number of sexual partners. It was not engaging in just one of these behaviors that marked them as floundering but rather a pattern of behavior that included high activity of all of these behaviors. In other words, they were focused on selfish, hedonistic, and leisurely behaviors.

What is so noticeable about this finding is that men made up 83% of this floundering group. Furthermore, men made up 77% of the other floundering group as well. This second group (labeled "poorly-adjusted group") consisted of individuals who, like the externalizing group, scored high on alcohol and drug use and number of sexual partners, but they also all scored high on depression and anxiety and low on self-esteem. Combined, of all of the men in the sample, 70% of them fell into one of the two floundering groups. Only 30% fell into the flourishing group (the group identified by their strong, internalized values related to kindness, honesty, and fairness, as well as low levels of anxiety and depression, low levels of alcohol, drug, video game, and pornography use, low numbers of sexual partners, and often, increased religiosity and self-esteem). In comparison, 80% of the college-age women in our study were classified as flourishing.

Although this study focused on non–Latter-day Saint emerging adults, the concern is that it might reflect all too well what might be occurring among some Latter-day Saint males as well. In our own samples of Latter-day Saint emerging adults, the amount of time spent playing video games is alarmingly high for a certain portion of young men. Specifically, 27% of young men report playing video games several days a week while 5% report playing daily and totaling anywhere from 10 to 24 hours a week (Nelson, 2012). Likewise, there are a number of Latter-day Saint young men who view pornography, with 35% reporting that they have viewed pornography during the past year (Nelson, Padilla-Walker, & Carroll, 2010). Although participation in hedonistic behaviors such as pornography is certainly wrong, it is not necessarily problematic to participate in some other forms of leisure activities (such as video games); it is the amount of time spent engaged in these activities that poses a threat to young men. It is this concern that Elder Ian S. Ardern (2011), a member of the Seventy, addressed in general conference: "I know our greatest happiness comes as we tune in to the Lord and to those things which bring a lasting reward, rather than mindlessly tuning in to countless hours of status updates, Internet farming, and catapulting angry birds at concrete walls. I urge each of us to take those things which rob us of precious time and determine to be their master, rather than allowing them through their addictive nature to be the master of us" (p. 32). Again, it is not the participation in some of these behaviors that is the problem. It is the amount of time that many young men spend engaged in leisure activities that is problematic. Obviously, behaviors that break the Word of Wisdom or the law of chastity need to be avoided at all costs, but engaging in other recreational pursuits that detract from preparation for adult roles should be done in moderation. Young men need to be cautious and use their time in a way that will fully prepare them for their ministry as husband, father, provider, and protector.

A Word to Young Women

In writing a few words directed specifically to young women, I would like to share the profound experience I had while writing this section of the chapter. I had finished writing what I thought would be the final version of this chapter (including the following paragraph) but felt that I ought to wait before submitting it to the editors of the book. Please read what I had written at that time and then I will continue with the experience.

Although there are similar issues faced by both men and women during emerging adulthood, there are some challenges that tend to be more gender specific. For young women, impediments to a successful transition to adulthood and preparation for marriage come in the form of lack of structure. Men have numerous developmental opportunities provided for them throughout adolescence (for instance, the duties and responsibilities of the Aaronic Priesthood) and into emerging adulthood. These opportunities for growth include missions at the beginning of emerging adulthood, the responsibilities and duties that come with receiving the Melchizedek Priesthood, and temple ordinances. For women, most of these growth-promoting forms of structure do not occur until marriage or age 21 (at which time they might choose to serve a mission). As a result, it is necessary that young women create opportunities for growth rather than succumbing to idleness during this period of their lives.

As I stated previously, I decided to wait before submitting to the editors of this book the version of this chapter that included the previous paragraph. It was just a few days later that President Thomas S. Monson declared the historic change in the age at which young women can serve missions. As a teacher of classes comprising mainly young women and as one whose research focuses on this period of life (and now as a father of a nineteen-year-old daughter), I have been so concerned about the young women of the Church for a very long time. Therefore, I cried tears of joy as I listened to a prophet of God make an announcement that blesses the lives of Latter-day Saint young women. It came as a further witness to me that he is a prophet of the Lord who receives revelation for our time. Given the challenges facing emerging adults in today's society in general, and Latter-day Saint young women in particular, it was an incredible experience to behold a prophet make a change that directly addresses what many young women today need at this time in their lives.

Because serving a mission is a priesthood responsibility for young men and an opportunity for young women, it is important to note that a mission

During emerging adulthood, it is necessary for young women to create opportunitites for growth—actively preparing themselves for whatever ministry they will enter rather than succumbing to idleness. Matt Reier, © Intellectual Reserve, Inc.

will not be right for all young women. Therefore, I still think it is important to reiterate that it is necessary for young women to create opportunities for growth (whether that be a mission, education, service experience, and so on) rather than succumbing to idleness. It is important that young women are actively engaged in the process of preparing themselves for *whatever* ministry they will enter. Too many young women have been letting valuable time for preparation lapse as they have passively waited for their ministry of wife and mother to begin. Elder Dallin H. Oaks (2006) directed the following to young single women, "If you are just marking time waiting for a marriage prospect, stop waiting. You may never have the opportunity for a suitable marriage in this life, so stop waiting and start moving. Prepare yourself for life—even a single life—by education, experience, and planning" (p. 14). By following this wise counsel, young women can prepare themselves (that is, in knowledge, physically, socially, and spiritually) for a lifetime of service, whether it be in a family, a career, their wards and stakes, or their communities. By ignoring this counsel and focusing too narrowly on a ministry (for instance, marriage) that might not come as soon as some might desire, they may, while just waiting, miss out on growth-promoting opportunities (such as education, missions, service opportunities, career training), and thereby may find themselves not only unprepared for marriage but unqualified for whatever ministry in which they may find themselves. A broad view of preparing for one's ministry will help young women be better prepared for whatever they will do, including, but not exclusive to, life as wife and mother.

Conclusion

I mentioned previously that my research has focused on identifying the characteristics of young people who flourish in emerging adulthood. We found that the criteria that distinguished those who were flourishing were that they tended to have a positive sense of self-worth; less alcohol and drug use; low levels of pornography and video game use; strong internalized values related to kindness, honesty, and fairness; and, for many, greater religiosity. Again, this was not a Latter-day Saint sample and yet the results reflect characteristics, behaviors, and relationships that capture the type of life that Latter-day Saint emerging adults need to be striving for in their efforts to prepare for marriage and other ministries. The characteristics of happy, flourishing young people include adhering to commandments such as the Word of Wisdom and law of chastity, using their time well, developing traits that will lead to stronger relationships with others (for example, kindness, honesty), and engaging

344

in spiritually strengthening activities (such as prayer, worship, service). As emerging adults follow the example of the Savior in preparing their minds, bodies, social skills, and spirits for their future ministries, they will, in the process, become the right person and, indeed, be better prepared for marriage.

References

Ardern, I. S. (2011, November). A time to prepare. *Ensign, 41*(11), 32.

Arnett, J. J. (1998). Learning to stand alone: The contemporary American transition to adulthood in cultural and historical context. *Human Development, 41*(5/6), 295–315.

Arnett, J. J. (2000). Emerging adulthood: A theory of development from the late teens through the twenties. *American Psychologist, 55*(5), 469–480.

Arnett, J. J. (2004). *Emerging adulthood: The winding road from the late teens through the twenties.* New York: Oxford University Press.

Bachman, J. G., Johnston, L. D., & O'Malley, P. M. (2009). *Monitoring the future: Questionnaire responses from the nation's high school seniors, 2008.* Ann Arbor, MI: Institute for Social Research.

Bachman, J. G., Johnston, L. D., O'Malley, P. M., & Schulenberg, J. (1996). Transitions in drug use during late adolescence and young adulthood. In J. A. Graber, J. Brooks-Gunn, & A. C. Petersen (Eds.), *Transitions through adolescence: Interpersonal domains and context* (pp. 111–140). Mahway, NJ: Erlbaum.

Ballard, M. R. (2012, May). That the lost may be found. *Ensign, 42*(5), 97–100.

Briere, J., & Gil, E. (1998). Self-mutilation in clinical and general population samples: Prevalence, correlates, and functions. *American Journal of Orthopsychiatry, 68*(4), 609–620.

Carroll, J. S., Willoughby, B., Badger, S., Nelson, L. J., Barry, C. M., & Madsen, S. D. (2007). So close, yet so far away: The impact of varying marital horizons on emerging adulthood. *Journal of Adolescent Research, 22*(3), 219–247.

Chadwick, B. A., Top, B. L., & McClendon, R. J. (2010). *Shield of faith: The power of religion in the lives of LDS youth and young adults.* Provo, Utah: BYU Religious Studies Center.

Cook, M. N. (2012, May). Seek learning: You have work to do. *Ensign 42*(5), 120.

Danziger, S., & Rouse, C. E. (2007). Introduction. In Sheldon Danziger & Cecilia E. Rouse (Eds.), *The price of independence: The economics of early adulthood* (1–24). New York: Russell Sage Foundation.

Davis, M. H., & Oathout, H. A. (1987). Maintenance of satisfaction in romantic relationships: Empathy and relational competence. *Journal of Personality and Social Psychology, 53*(2), 397–410.

Favazza, A. R. (1996). *Bodies under siege: Self-mutilation and body modification in culture and psychiatry* (2nd ed.). Baltimore, MD: Johns Hopkins University Press.

Glenn, N., & Marquardt, E. (2001). *Hooking up, hanging out, and hoping for Mr. Right: College women on dating and mating today.* New York: Institute for American Values.

Gratz, K. L., Conrad, S. D., & Roemer, L. (2002). Risk factors for deliberate self-harm among college students. *American Journal of Orthopsychiatry, 72*(1), 128–140.

Hinckley, G. B. (1995, December). Excerpts from recent addresses of President Gordon B. Hinckley. *Ensign, 25*(12), 66–67.

Hinckley, G. B. (1997). *Teachings of Gordon B. Hinckley* (pp. 328–329). Salt Lake City: Deseret Book.

Hinckley, G. B. (1999, February). Life's obligations. *Ensign, 29*(2), 2.

Hinckley, G. B. (2001, May). How can I become the woman of whom I dream? *Ensign, 31*(5), 95.

Hinckley, G. B. (2007, September). Seek learning. *New Era, 37*(9), 2–4.

Holland, J. R. (2005, November). To young women. *Ensign, 35*(11), 29.

Holman, T. B. (2002, September). Choosing—and being—the right spouse. *Ensign, 32*(9), 62–67.

Lefkowitz, E. S., & Gillen, M. M. (2006). "Sex is just a normal part of life": Sexuality in emerging adulthood. In J. J. Arnett & J. L. Tanner (Eds.), Emerging adults in America: Coming of age in the 21st century (235–256). Washington, DC: American Psychological Association.

Meeks, B. S., Hendrick, S. S. & Hendrick, C. (1998). Communication, love, and relationship satisfaction. *Journal of Social and Personal Relationships, 15*(6), 755–773.

Monson, T. S. (2011, May). Priesthood power. *Ensign, 41*(5), 66–69.

Muehlenkamp, J. J., & Gutierrez, P. M. (2004). An investigation of differences between self-injurious behavior and suicide attempts in a sample of adolescents. *Suicide and Life-Threatening Behavior, 34*(1), 12–24.

Nelson, L. J. (2012). *Behaviors of Latter-day Saint emerging adults: Analyses from Project READY.* Unpublished results. School of Family Life. Brigham Young University, Provo, UT.

Nelson, L. J., & Barry, C. M. (2005). Distinguishing features of emerging adulthood: The role of self-classification as an adult. *Journal of Adolescent Research, 20*(2), 242–262.

Nelson, L. J., & Padilla-Walker, L. M. (2012). *Flourishing and floundering: A cluster analysis of emerging adult college students.* Manuscript submitted for publication.

Nelson, L. J., Padilla-Walker, L. M., & Carroll, J. S. (2010). "I believe it is wrong but I still do it": A comparison of religious young men who do versus do not use pornography. *Psychology of Religion and Spirituality, 2*(3), 136–147.

Nelson, L. J., Padilla-Walker, L. M., Carroll, J. S., Madsen, S. D., Barry, C. M., & Badger, S. (2007). "If you want me to treat you like an adult, start acting like one!" Comparing the criteria that emerging adults and their parents have for adulthood. *Journal of Family Psychology, 21*(4), 665–674.

Oaks, D. H. (2006, June). Dating versus hanging out. *Ensign, 36*(6), 14.

Oaks, D. H. (2011, May). Desire. *Ensign, 41*(5), 42–45.

Pew Research Center (2007, January 9). *How young people view their lives, futures, and politics: A portrait of "Generation Next."* Retrieved from http://www.people-press.org/files/legacy-pdf/300.pdf.

Pascarella, E. T. & Terenzini, P. T. (1991). *How college affects students: Findings and insights from twenty-years of research.* San Francisco, CA: Jossey-Bass Publishers.

Prager, Karen J. (2000). Intimacy in personal relationships. In C. Hendrick & S. S. Hendrick (Eds.), *Close relationships: A sourcebook* (pp. 229–242). Thousand Oaks, CA: Sage.

Rabow, J., Choi, H., & Purdy, D. (1998). The GPA perspective: Influences, significance, and sacrifices of students. *Youth & Society, 29*(4), 451–470.

Ravert, R. D. (2009). "You're only young once": Things college students report doing now before it is too late. *Journal of Adolescent Research, 24*(3), 376–396.

Regnerus, M., & Uecker, J. (2011). Premarital sex in America: How young Americans meet, mate, and think about marrying. New York: Oxford University Press.

Schulenberg, J. E., & Maggs, J. L. (2001). A developmental perspective on alcohol use and heavy drinking during adolescence and the transition to adulthood. *Monitoring the Future Occasional Paper No. 51.* Ann Arbor, MI: Institute for Social Research, University of Michigan.

Scott, R. G. (2011, May). The eternal blessings of marriage. *Ensign, 41*(5), 94–97.

Sprecher, S., & Hendrick, S. S. (2004). Self-disclosure in intimate relationships: Associations with individual and relationship characteristics over time. *Journal of Social and Clinical Psychology, 23*(6), 857–877.

The Renfrew Center Foundation for Eating Disorders. (2013). *Eating disorders 101 guide: A summary of issues, statistics and resources.* The Renfrew Center Foundation for Eating Disorders, Retrieved from http://www.docstoc.com/docs/15314778 /Eating-Disorders-Statistics

Troy, Adam B. (2000). Determining the factors of intimate relationship satisfaction: Interpersonal communication, sexual communication, and communication affect. *Colgate University Journal of the Sciences*, 221–230.

Twenge, J. M. (2006). *Generation me: Why today's young Americans are more confident, assertive, entitled—and more miserable than ever before.* New York: Free Press.

US Census Bureau. (2010, September). *Income, poverty and health insurance coverage in the United States: 2009, Current Population Reports* (Series P60-238, and Detailed Tables—Table PINC-04). Retrieved from http://www.census.gov /compendia/statab/2012/tables/12s0703.pdf

US Census Bureau. (2010). U.S. Census Bureau reports men and women wait longer to marry. Retrieved from http://www.census.gov/newsroom/releases/archives /families_households/cb10-174.html

Whitehead, B. D., & Popenoe, D. (2001). Who wants to marry a soul mate? In *The National Marriage Project, the State of our Unions 2001* (pp. 6–16). Piscataway, NJ: The National Marriage Project.

LARRY J. NELSON & LAURA M. PADILLA-WALKER

12

Parenting Lasts *More Than 18 Years:*
Parenting Principles and Practices for Emerging-Adult Children

A LOOK at the parenting section of a bookstore or library provides parents with shelves of books aimed at helping them parent infants, young children, and adolescents. Notably lacking are books on how to parent children who are 18 and older. Because 18- to 27-year-olds are no longer children but are still not quite adults, these young people are called "emerging adults." The need to be heavily involved in the parenting of emerging adults is a relatively new phenomenon. In past decades, marriage, parenthood, and the beginning of careers tended to, on average, occur in the late teens or early twenties (Schlegel & Barry, 1991). However, as the average age of marriage has risen (28 for males and 26 for females in the United States; US Census Bureau, 2010), and the number of jobs available to those without higher education has decreased, more and more young people are single, living at home, and financially dependent on parents well into their twenties. As a result, compared to past generations, there is a greater need for many parents to remain engaged in the parenting process longer than previously expected.

Based on our discussions with parents, many parents report that parenting emerging adults is more challenging than guiding toddlers through the "terrible twos" or adolescents through the "terrible teens" because the stakes are higher and the issues much more complex. Indeed, the challenges facing today's young people as they make the transition to adulthood leave even the best of parents wanting to help their children but not really knowing the best way to do so. The purpose of this chapter is to identify parenting principles and practices that are adapted to fostering healthy outcomes in emerging-adult children. We will describe the period of life known as emerging adulthood (ages 18 to the mid-to-late twenties) so as to better understand the context for parenting children in this stage of life. Next, we will present specific parenting principles and practices that have been identified as important in parenting children at every stage of life. Then we will specifically examine these principles and practices as they apply to parenting emerging-adults. We will give special attention to the problematic potential that parental control may play during this period of life. Conversely, we will highlight for the reader the importance of focusing on the parent-child relationship and provide examples of practices that promote that important relationship during emerging adulthood. Finally, we will provide a word of comfort and support for parents as they undertake the challenge of parenting during one of the most important periods of development in the lives of their children.

The New Stage of Emerging Adulthood

One of the defining features of emerging adulthood is that young people feel a sense of being in between—no longer an adolescent but not yet an adult (Arnett, 2004). When asked whether they feel like they have reached adulthood, most young people between the ages of 18 and 27 tend to respond with "no" or "in some respects yes, in some respects no" (see Arnett, 1998; Nelson & Barry, 2005). In a recent study (Nelson et al., 2007), we found that 16% of the emerging adults answered "yes," 13% answered "no," and 72% answered "in some ways yes, in some ways no." Interestingly, their parents felt the same way about their emerging adults. We asked them, "Do you think that your child has reached adulthood?" For fathers, 19% answered "yes," 16% answered "no," and 65% answered "in some ways yes, in some ways no." For mothers, 16% answered "yes," 16% answered "no," and 68% answered "in some ways yes, in some ways no."

In order to better understand why 18- to 27-year-olds are not generally considered adults, researchers have asked what the criteria for adulthood are according to today's young people and their parents. Initial studies in this area (Arnett, 1998; Nelson & Barry, 2005) documented that contemporary emerging adults tend to view necessary criteria for adulthood as the following: (a) being independent and self-reliant (for example, accepting responsibility for the consequences of one's actions, becoming financially independent of parents), (b) being able to form mature relationships (that is, becoming less self-oriented and developing greater consideration for others), (c) being able to comply with societal norms (for example, avoiding drunk driving and committing petty crimes), and (d) being able to provide for and care for a family (for example, becoming capable of caring for children).

When we compared young people's answers to their parents', we found that parents emphasized similar characteristics as requisite for adulthood (Nelson et al., 2007). Interestingly, items such as marriage, parenthood, finishing education, and purchasing a home ranked very low by both emerging adults and their parents. This is likely because many young people realize that "doing" something (for example, graduating from high school) does not automatically make one an adult. Instead, the criteria endorsed by young people show that they likely understand one's transition to an adult by *becoming* ready to marry, care for children, and take on other responsibilities.

It is important to note that this perspective is no different among members of The Church of Jesus Christ of Latter-day Saints. In a study of young, active Latter-day Saints, only 24% of participants considered themselves to be adults (Nelson, 2003). The criteria they rated as most necessary for adulthood included "accept responsibility for the consequence of your actions," "decided on personal beliefs/values independently of parents and other influences," "become less self-oriented, develop greater consideration for others," and "learn always to have good control of your emotions." Out of 48 items on the list, serving a mission for men was 28th, settling into a long-term career was 37th, marriage ranked 39th, finishing education was 41st, having a child ranked 45th, and serving a mission for women ranked 46th. These findings show that many Latter-day Saint young people, like their peers, understand that becoming an adult takes much more than just reaching a certain age or accomplishing a certain task (for example, getting married). They realize that it takes much more than just finding someone, getting married in the temple, and living happily ever after. They know it is less about simply taking on adult roles and more about becoming prepared to take on those roles.

For emerging adults, parents are important in the process of developing the skills and abilities to take on adult roles. Some parents may not understand how instrumental they can and need to be in their emerging-adult children's lives as their children are making the transition to adulthood. Some parents may take the approach that once children reach the age of 18, they are on their own. Unfortunately, many parents who take this approach may underestimate the challenges of preparing to step into adulthood in today's society. Latter-day Saint emerging adults are trying to successfully make the transition to adulthood in a society in which typical 18- to 27-year-olds (a) are becoming increasingly devoted to individualistic-oriented rather than other-oriented goals; (b) are experimenting with work, relationships, and worldviews; (c) lack specific transitional roles that prepare them for adult roles; (d) are entering into increasingly intimate, non-marital relationships; and (e) are engaging in relatively high rates of risky behaviors such as unprotected sexual intercourse, illegal drug use, and drunk driving (see Arnett, 2000). Indeed, emerging adults who are not Latter-day Saints report that emerging adulthood is a time to experience a carefree lifestyle filled with traveling and adventure; participating in social events; experimenting with alcohol, tobacco, and drugs; engaging in multiple sexual experiences; and, in general, taking advantage of one's independence (Ravert, 2009). It is within this carefree culture that our young people are attempting to find their way towards righteous goals.

The challenges facing our young people are not just in the form of temptation all around them. Rather, the challenges are practical as well. Gone are the days in which, on average, a high school diploma is enough to get a job that can provide for a family (Danziger & Rouse, 2007). It takes time and money to acquire the skills and education needed to become self-reliant. Many adults think that emerging adults enjoy "living off" their parents. However, financial independence is a goal of most young people (Arnett, 1998; Nelson & Barry, 2005; Nelson et al., 2007), but the process of getting there is daunting, especially in today's economic climate.

The process of becoming an adult capable of caring for himself or herself as well as others is a daunting task in a society that promotes individualism, self-indulgence, and putting off responsibility and commitment. It is likewise challenging because of the need for education or specialized training compounded by both the high costs of higher/specialized education and the high costs of living while trying to pay for and attain that education. Things are made even worse for young people if they have to make this transition alone. Just as when they were young, emerging adults need their parents' support and involvement during this important period of their lives. Emerging adults who are left to tackle these challenges on their own tend to struggle during emerging adulthood and be less prepared to successfully transition into adult roles such as spouse, parent, and provider. We will now explore principles and practices that might assist parents of emerging adults.

Parenting Principles and Practices

Researchers have identified three important features of parenting: (a) support shown to a child (for example, acceptance, warmth, affection, involvement, nurturance) aimed at forming an emotional connection with the child, (b) behavioral control (such as, limit setting, supervision, reasoning about consequences) of the child aimed at promoting mature behavior, and (c) autonomy granting (for example, giving choices, allowing the child input on rule making, permitting the expression of ideas, avoiding intrusive behavior) aimed at fostering emotional and psychological self-reliance (Hart et al., 2003). Each aspect of parenting has been found to be linked to specific child outcomes, but the unique balance, or ratio, of each feature of parenting appears to be especially important. In other words, researchers have identified potential combinations of support, control, and autonomy granting that appear to be more or less adaptive across childhood and adolescence. For example, parenting that reflects an appropriate combination of support and behavioral control has been linked to numerous indices of social, emotional, cognitive, and academic well-being and functioning from early childhood through adolescence (see Aunalo et al., 2000; Bean et al., 2006; Eccles et al., 1997; Hart, Yang, Nelson, Jin, Bazarskaya, & Nelson, 1998; Steinberg et al., 1994). Conversely, the combination of high levels of control and the absence of support has been linked repeatedly to negative child outcomes such as anxiety, withdrawal, unhappiness, aggression, anger, defiance, hostility, low self-esteem, poor school performance, and deviant behaviors (see Baumrind, 1967, 1971; Hart, Nelson, Robinson, Olsen, & McNeily-Choque, 1998; Hart et al., 2003; Lamborn et al., 1991; Steinberg et al., 1994).

This research shows that the balance between support, control, and granting autonomy to the child is central to increasing the chances for positive outcomes in children. However, it is important to understand that this balance changes depending on the age of the child. For toddlers, there will be many more limits imposed on them than adolescents. Adolescents should be given much more freedom to make choices than preschoolers should. Not only does the balance between the key aspects of parenting change, but so do the forms they take. For example, parents show support to toddlers by reading them bedtime stories, helping them up when they fall, showering them with general verbal praise, and giving hugs and kisses. Support evolves in childhood into helping with homework, driving to soccer games, attending recitals, and giving specific compliments as well as physical affection. Additional changes will occur in adolescence to include greater levels of discussion, verbal give-and-take, and listening intently to teenagers' concerns and problems. The question for many parents is what the balance should be between support, control, and autonomy granting in emerging adulthood.

Balancing Support and Control in Emerging Adulthood

In order to be prepared to parent in emerging adulthood, it is necessary to understand that (a) support, control, and autonomy granting are still important, (b) the balance between them must change, and (c) the form that each takes will change to fit the development or age of the child. In a recent study, we identified different approaches to parenting emerging adults and determined which were the most effective at promoting positive outcomes for emerging adults (Nelson et al., 2011). We found that emerging adults with the most positive outcomes (that is, the lowest levels of risk behaviors, depression, and anxiety as well as the highest levels of kindness, self-worth, and closeness to parents) were those who had parents who displayed high levels of support and communication with their children, but also allowed for high levels of autonomy. In addition, these parents displayed low levels of control. It seems that these parents were still quite involved in the lives of their children, but in a very supportive and autonomy-promoting manner.

In contrast, the parents whose children had the most negative outcomes were those parents who displayed high levels of control and low levels of support. As mentioned previously, the use of parental control in the absence of parental support is rarely effective, and this seems to be even more marked during the emerging adult years when there is a clear expectation for increased autonomy. Indeed, it has been suggested that perhaps any amount of parental control is seen as inappropriate for college-age children, even when parental support is present (Padilla-Walker & Nelson, in press). However, parental control should be distinguished from parental involvement, although there is often a fine line between the two, especially when involvement borders on *over*involvement. In order to demonstrate the difference between parental control and parental involvement we will first examine three forms of parental control that have been found among parents of emerging adults, and then we will identify parental practices that reflect appropriate involvement and support that lead to a positive parent-child relationship during emerging adulthood.

Behavioral Control

Behavioral control during emerging adulthood generally looks slightly different than behavioral control at earlier ages. At younger ages, behavioral control might take the form of time-outs, grounding, revoking television/computer/video game privileges, and so forth. Such techniques are age-inappropriate for emerging adults even if they live at home. Unfortunately, many parents still try to control the behavior of their emerging adults. For example, if parents are financially involved in the lives of their emerging adults, they often are seen by their emerging adults as having some legitimate authority in decisions (Padilla-Walker et al., 2012). However, some parents use this financial leverage as a means to control emerging-adult children inappropriately (Nelson et al., 2011). For example, some parents will say they will help pay for an emerging adult's college tuition only if he or she declares a major of the parents' choosing.

Other examples of parental attempts at controlling emerging-adult children include conditional promises such as "if you go on a mission, I will buy you a new car," as well as yelling, anger, and other forms of verbal hostility. Certainly parents have the right to hold certain expectations of their student (for example, attend class, do one's best, maintain a realistic GPA) if they are providing financial support. Of course, adherence to family rules and serving a mission are desirable outcomes. However, the problem hinges on the element of control being exercised by the parent(s) in these examples. Once while teaching a lesson on this topic at church, one of the authors of this chapter was asked by a member of the class, "Isn't it okay to make your children do something as long as it is right and for their own good?" With as much sensitivity and kindness as the author/teacher could muster, he pointed out just how much that proposal sounded like one presented by another individual in the great, premortal council in heaven. He then suggested that since Heavenly Father rejected that proposal then, we should not embrace it now.

As pointed out previously, depending on the age of the child and the context, parents will indeed exercise varying levels of control in order to protect their children. However, as a general rule, forcing individuals to behave a certain way is not a Christlike characteristic, nor is it an effective parenting practice. Research shows that these forms of control are linked to negative outcomes (such as low self-worth, high depression, anxiety, impulsivity) for emerging adults and tend to hurt the parent-child relationship (Nelson et al., 2011). It is as Brigham Young (*Teachings of Presidents of the Church,* 1997) said, "Kind looks, kind actions, kind words, and a lovely, holy deportment towards [them] will bind our children to us with bands that cannot be easily broken; while abuse and unkindness will drive them from us" (p. 166). Indeed, frequent and harsh attempts by parents to control the behavior of their emerging-adult children tend to harm young people rather than help them. Such behaviors also jeopardize the parent-child relationship, which, as we will discuss, is the most important aspect of parenting emerging-adult children.

Psychological Control

Unfortunately, sometimes because parents are unable to behaviorally control their children at this age, they turn to psychological control as a means of staying involved. Psychological control is a parent's attempt to control his or her child's thoughts and psychological world and is associated with a host of negative outcomes at all ages (see Barber, 1996; Barber & Harmon, 2002), but particularly during emerging adulthood (for example, Luyckx et al., 2007; Nelson et al., 2011; Urry et al., 2011). Psychological control includes parents inducing guilt if the child does not do what is desired ("After everything I've done for you, this is all that you're going to do for me?"), ignoring the child if behavior is seen as unacceptable (referred to as love-withdrawal), and trying to change how the child thinks or feels about something through manipulation. Although many seemingly negative aspects of parenting can be positive when done in a loving manner, research has never linked psychological control to positive outcomes in children at any age. Instead, as noted, it has been linked repeatedly to negative outcomes in children, adolescents, and emerging adults (see Barber, 2002; Barber et al., 2005; Nelson et al., 2011).

Not only is there no empirical support endorsing the use of psychological control, but there are no examples in the scriptures of our Savior or Heavenly Father trying to lead us by controlling us psychologically or guilting us into good behavior. Though guilt is the natural result of sinning and "godly sorrow" (see 2 Corinthians 7:10) and leads us to want to do better, it is unhealthy for parents to try to use guilt to psychologically control their children. A loving approach to parenting is always done via patience and long-suffering rather than guilt induction or love-withdrawal. Even when (or we might say *especially* when) children might not be making decisions that are in their best interests, we should not withdraw our love and support as a way of manipulating them into course corrections. In a conference talk by Elder Dallin H. Oaks called "Love and Law," he suggested that when children are making decisions with which parents do not agree, parents do not need to endorse those decisions, but should always maintain a loving relationship with their children. Elder Oaks (2009) said:

> If an adult child is living in cohabitation, does the seriousness of sexual relations outside the bonds of marriage require that this child feel the full weight of family disapproval by being excluded from any family contacts, or does parental love require that the fact of cohabitation be ignored? I have seen both of these extremes, and I believe that both are inappropriate. Where do parents draw the line? That is a matter for parental wisdom, guided by the inspiration of the Lord. There is no area of parental action that is more needful of heavenly guidance or more likely to receive it than the decisions of parents in raising their children and governing their families. This is the work of eternity. As parents grapple with these problems, they should remember the Lord's teaching that we leave

Elder Dallin H. Oaks said, "There is no area of parental action that is more needful of heavenly guidance or more likely to receive it than the decisions of parents in raising their children and governing their families." Craig Dimond, © Intellectual Reserve, Inc.

the ninety and nine and go out into the wilderness to rescue the lost sheep. (p. 28)

Because the Lord's commandments are unchanging and nonnegotiable, parents may have to chastise a child for his or her behavior. But a child's choices should not detract from a parent's love for the child or the communication of that love. Love-withdrawal, using guilt to control, and manipulation are neither in harmony with principles of righteousness nor found in any examples from Deity. Although our blessings and privileges may change as we disobey God's laws, his love for us does not decrease. Parents should follow this example in regard to parenting their emerging-adult children. To reiterate, parents might disapprove of and even chasten emerging adults for their behavior, but it should be done with persuasion, gentleness, and love unfeigned rather than any form of manipulation (for example, guile) or control (see D&C 121:41–42).

Helicopter Parenting

A final way that parents sometimes mistakenly attempt to control their children during emerging adulthood is called helicopter parenting. This approach consists of parents "hovering" over their emerging-adult children, making important decisions for them such as where they should live, whom they should date, and what classes they should take. It is unclear how much of this parental help is solicited by emerging adults. But it is clear that while helicopter parenting is not as destructive as behavioral or psychological control, helicopter parenting may be growth-inhibiting for emerging adults and may delay their ability to transition into healthy adult roles (Padilla-Walker & Nelson, 2012).

Helicopter parenting is a form of overinvolvement and is often well-intentioned on the part of parents. Instead of providing parental input or guidance, helicopter parents continue to solve problems for their emerging-adult children. Rather than calling a professor because of a late assignment

Rather than doing things for your young adult, it is more appropriate to help them succeed by themselves and act as a sounding board as they are making decisions. Mark A. Philbrick, © 2012 BYU Photo.

or filling out a job application for your emerging adult, it is more appropriate to help him or her (as needed) succeed at doing it by him or herself. It is also more appropriate to act as a sounding board as decisions are being made instead of making decisions for your emerging adult.

This approach is reminiscent of how the Lord dealt with the brother of Jared as he was preparing for his journey to the promised land. In the early stages of preparation, the Lord solved problems for the brother of Jared. For example, he gave him a solution for the problem of no air in the barges (much like parents sometimes provide solutions for their children during childhood and the teen years). However, when the brother of Jared asked the Lord for help a second time, with the problem of not having light in the barges, the Lord responded, "What will ye that I should do?" It certainly would have been easier for the Lord to solve the problem. But he consecrated the brother of Jared's decision, as we should our children's decisions, even if they are not the solutions we might have thought of initially. In a recent conference talk, Elder Larry Y. Wilson (2012) said: "Wise parents prepare their children to get along without them. They provide opportunities for growth as children acquire the spiritual maturity to exercise their agency properly. And yes, this means children will sometimes make mistakes and learn from them" (p. 104).

In summary, parental attempts at controlling emerging-adult children are inconsistent with gospel principles, tend to place the emerging adults at risk of negative outcomes, and harm the parent-child relationship at a time when emerging-adult children need supportive parents. Control just is not the Lord's way. Elder Wilson (2012) again underscored this point when he cautioned:

> [The scriptures say] we must lead by "principles of righteousness." Such principles apply to all leaders in the Church as well as to all fathers and mothers in their homes. We lose our right to the Lord's Spirit *and* to whatever authority we have from God when we exercise control over another person in an unrighteous manner. We may think such methods are for the good of the one being "controlled." But anytime we try to compel someone to righteousness who *can* and *should* be exercising his or her own moral agency, we are acting unrighteously. When setting firm limits for another person *is* in order, those limits should always be administered with loving patience and in a way that teaches eternal principles. (p. 103)

Taking this approach will help parents of emerging-adult children to be involved and will foster a stronger relationship, but in a manner that promotes autonomy rather than a manner that might hinder growth and independent decision making.

Indeed, in counseling parents to be careful not to be controlling in their interactions with their emerging adults, some might mistakenly think we are suggesting that parents abdicate their responsibilities as parents. Absolutely not! While we need to allow greater autonomy to our emerging-adult children, and our approach to parental support may change, our children still consistently need our support and involvement in their lives. Parents still have a solemn responsibility to care for their children, even if those children are in the process of becoming adults. The point we are trying to stress is *how* that is done especially in emerging adulthood. In "The Family: A Proclamation to the World," parents are told that this sacred duty of rearing children needs to be done in *love and righteousness*, not control and manipulation. Therefore, we will now focus on the positive things parents can do in providing support and staying involved in ways that foster a positive parent-child relationship during this period of life.

Fostering a Positive Parent-Child Relationship through Parental Support and Involvement

Concerned parents would still like to have, if not control, at least some knowledge of what is going on in their children's lives. Ultimately, the best way to stay informed about a child's behavior and stay involved in his or her life during this time period, without being controlling, is to maintain a strong relationship that will promote open communication. This is important at younger ages as well, but becomes even more essential as children leave their parents' home. The main way that parents will be informed of their child's whereabouts or activities once the child has left home will be if the child chooses to tell them. Our work shows this only happens if there is a good relationship between the parent and the child (Urry et al., 2011). Thus it is important that parents open these lines of trust and communication early in the parent-child relationship—long before emerging adulthood—so that child disclosure to parents is a normal and frequent occurrence. This will likely lead to emerging adults who seek their parents out for advice and guidance rather than needing to be hounded or controlled by parents.

While young people may be striving for greater independence and self-reliance, this does not mean that they want to distance themselves from parents (unless, again, the parents tend to be too controlling). Numerous studies have shown that a major desire of emerging adults is to

Emerging adults want to develop a stronger, more mature and equal relationship with their parents. © Arekmalang.

develop a stronger, more mature and equal relationship with parents (for example, Arnett, 1998; Nelson & Barry, 2005; Barry & Nelson, 2005). Thus the most effective thing parents can do is focus on the relationship. A recent study of ours (Urry et al., 2011) illustrates this point well. We found that emerging adults who reported a good relationship with mothers told their parents what they were doing, *and* they engaged in fewer negative behaviors.

Again, parents may ask how to foster that relationship. To reiterate, it comes via warmth, support, love, concern, and communication. To let their emerging adults know they care, parents should check in with them, which shows love and concern. Checking *in* is different than checking *up* on them, which reflects attempts at behavioral control. Ask emerging adults how they are doing, not where they were the night before. Parents should *encourage* their emerging adults in the decision-making process. It is time for emerging adults to be learning how to make important decisions on their own. So, instead of deciding for your emerging adult, here are some ways you can provide guidance and support while allowing your child to exercise autonomy in making his or her own decisions. First, ask your emerging adult where he or she is in the decision-making process. Listen to the issues being weighed by your child and empathize with how he or she is feeling about the situation. Then, *if asked*, provide additional points the emerging adult might consider in the decision-making process. Finally, express support and confidence in the emerging adult's ability to make the right decision. When your emerging adult does make a decision, congratulate him or her on it. *Do not* say things like "that isn't what I would have done," or, if things don't go well, "I told you so." In general, reciprocate your emerging adult's willingness to talk with you by listening more than talking. Additionally, still make attempts to spend time with your emerging adult, whether that be a set "date" for lunch, watching a favorite show or sporting event together, or catching up on the phone. Finally, do not forget expressions of love and affection verbally (such as, "I miss you," "I love you," "I'm proud of you"), physically, and, yes, electronically. A text

A supportive text message from Mom and Dad during a hard moment can mean a lot. Courtesy of Maddie Lee and Rachel Ishoy.

message from Mom and Dad just before a hard exam or after a long shift at work can mean a lot.

A Final Word of Comfort and Support to Parents

Allowing children the autonomy to make more and more decisions on their own can be challenging for many parents. Many parents of emerging adults are worried that their emerging adults will fail, but there may simultaneously be just as much or more heartache knowing they may succeed, which means transitioning out of the home and away from us as parents. The first author's own daughter recently joined the ranks of emerging adulthood. Therefore, the author is numbered with those countless parents who stand with excitement and awe as well as fear and worry as they watch their children embark on adulthood. Certainly the emotions he experiences as he watches his daughter "stretch her wings" include trepidation and concern over whether she will make the right choices that lead to success in adult roles. But the emotions are even stronger realizing that his little girl is growing up and that he has to prepare to let her do so. Parenting an emerging adult is certainly not an easy time for parents, but we need to make sure that we provide the support and autonomy that will allow our children the best chances to grow.

Again, it can be hard not to be controlling during this time because parents want to see their children succeed. We do not want to see those we love get hurt. What must it have been like for Lehi to see his sons Laman and

Lemuel make the poor decisions they made? What must Alma and Mosiah have thought as their sons were out defying everything they had ever been taught? What must our Heavenly Father have felt like as he watched a third part of his children leave his presence in the premortal life? How does he feel now as he watches even more enter paths that lead away from him? It is hard, but agency is essential to the plan! We cannot force our children to do anything. Elder Robert D. Hales (1999) has counseled:

> Act with faith; don't react with fear. When our teenagers begin testing family values, parents need to go to the Lord for guidance on the specific needs of each family member. This is the time for added love and support and to reinforce your teachings on how to make choices. It is frightening to allow our children to learn from the mistakes they may make, but their willingness to choose the Lord's way and family values is greater when the choice comes from within than when we attempt to force those values upon them. The Lord's way of love and acceptance is better than Satan's way of force and coercion, especially in rearing teenagers. (p. 34)

While this counsel was directed at parents of teenagers, the principles contained therein apply even more so to emerging adults because it is a time in which even greater autonomy is expected and needed by emerging-adult children. So while we cannot force and control (because those techniques belong to the proposal rejected already in the premortal life), there are things we can do as parents. First, we can have faith in the principles we have taught our children. We can only hope there are a lot more young people like Alma the Younger and the sons of Mosiah, who eventually return strong, than there are like Laman and Lemuel who do not. It is interesting to consider the additional 60 young men who joined Helaman's band of 2,000 stripling warriors. Why did they join their brethren later? Were they not old enough to begin with or did they possibly have some personal struggles to overcome first? Indeed, how many poor choices were made as part of

Our young people, like the stripling warriors, will be strengthened to make it because of wonderful mothers (and fathers and leaders) who taught them well and then let them make decisions for themselves. Friberg Fine Art Prints, © Intellectual Reserve, Inc.

the learning process by the young men who would eventually become the stripling warriors that we read about? Our young people, like the stripling warriors, will be strengthened to make it because of wonderful mothers (and fathers and leaders) who taught them well and then let them make decisions for themselves.

Second, if emerging adults do wander off the path, or simply struggle along the way, we can know that the Lord is mindful of them. More than just "mindful," we need to remember our children are his children. Elder Orson F. Whitney (1929) reminds us:

The Shepherd will find his sheep. They were his before they were yours—long before he entrusted them to your care; and you cannot begin to love them as he loves them. They have but strayed in ignorance from the Path of Right, and God is merciful to ignorance. Only the fullness of knowledge brings the fullness of accountability. Our Heavenly Father is far more merciful, infinitely more charitable, than even the best of his servants, and the Everlasting Gospel is mightier in power to save than your narrow finite minds can comprehend. (p. 110)

Likewise, President Faust (2003) has reminded us of the doctrine Joseph Smith taught about the power of temple sealings to bring wayward children back to their families.

The Prophet Joseph Smith declared—and he never taught more comforting doctrine—that the eternal sealings of faithful parents and the divine promises made to them for valiant service in the Cause of Truth, would save not only themselves, but likewise their posterity. Though some of the sheep may wander, the eye of the Shepherd is upon them, and sooner or later they will feel the tentacles of Divine Providence reaching out after them and drawing them back to the fold. Either in this life or the life to come, they will return. They will have to pay their debt to justice; they will suffer for their sins; and may tread a thorny path; but if it leads them at last, like the penitent Prodigal, to a loving and forgiving father's heart and home, the painful experience will not have been in vain. Pray for your careless and disobedient children; hold on to them with your faith. Hope on, trust on, till you see the salvation of God. (p. 62)

We need to remember that Alma the Younger and the sons of Mosiah came back stronger after they had endured their trials. It is never better to sin and we are not made stronger through sin. But we can learn from the trials which are part of natural life experiences. As unlikely as that may seem at times in the lives of some of our children, we must allow them their agency and then have faith that they will return to righteousness or persevere in righteousness.

Conclusion

Emerging adulthood is not always easy for young people. It is a challenging period for parents as well, but parents need to avoid controlling behaviors, whether that be forcing decisions upon their emerging adults (that is, behavioral control), withholding love or inducing guilt (psychological control), or doing things for them that they should be doing themselves (helicopter parenting). All of these forms of control are not in line with gospel principles and hinder a healthy and positive transition to adulthood by our young people. For our children to be successful, parents must be warm, supportive, and encouraging. They need to foster open communication. They need to allow their children the opportunity to make decisions for themselves while still being there to lend a listening ear, provide appropriate counsel, teach gospel principles and standards, and express love for and confidence in them. In sum, emerging adults want a strong relationship with their parents. So foster that relationship. Work together in forging a new and stronger relationship.

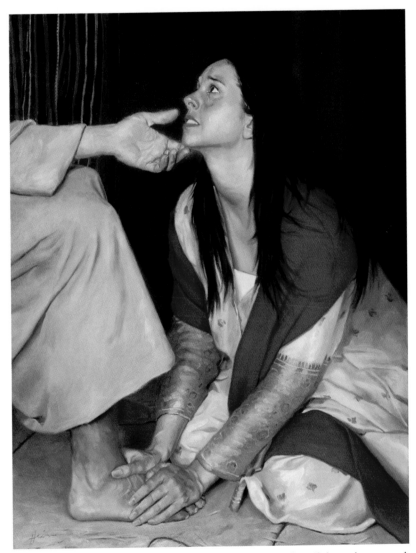

The Lord is mindful of each of us. If emerging adults wander off the path or struggle along the way, he is right there, ready to help and love them; they are his children. Jeff Hein, © Intellectual Reserve, Inc.

In doing so, remember to do exactly like the Lord does with all of us—allow them their agency and love them completely.

References

Arnett, J. J. (1998). Learning to stand alone: The contemporary American transition to adulthood in cultural and historical context. *Human Development, 41*(5–6), 295–315.

Arnett, J. J. (2000). Emerging adulthood: A theory of development from the late teens through the twenties. *American Psychologist, 55*(5), 469–480.

Arnett, J. J. (2004). *Emerging adulthood: The winding road from the late teens through the twenties.* New York: Oxford University Press.

Aunola, K., Stattin, H., & Nurmi, J. (2000). Parenting styles and adolescents' achievement strategies. *Journal of Adolescence, 23*(2), 205–222.

Barber, B. K. (1996). Parental psychological control: Revisiting a neglected construct. *Child Development, 67*(6), 3296–3319.

Barber, B. K. (2002). *Intrusive parenting: How psychological control affects children and adolescents.* Washington, DC: American Psychological Association.

Barber, B. K., & Harmon, E. L. (2002). Violating the self: Parental psychological control of children and adolescents. In Barber, B. K. (Ed.). *Psychological control of children and adolescents.* Washington, DC: American Psychological Association, 15–52.

Barber, K. K., Stolz, H. E., & Olsen, J. A. (2005). Parental support, psychological control, and behavioral control: Assessing relevance across time, culture, and method. *Monographs of the Society for Research in Child Development, 70*(4).

Barry, C. M., & Nelson, L. J. (2005). The role of religion in the transition to adulthood for young emerging adults. *Journal of Youth and Adolescence, 34*(3), 245–255.

Baumrind, D. (1971). Current patterns of parental authority. *Developmental Psychology, 4*(1), 1–103.

Baumrind, D., & Black, A. E. (1967). Socialization practices associated with dimensions of competence in preschool boys and girls. *Child Development, 38*(2), 291–327.

Bean, R. A., Barber, B. K., & Crane, D. R. (2006). Parental support, behavioral control, and psychological control among african american youth: The relationships to academic grades, delinquency, and depression. *Journal of Family Issues, 27*(10), 1335–1355.

Danziger, S. & Rouse, C. E. (Eds.). *The price of independence: The economics of early adulthood*. New York: Sage, 1–24.

Eccles, J. S., Early, D., Frasier, K., Belansky, E., & McCarthy, K. (1997). The relation of connection, regulation, and support for autonomy to adolescents' functioning. *Journal of Adolescent Research, 12*(2), 263–286.

Faust, J. E. (2003). Dear are the sheep that have wandered. *Ensign, 33*(5), 62.

Hales, R. D. (1999). Strengthening families: Our sacred duty. *Ensign, 29*(5), 32–34.

Hart, C. H., Nelson, D. A., Robinson, C. D., Olsen, S. F., & McNeilly-Choque, M. K. (1998). Overt and relational aggression in Russian nursery-school-age children: Parenting style and marital linkages. *Developmental Psychology, 34*(4), 687–697.

Hart, C. H., Newell, L. D., & Olsen, S. F. (2003). Parenting skills and social-communicative competence in childhood. In Greene, J. O. & Burleson, B. R. (Eds.). *Handbook of communication and social interaction skills*. Mahwah, NJ: Erlbaum, 753–797.

Hart, C. H., Yang, C., Nelson, D. A., Jin, S., Bazarskaya, N., Nelson, L. J., et al. (1998). Peer contact patterns, parenting practices, and preschoolers' social competence in China, Russia, and the United States. In Slee, P. & Rigby, K. (Eds.). *Children's peer relations*. London: Routledge, 3–30.

Lamborn, S. D., Mounts, N. S., & Steinberg, L. (1991). Patterns of competence and adjustment among adolescents from authoritative, authoritarian, indulgent, and neglectful families. *Child Development, 62*(5), 1049–1065.

Luyckx, K., Soenens, B., Vansteenkiste, M., Goossens, L., & Berzonsky, M. D. (2007). Parental psychological control and dimensions of identity formation in emerging adulthood. *Journal of Family Psychology, 21*(3), 546–550.

Mounts, N. S. (2004). Contributions of parenting and campus climate to freshmen adjustment in a multiethnic sample. *Journal of Adolescent Research, 19*(4), 468–491.

Nelson, L. J. (2003). Rites of passage in emerging adulthood: perspectives of young Mormons. *New Directions for Child and Adolescent Development: Cultural Conceptions of the Transition to Adulthood, 100*, 33–49.

Nelson, L. J., & Barry, C. M. (2005). Distinguishing features of emerging adulthood: The role of self-classification as an adult. *Journal of Adolescent Research, 20*(2), 242–262.

Nelson, L. J., & Padilla-Walker, L. M. (2012). *Flourishing and floundering: Multiple trajectories of emerging adult college students.* Manuscript submitted for publication.

Nelson, L. J., Padilla-Walker, L. M., Carroll, J. S., Madsen, S. D., Barry, C. M., & Badger, S. (2007). "If you want me to treat you like an adult, start acting like one!" Comparing the criteria that emerging adults and their parents have for adulthood. *Journal of Family Psychology, 21*(4), 665–674.

Nelson, L. J., Padilla-Walker, L. M., Christensen , K. J., Evans, C. A., & Carroll, J. A. (2011). Parenting in emerging adulthood: An examination of parenting clusters and correlates. *Journal of Youth and Adolescence, 40*(6), 730–743.

Oaks, D. H. (2009). Love and law. *Ensign, 39*(11), 29.

Olsen, S. F., Yang, C., Hart, C. H., Robinson, C. C., Wu, P., Nelson, D. A., Nelson, L. J., Jin, S., & Jianzhong, W. (2002). Mothers' psychological control and preschool children's behavioral outcomes in China, Russia, and the United States. In Barber, B. K. (Ed.), *Psychological control of children and adolescents.* Washington, DC: American Psychological Association, 235–262.

Padilla-Walker, L. M., Nelson, L. J., & Knapp, D. J. *"Because I'm still the parent, that's why!" Parental legitimate authority during emerging adulthood.* Manuscript submitted for publication.

Padilla-Walker, L. M., & Nelson, L. J. (2012). Black Hawk down? Establishing helicopter parenting as a distinct construct from other forms of parental control during emerging adulthood. *Journal of Adolescence, 35*(5), 1177–1190.

Ravert, R. D. (2009). "You're only young once": Things college students report doing now before it is too late. *Journal of Adolescent Research, 24*(3), 376–396.

Schlegel, A. & Barry, H. (1991). *Adolescence: An anthropological inquiry.* New York: Free Press.

Steinberg, L., Lamborn, S. D., Darling, N., Mounts, N. S., & Dornbusch, S. M. (1994). Over-time changes in adjustment and competence among adolescents from authoritative, authoritarian, indulgent, and neglectful families. *Child Development, 65*(3), 754–770.

Taylor, J. (1851, November). *Millennial Star,* 15.

Teachings of Presidents of the Church: Brigham Young (1997). Salt Lake City: Intellectual Reserve, 166.

Urry, S., Nelson, L. J., & Padilla-Walker, L. M. (2011). *Mother knows best: Correlates of child disclosure and maternal knowledge in emerging adulthood.* Manuscript submitted for publication.

US Census Bureau, 2010.

Whitney, O. F. (1929). Prophets' promises to parents of wayward children. In Conference Report, April 1929, 110.

Wilson, L. Y. (2012). Only upon the principles of righteousness. *Ensign, 42*(5), 103–104.

Contributors

Bruce A. Chadwick is professor emeritus of sociology at Brigham Young University (BYU). He is the former director of the Family Studies Program and the Center for the Study of the Family at BYU. He is a past recipient of the prestigious Karl G. Maeser Distinguished Research Award and the Maeser Professorship in General Education. He received his PhD from Washington University in St. Louis and has published numerous books and scores of articles on family and sociological issues. He coauthored with Brent L. Top the books *Rearing Righteous Youth of Zion, Ten Secrets Wise Parents Know,* and *Shield of Faith: The Power of Religion in the Lives of LDS Youth and Young Adults.*

David C. Dollahite is a professor in the School of Family Life at BYU. His teaching and research focuses on religion and family life among Christian, Jewish, and Muslim families. He obtained a master's degree in marriage and family therapy from BYU and a doctorate in family science from the University of Minnesota. He has published over 60 scholarly articles and chapters and has edited or coedited four books: *Generative Fathering, Successful Marriages and Families, Helping and Healing Our*

Families, and *Strengthening Our Families*. In addition to his work at BYU, he works as a family life coach by helping good men to become great husbands and fathers.

Jenet Jacob Erickson is an adjunct faculty member in the School of Family Life at BYU. She received a PhD in family social science in 2007 from the University of Minnesota. Her academic research focuses on the maternal well-being in the sphere of work and family life, the influence of non-maternal child care on children's development, and the role of family routines and rituals in family well-being. She was a full-time faculty member at BYU from 2007 until 2010, when she chose to be a full-time wife and mother to her two-year-old daughter and an infant son.

Michael A. Goodman is an associate professor of Church history and doctrine at BYU, where he teaches courses in LDS Marriage and Family. He holds a PhD in marriage, family, and human development from BYU. Prior to joining the faculty at BYU, he was an instructor and manager of college curriculum for Seminaries and Institutes.

Craig H. Hart is a professor in the School of Family Life at BYU. He has served as department chair of Marriage, Family, and Human Development; associate dean in the College of Family, Home, and Social Sciences; and is currently associate academic vice president at BYU. He received his PhD from Purdue University. He has also authored or coauthored numerous scientific papers on parenting and familial linkages with children's social development and on developmentally appropriate practices in early childhood education. His work has appeared in leading developmental science journals, such as *Child Development* and *Developmental Psychology* and in early childhood education research journals, including *Early Childhood Research Quarterly*, as well as Latter-day Saint publications.

Julie H. Haupt has been an adjunct professor in the School of Family Life at BYU for 25 years. She has contributed to academic journal articles, independent study materials, and film projects in the area of family studies. Professor Haupt also served as the managing editor to a previous Deseret Book publication on the family proclamation.

E. Jeffrey Hill is an associate professor in the School of Family Life at BYU. His research deals with finding harmony and peace while integrating work, family, and community responsibilities. He received a doctorate in family and human development from Utah State University. Before coming to BYU, he was an expert on work and family subject matter at IBM for two decades, where he pioneered many flexible work options, including flextime, telecommuting, part-time employment, and parental leave. He has published four books and more than sixty articles and book chapters, including articles in the *Ensign*.

Debra Theobald McClendon currently works in private practice and is an adjunct faculty member in the Department of Psychology at BYU. She is a licensed psychologist in the state of Utah and has a master's degree in Marriage and Family Therapy and a PhD in Clinical Psychology. Her clinical work is primarily with young adults and adults through individual, couple, and group therapy. She often treats depression, anxiety, marriage/relationships, and trauma/crisis issues. She has published research in the areas of group psychotherapy and the use of outcome measures for children and adolescents in outpatient psychological treatment.

Richard J. McClendon is an associate director of Institutional Assessment and Analysis at BYU. He has taught as an adjunct professor in the Department of Sociology at BYU and as an adjunct professor in the Department of Religious Education. Prior to coming to BYU, he taught for many years in Seminaries and Institutes. He received his PhD in sociology at BYU and is the author of several publications focusing on LDS families, marriage, returned missionaries, and education. He coauthored with Bruce A. Chadwick and Brent L. Top the book *Shield of Faith: The Power of Religion in the Lives of LDS Youth and Young Adults.*

Steven P. Moody is currently working as a therapist in private practice in Irvine, California, at Huisken & Moody Counseling Services, specializing in both relationships and addictions. He received his bachelor's degree in psychology and social behaviors from the University of California, Irvine. He went on to receive his master's degree in clinical social work from the University of Southern California (USC). At USC, his clinical focus was on working with families, including marital therapy and relationships. Steven has worked as a therapist for the Orange County Department of Education, where he worked with incarcerated youth at locations including Juvenile Hall and the Youth Guidance Center. He has also worked as a part-time counselor with LDS Family Services.

Larry J. Nelson is an associate professor in the School of Family Life at BYU. He holds a master's degree in family sciences from BYU and a PhD in human development from the University of Maryland. He is the author of numerous articles in academic journals and faith-based publications on emerging adults.

Lloyd D. Newell received a PhD in marriage, family, and human development from BYU, where he is a professor of Church history and doctrine and an associated faculty member in the School of Family Life. He is the author of more than a dozen books and numerous articles. He has served as announcer and writer for the weekly Mormon Tabernacle Choir inspirational broadcast, *Music and the Spoken Word*, since 1990.

Mark D. Ogletree is an associate professor of Church history and doctrine at BYU. Prior to joining the faculty, he was with Seminaries and

Institutes for over 20 years. He holds a master's degree in mental health counseling from Northern Arizona University and a PhD in family and human development from Utah State University. He has also been in private practice in marriage and family counseling in both Texas and Utah and has written several books on marriage and family.

Jeffrey S. Reber is an associate professor in the Department of Psychology at BYU, where he earned a doctoral degree in psychology with a dual emphasis in social psychology and theoretical/philosophical psychology. He has published numerous scholarly articles and book chapters on the relationship between religion and psychology and on interpersonal relationships. He is a licensed professional counselor and worked for several years as a part-time counselor with LDS Family Services. He is coeditor of a textbook on critical thinking about psychology, and he and Steven Moody are the authors of *Are We Special? The Truth and the Lie About God's Chosen People.*

Brent L. Top is the dean of Religious Education at BYU and a professor of Church history and doctrine. In addition to teaching classes in LDS marriage and family, he has authored numerous articles and book chapters in both academic journals and LDS publications. Professor Top previously served as associate dean of Religious Education and held an endowed professorship in Moral Education. He is also the author of numerous articles and more than a dozen books on LDS doctrine and scriptures.

Laura M. Padilla-Walker is an associate professor in the School of Family Life at BYU. She received her PhD in developmental psychology from the University of Nebraska–Lincoln in 2005. Professor Walker has published several articles in top tier academic journals in the field of parenting and moral development. Her research has also been highlighted by the *New York Times*, CNN, ABC, CBS News, *US News and World Report*, and other news outlets.

Index

marriage and time management
    and, 52, 54–55
  parenting responsibilities of, 68–69
  statistics on marriage and divorce
    among, 96–97
learning, through nurturing, 170–71
Lehi, dream of, 246–48
life harmony
  balance through, 2
  fishing village story, 18–19
  through bundling activities, 8–10
  through centering on Jesus Christ,
    16–18
  through focusing on important
    things, 10–12
  through increased energy, 3–5
  through increased quality time, 5–8
  through simplicity, 14–16
  through work flexibility, 12–14
limits
  and avoiding coercion or permis-
    siveness, 136–39
  in child-rearing, 117–18
  importance of, 130–33
  and seeking Spirit's guidance,
    133–36
  setting and enforcing, 139–45
love
  benefits of, for children, 148–50
  in child-rearing, 117–18, 132–33,
    145–46
  in discipline, 136–38
  expressing, through rituals, 87–88
  expressing, through talk rituals,
    76–79

expressing, to emerging adults,
    365–66
  expressing, with greeting and good-
    bye rituals, 73–76
  of fathers, 215
  feeding, 57
  Heavenly Father as example of,
    146–48
  of mothers, 175–82
  presiding in, 198
  showing support and, 150–52
  withdrawing, 357–60
manipulation, of emerging adults,
    356–57, 358, 360
marriage. *See also* divorce
  American Families of Faith Project
    and, 31–35
  commitment in, 26–29
  current state of, 25–26, 164–65
  emerging adults' preparation for,
    322–23
  emerging adults' views on, 320
  LDS beliefs and commitment in,
    36–38
  loyalty to God and, 99–111
  marital commitment and doctrine
    of eternal, 39–46
  ongoing difficulties in, 112–14
  and origins of time famine, 61–70
  as partnership, 211–16
  religion and commitment in, 29–35
  religion's influence on, 23–25
  rituals and strengthening, 70–88
  time famine's effect on, 56–61
  time management and, 51–55
  waiting for, 343–44